Contemporary Scottish Women Writers

Edited by

Aileen Christianson

and

Alison Lumsden

Edinburgh University Press

Edinburgh University Press Ltd
22 George Square, Edinburgh

Typeset in Garamond
by Initial Typesetting Services, and
printed and bound in Great Britain by MPG Books Ltd, Bodmin

A CIP Record for this book is available from the British Library

ISBN 0 7486 0979 2 (paperback)

Contents

Acknowledgements

The editors would like to thank Jackie Jones, who commissioned this book, and Carol Macdonald, who has given us careful and cheerful editing support, both of Edinburgh University Press. We would also like to thank Carol Anderson, Anne Mason, Glenda Norquay, Wayne Price and the staff of the Issue Desk at the National Library of Scotland.

Aileen Christianson
Alison Lumsden

Introduction

Alison Lumsden and Aileen Christianson

The first issue of *Cencrastus* in 1979 made reference to the paucity of women writers in Scotland.[1] There were, in fact, Scottish women writing in the 1970s and 1980s: poets (for example, Valerie Gillies and Liz Lochhead; for further details, see Chapter 1); novelists (Muriel Spark, Jessie Kesson and Emma Tennant, for example); short story writers such as Elspeth Davy; and dramatists such as Joan Ure. The 1990s have seen the addition of many new Scottish women writing from a more confident assumption that being female and being Scottish are linked and culturally positive. The breadth of the work of contemporary Scottish women writers now ensures the redrawing of the literary map of Scotland, allowing for these writers a natural assumption of place in a culture previously more accessible to male Scottish writers. Women writers have become fully part of 'the bedrock' of this 'small / and multitudinous country'.[2]

The political debates surrounding the 1979 referendum for a devolved Scottish Parliament, and the failure of the campaign for implementation, may ironically have been the watershed for Scottish writing generally, as Gavin Wallace suggests in his introduction to *The Scottish Novel since the Seventies*:

> The intellectual wasteland to which many believed Scotland had been reduced in 1979 was, however, not barren for long – if, in fact, it ever had been. The late 1970s and 1980s witnessed the beginnings of a third and infinitely more radical phase in twentieth-century Scottish literature ... The considerable impact of this bold enlargement of Scottish creative potential remains symbolised by the publication in 1981 of Alasdair Gray's novel *Lanark*.[3]

Much has happened since that watershed and, indeed, since the rejuvenation of Scottish writing described in Wallace and Stevenson's collection of critical essays (1993). The political climate has, of course, altered dramatically with Scotland's achievement of a devolved Parliament in May 1999, an event for which many of us demonstrated (during the meeting of the European Heads of Government in Edinburgh, December 1992), with hope rather than belief in its happening. In terms of writing, there has also been a spate of new women writers to join those who were already publishing (and who have continued to develop). Another study, Christopher Whyte's *Gendering the Nation*, published in 1995, raised interesting issues about sexuality, gender and nation, giving 'notice that Scottish texts are being read in new, disruptive and not infrequently discordant ways'.[4]

In addition, the publicaton of Gifford and McMillan's *A History of Scottish Women's Writing* (1997) has provided a literary map on which contemporary Scottish women's writing may be located, recovering a rich tradition. The study also reintroduces writers into the critical debate, as the editors themselves suggest in their introduction:

> Overall, we do feel that this volume succeeds in being celebratory in the sense that it opens up possibilities of reading: it aims to reveal and release texts, not to fix and preserve them. And above all it hopes to introduce the work of both known and forgotten writers to an audience within and far beyond Scotland.[5]

Anderson and Christianson's collection *Scottish Women's Fiction 1920s to 1960s* (2000) provides more detailed discussion of specific works by earlier twentieth-century women writers.[6] Given these developments and with these previous collections providing a cultural framework, the time is appropriate for a new collection of essays devoted to contemporary Scottish women's writing. Indeed, the increasing interest in Scottish literature and culture generally in schools (the inclusion of a compulsory Scottish text in Higher Still is a significant landmark), in universities and in the wider public sphere almost necessitates such a study.

Any work which takes as its parameters the terms 'Scottish' and 'women' must make some attempt to explain its critical paradigms. Clearly there is a sense in which both denote a degree of 'marginality', an exclusion from the dominant discourse of white male 'Britishness'. Benedict Anderson suggests a close relationship between race and gender when he writes that one of the paradoxes of theories of nationalism is that 'in the modern world everyone can, should, will "have" a nationality, as he or she "has" a gender' (although he nowhere examines the role of gender in nationhood).[7] However, we must be wary of *assuming* that peripheralisation of nation can be straightforwardly equated with that of gender. Anderson argues that 'Communities are to be distinguished, not by their falsity / genuineness, but by the style in which they are imagined' (6), but what is frequently interesting about the women writers discussed here is the way in which their work *cuts across* patriarchal constructions of Scotland to suggest alternative 'imaginings' or constructions of nationhood and their relationship to it than those offered by their male counterparts. Frequently, it is women writers within national cultures who seemingly disrupt homogeneity.

The notion of a study which takes as its terms of definition 'nation' and 'gender' is also problematised by post-colonial theory which calls into question the idea of nation itself, reminding us that national identities, like their boundaries, are not *essential* but simply constructed. Homi Bhabha argues: 'The very concepts of homogeneous national cultures, the consensual or contiguous transmission of historical traditions, or "organic" ethnic communities – *as the grounds of cultural comparativism* – are in a profound process of redefinition.'[8] Bhabha's thesis is exemplified by the break-up of the Soviet Union during the 1990s into smaller and smaller 'national' regions. Now that a greater degree of autonomy has been achieved in Scotland and what many would regard as the common political goal attained, what begins to emerge is a sense, or a reminder, of Scotland's own lack of homogeneity. Within its compact national boundaries there are significant geographical and cultural differences between Highland and Lowland Scotland, north-east, east and west, mainland and (diverse) islands. Helen Kidd nicely complicates the idea of 'site' and 'topos' as 'mutable and movable' in relation to Scotland's complicated regional differences, 'the site' being 'split – not into two – but into many', in her 'Writing Near the Fault Line: Scottish Women Poets and the Topography of Tongues'.[9] A question for the twenty-first century, perhaps, is how Scotland, 'this most complicated and self-ironising of nations',[10] will hold together in its devolved state.

What rationale is there, then, for a collection of essays which takes as its terms of reference contemporary Scottish women's writing? Clearly, as with all studies of Scottish Literature, there is an implication that whatever diversities may exist within Scotland itself, these writers have more in common than they would with those of another nation. Similarly, there is an assumption that as women writers they share certain agendas and influences, and interrogate the 'space' of Scotland in their own way. This book places contemporary Scottish women writers together with the understanding that while the terms 'Scottish' and 'women' may be fluid and, to a degree, problematic, nevertheless these categories contain potential as paradigms in which to consider these writers' work.

With an awareness of the problems attached to its terms of reference, then, the aim of this book has been to employ them eclectically. When deciding who should be discussed in this collection, 'Scottishness' has been interpreted in the widest possible sense; writers who live and work within Scotland and who engage directly with its parameters in their work – Janice Galloway and Laura Hird, for example – are included, alongside those who no longer live here – Muriel Spark, Sharman Macdonald, Candia McWilliam and Ali Smith. It was also the intention of the editors that the critical approaches taken towards these writers should be wide-ranging. Several of the writers here – Dilys Rose or A. L. Kennedy, for example – resist being labelled in terms of their nationality or gender, suggesting that to them such categories are limiting. With this in mind, there was no overall mandate that contributors to this volume should address any of the writers purely in these terms. In fact, we encouraged a diversity of approach and length, rather than enforcing or attempting what might become a misleading homogeneity. Rather than 'subsuming emergent cultural differences ... under the all-overshadowing tartan umbrella of what is traditionally perceived to be truly or typically Scottish', as Schoene-Harwood puts it, we hope that these chapters can be 'read and appreciated as contributions to the heterogeneous canons of feminist, gay ... or working-class literatures written in English'.[11] However, several of the chapters do take a paradigm of nation or gender at least as a starting point of their discussions. The results are often fruitful, foregrounding concerns in the work of these women writers that might otherwise have gone unrecognised (or have been underemphasised).

In spite of attempts to be eclectic, a book such as this is also governed by what is possible. While it was the intention of the editors to include chapters on several other writers, this proved difficult for a variety of reasons. Gaps and omissions, if inevitable, are still noticeable. Writing in Gaelic is considered, as one of Scotland's three languages, only in Chapter 1, 'Scottish Women's Poetry 1972–1999', and those Gaelic writers available in parallel texts have also been listed in the 'Selective Bibliography of Other Scottish Women Writers'. This results partly from the fact that those critics who are fluent in Gaelic and English may choose not to contribute, but it also reflects an acceptance by the editors, Scots- and English- but not Gaelic-speaking, that an honest representation of current writing in two of the languages in Scotland is better than a token addition of a further chapter on contemporary Gaelic women's writing, perhaps repeating what Meg Bateman has already well discussed in 'Poetry in the Modern Idiom', in her 'Women's Writing in Scottish Gaelic since 1750'.[12]

Other omissions result from the fact that a planned chapter has not come to fruition. We had intended that the writers Margaret Elphinstone and Ellen Galford would be considered in what has become a ghost chapter on Scottish fantasy. Elphinstone, in her critical article 'Contemporary Feminist Fantasy in the Scottish Literary Tradition',[13] draws attention to the problems of situating her own novels generically and also to the subversive possibilities in the feminist fantasies of Sian Hayton's fiction (also unrepresented; for their novels, see 'Selective Bibliography'). All three are writers who, as adults, came to Scotland from English and North American backgrounds but whose writing engages with Scotland. Both Galford and Elphinstone use fantasy to discuss Scottish reality, and placing Galford's novels within genre is also difficult. Galford has talked of the difficulties bookshops have with physically situating her novels: Scottish, lesbian, Jewish, fantasy, political satire, historical fiction – there is no bookshelf category encompassing them all.[14] All of Galford's fiction comes from the refreshing perspective of lesbian as norm, her narrators time-travelling, sceptical and chatty. Her two novels set in Scotland, *The Fires of Bride* and *Queendom Come*, contain satirical interrogations of attitudes to religion, sexuality and gender and all her novels are radical in their sweep and flexibility. It is the accident of her birth in New Jersey which seems to prevent her being read as a Scottish writer, when many of her concerns, in fact, place her within contemporary Scottish cultural contexts.

Elphinstone discusses the paradox of writing her early fiction as pastiche or as 'about where I live' yet having it published and reviewed as science fiction or as Scottish fantasy. Placing herself within a Scottish critical tradition, she writes of having used Gregory Smith's model of the 'polar twins of the Scottish Muse'.[15] She now voices more overtly feminist connections:

> I totally part company with my former self. But then, ten years ago I hadn't read Cixous ... what she did do for me was put me off hierarchical binary oppositions for life. Away with this real / fantastical juxtaposition! Life is infinitely more complicated than that, and all I can say these days, when I look at the fantastic in my own writing, is that since no paradigm of reality ever does add up, I don't bother too much about boundaries ... my rejection of anti-syzygies in any shape or form is that they imply a really boring fixed boundary between one state and another, whereas to me one of the interesting things about fiction is that it avoids having to establish set differences between fact and imagination, or evidence and truth.[16]

A critique of binary, oppositional modes is also recurrent in several of the chapters in this collection, as they interrogate ideas of what Jackie Kay calls 'inherent contradiction'. Lumsden, for example, foregrounds Kay's wish to embrace difference – 'contain both things, being Black and being Scottish'[17] – while Christianson believes Spark's work provides positive conjunctions between the apparently incompatible.

Shena Mackay, born in Scotland but raised and educated in England, is another missing writer. While her fiction is generally set in south-east England, her novel *Dunedin* (1992) and short stories *The Laughing Academy* (1993) both gained Scottish Arts Council awards. Her work is present in Scottish collections,[18] and she is classified as an 'Anglo-Scot' by Flora Alexander.[19] Her recurring interest in border-crossings, the significance of the past, and the nature of identity is most notable in *Dunedin*, the opening and closing sections of which focus on a group of Scottish settlers in early twentieth-century New Zealand. Her intensely visual prose frequently concerns temporal and cultural borderlands, possibly linking her work to Scottish traditions; her sharply satirical wit invites comparisons with Muriel Spark. But she remains very much herself, both illustrating and exploring the slipperiness of identity. Her relationship to Scottish literature seems less certain than that of Spark, Elspeth Barker or Candia McWilliam, all of whom are discussed in this book.[20]

In the chapters on writers who have been discussed, several points clearly emerge. First of all, what is apparent is the volume of work by Scottish women writers today. Indeed, so great is this volume that the general chapters – on poetry, on drama and on short stories – have had, by necessity, to be selective. What also emerges is that contemporary Scottish women writers are offering both a continuity with past tradition and a break from it, Carol Anderson's chapter on female Gothic neatly illustrating this relationship. Similarly, several of the chapters also suggest where they overlap today with their male counterparts and where they diverge; for example, Lynne Stark's discussion of Agnes Owens. What perhaps is most notable about Scottish women writers today is their diversity; they write in a number of styles and genres and take as their subject-matter a wide variety of themes. Such a body of work means, similarly, that it is impossible to write critically of this work in only one way. There is 'no one version',[21] either of women's writing in Scotland today or of critical response to it.

Such multiplicity within Scottish women's writing is encouraging and exciting. There is, inevitably, a varying range of talent represented in this book but only time can tell who of these writers will consolidate their current reputations by achieving enduring aesthetic as well as cultural value. For now, it is important to celebrate the plurality within Scottish women's writing. We hope that this diversity will equally be embraced within the new Scotland. Kathleen Jamie wrote her poem 'Lucky Bag' for the hoarding around the new Museum of Scotland (that container of disparate artefacts of Scottish cultural history) as it was being built in Edinburgh, 1997–8. The poem incorporates many versions of representative Scottishness and ends:

> yer Scottish lucky-bag, one for each wean;
> please form an orderly   rabble.[22]

May its celebratory inclusiveness represent the spirit in which these chapters are offered.

Notes

1. William Findlay, 'Interview with Margaret Atwood', *Cencrastus*, no. 1 (Autumn 1979), pp. 2–6 (4).
2. Liz Lochhead, 'Five Berlin Poems', *Bagpipe Muzak* (Harmondsworth: Penguin, 1991), p. 78.
3. Wallace, 'Introduction', in Gavin Wallace and Randall Stevenson (eds), *The Scottish Novel since the Seventies: New Visions, Old Dreams* (Edinburgh: Edinburgh University Press, 1993), pp. 1–7 (3).
4. Christopher Whyte (ed.), *Gendering the Nation Studies in Modern Scottish Literature* (Edinburgh: Edinburgh University Press, 1995), p. xvi.
5. Douglas Gifford and Dorothy McMillan, 'Introduction', in Gifford and McMillan (eds), *A History of Scottish Women's Writing* (Edinburgh: Edinburgh University Press, 1997), p. xxii. The 716 pages of this collection are the best response to William Findlay's view that 'there are and have been very few women writers in Scotland' (1979; see note 1).
6. Carol Anderson and A. Christianson (eds), *Scottish Women's Fiction 1920s to 1960s: Journeys into Being* (East Linton: Tuckwell Press, 2000). The writers are Catherine Carswell, Rebecca West, Nan Shepherd, Willa Muir, Nancy Brysson Morrison, Naomi Mitchison, Jessie Kesson and Muriel Spark.
7. Benedict Anderson, *Imagined Communities* (1983; London: Verso, 1991), p. 5; see also A. Christianson, 'Imagined Corners to Debatable Land: Passable Boundaries', *Scottish Affairs*, 17 (Autumn 1996), pp. 120–34 (121).

8. Homi K. Bhabha, *The Location of Culture* (London and New York: Routledge, 1994), p. 5.
9. In Vicki Bertram (ed.), *Kicking Daffodils Twentieth-Century Women Poets* (Edinburgh: Edinburgh University Press, 1997), pp. 95–110 (95, 95–7).
10. Candia McWilliam, 'All the Dead Dears', *Sunday Review. Independent on Sunday*, 17 September 1995, p. 32.
11. Berthold Schoene-Harwood, '"Emerging as the Others of Our Selves" – Scottish Multiculturalism and the Challenge of the Body in Postcolonial Representation', *Scottish Literary Journal*, 25.1 (May 1998), pp. 54–72 (55).
12. In Gifford and McMillan (eds) (1997), pp. 659–76 (667–75).
13. Margaret Elphinstone, 'Contemporary Feminist Fantasy in the Scottish Literary Tradition', in Caroline Gonda (ed.), *Tea and Leg-Irons: New Feminist Readings from Scotland* (London: Open Letters, 1992), pp. 44–59.
14. 'Mythdemeanours: Celtic Twilights and Lesbian Dawns', in 'Myths and Peripheries: The Hidden Ot(her) in Scottish Literature', MLA session, December 1993, Toronto, Canada.
15. Elphinstone, p. 48; G. Gregory Smith, *Scottish Literature Character and Influence* (London: Macmillan, 1919), p. 20.
16. Letter to editors (13 December 1999) about her most recent novel, *The Sea Road* (Edinburgh: Canongate, 2000).
17. Gillean Somerville-Arjat and Rebecca E. Wilson (eds), *Sleeping with Monsters* (Edinburgh: Polygon, 1990), p. 121.
18. For example, Harry Ritchie (ed.), *New Scottish Writing* (London: Bloomsbury, 1996).
19. 'Contemporary Fiction III: The Anglo-Scots', in Gifford and McMillan (eds) (1997), pp. 630–40. Emma Tennant, Alison Fell, Sara Maitland and Candia McWilliam are the other 'Anglo-Scots' discussed.
20. These thoughts on Mackay are from a conversation with Carol Anderson, for which thanks.
21. Margaret Laurence, *The Diviners* (Toronto: McClelland & Stewart, New Canadian Library, 1978), p. 350; cited in Coral Ann Howells, *Private and Fictional Words Canadian Women Novelists of the 1970s and 1980s* (London: Methuen, 1987), p. 10.
22. Kathleen Jamie, *Jizzen* (London: Picador, 1999), p. 42.

PART ONE

Contemporary Scottish Women Poets and Playwrights

CHAPTER ONE

Scottish Women's Poetry 1972–1999: Transforming Traditions

Margery Palmer McCulloch

You called me a poet ... but no man ever said I was a poet.[1]

This chapter explores poetry by women writing in all three of Scotland's languages – English, Scots and Gaelic – in the final quarter of the twentieth century, from the publication of Liz Lochhead's *Memo for Spring* in 1972 to Kate Clanchy's *Samarkand* in 1999.[2] The focus is primarily on poets living and working in Scotland although expatriate writers such as Clanchy and Carol Ann Duffy are also included. The chapter is divided into three sections, corresponding approximately with the birth dates of the writers and the three decades from the 1970s. Since Liz Lochhead, Jackie Kay and Kathleen Jamie are discussed elsewhere, their work will be given only passing mention here. Lochhead is, however, inevitably a presence throughout, since she has been an influential mould-breaker in so many ways from 1972 until the present, anticipating with *Memo for Spring* the feminist discourses of the later 1970s.

Whose Tradition? Which Tradition?: Poetry in the 1970s

Among reasons advanced for the relative absence of women from poetry in the past has been the 'high art' nature of poetry itself, its privileging of literary language and forms which contrasted with women's domestic lives and lack of higher education. In addition, romanticism gave the poet a transcendent, universal status, the lyric voice traditionally being a male one. How, then, could a woman, to whom society had allocated a private role, aspire to the public voice of the poet? And when, in our century in particular, she has so aspired, what language is she to use; whose tradition is she to follow? Such questions have been prominent in feminist literary discourse from the 1970s onwards and in Scotland they are complicated by the fact that there are three languages and at least three literary traditions to be considered.

My first group of English-language poets, who, like Lochhead, began to publish in the 1970s, are transitional writers. All university-educated, they chose to use existing models, modifying them where necessary for their own purposes, rather than to break openly with the predominantly male poetry tradition which they had, understandably, internalised and learned from.

Janet Caird (b. 1913) is the oldest of these writers and perhaps the least well-known to a contemporary readership. She is interesting for the way in which education and literary influences from an earlier period have interacted with female experience in our own time to produce a distinctive poetry. Born in Malawi, Caird was educated at Edinburgh University, the Sorbonne in Paris and the University of Grenoble; she began to publish poetry only in her sixties. Like many women of her generation, she did not consider herself a feminist in' present-day terms and her education enabled her to enjoy intellectual and artistic pursuits alongside her domestic responsibilities. Yet her poetry is informed by an awareness of the restrictions under which women have lived and to some extent still live. Caird studied literature under Sir Herbert Grierson at a time contemporary with modernism and this influence can be seen in her work. Her poems are short in length, economical in statement and image; it is a poetry which has the intensity and concentration of Pound's *imagism*, yet which encourages the reader to make the leap beyond the concrete visual image to the 'message' within. In 'Red Tulips', for example, the poem's speaker, asked why she always chooses red tulips for her jug and garden, tells of her childhood home with its 'bed of red tulips, / and a small girl for whom they, / warm in sunlight, / were the most beautiful things she had ever seen'. And then come the final lines: 'This was before the world shook, / and a chasm split her landscape'.[3] Carol Ann Duffy has written that 'all childhood is an emigration',[4] but here the imagery seems to speak of an emotional rupture between childhood and adulthood which is especially critical for a female child. The tree imagery of 'Bonsai' speaks of a restricted existence for the adult woman: 'Roots clipped; / branches bound; / cherished and manipulated' she now 'sits in the parlour among old china cups, / and sees through the window-pane / the trees of the forest march on the sky-line'.[5] Caird's late entry into poetry has also allowed her to explore the experience of growing old. In 'Ageing', the metaphor is that of the cat 'laying a lethargic paw over fingers, / brushing fur across eyes' but whose 'claws dig deep / and the bite is mortal' (*Narrow Path*, 9). 'Time's meanest jest' is 'to leave the will but lock away the tools / for making' (*John Donne*, 17). There is a philosophical framework behind all her poems. In 'John Donne, You Were Wrong ...', her perception is that essentially 'we are all islands', our human relationships 'lighthouses, beacons, [which] criss-cross the dark ... small skiffs beached on the shingle [which] must soon drift on / under the tyranny of the tide' (*John Donne*, 50). Caird's poetry is a good example of how a woman born in an earlier period, fortunate to have the kind of education which made her at ease with poetic forms developed by a male poetry tradition, has been able to use these forms in a more feminist age, adapting them to deal with present-day concerns.

Adapting existing poetic forms has been the practice also of Tessa Ransford and Valerie Gillies. In *Sleeping with Monsters*, Ransford comments that a passion for ideas has been the inspiration for her poetry, but ideas have to find an 'objective correlative' in order to be transformed into poetry.[6] She believes strongly that poets are not 'born' but that they have to learn their craft, one of the reasons behind the School of Poets which she started on her return from Pakistan in 1968. Her language studies at university introduced her to the poetry of Rilke and Hölderlin and her own practice was to imitate these poets and English poets she admired such as Donne, Hopkins and Lawrence, learning much in particular from the translations she made of Hölderlin. She has a clear view of the kind of poet she thinks she is: meditative, contemplative, not visual – 'I'm not good at remembering details of things I've seen. It's more the analogy I'm looking for.' And unlike Lochhead and many of the younger poets: 'I tend to write about myself. I'm not very good at projecting myself into other people' (*Monsters*, 194–5).

Ransford is therefore very much a poet in an age of transition, ambitious to be recognised as a poet, aware of the obstacles women have to face in the attempt to enter poetry and yet drawn by training and personal psychology to write in the tradition of male poets who appeal to her intellect and her sense of the importance of philosophical contemplation. Her meditative poems could be seen as belonging with the work of Edwin Muir who also was deeply influenced by Hölderlin. Later collections such as *Medusa Dozen* (1994) and *When It Works It Feels Like Play* (1998) show the impact of feminism, with the latter in particular bringing together generations of female experience and exploring in a fresh way the relationship between motherhood and artistic creativity.[7]

Several of the poems in Valerie Gillies's first collection *Each Bright Eye* were meditations on her experience of India when studying at the University of Mysore.[8] Others remembered her childhood at her grandfather's farm – 'a kind of adult life in miniature' (*Monsters*, 54). From the first, however, one has a strong sense of an everyday speaking voice in Gillies's poetry as opposed to a literary voice. Gillies is clear she does not want to be categorised as a 'female poet', but does not seem to have thought acutely about the implications of gender in poetry:

> there's neither man nor woman, there's only the maker … I like to think there are things I've written where you wouldn't know whether it was a woman or a man writing, and then there are other things, to do with children, or love poems. Yet men write poems about children as well … I suppose I've a lot of male heroes in my poems. (*Monsters*, 56)

Ironically, some of the best poems in her first collection are about her children or that most female of occupations, 'Shopping', while 'Infertility Patient' in *Sleeping with Monsters* (58–9) is powerful. Later collections such as *The Ringing Rock* (1995) contain poems of landscape and estuary, sharply observed and communicated.[9] Gillies is interested in making connections between poetry and other art-forms and collaborates with visual artist Will Maclean and clarsach player and composer Savourna Stevenson.

For poets such as Sheena Blackhall and Ellie McDonald, on the other hand, *tradition* means the Scots-language poetry tradition of the north-east. Blackhall and McDonald are both aware that they come from a strong Scots-language heritage, a heritage in which women have for centuries played a public role in the transmission of poetry. They also are therefore hostile to terminology such as 'woman poet'. Blackhall comments: 'I find my hackles go straight up when people write "poetess". I don't want to be judged as a woman. I hate that. ... And when people say, "Oh, woman writer", it's as if they're making allowances for you.' McDonald agrees: 'I don't believe in female poets and male poets. Creativity's a thing in itself. I feel as close to a male poet as I would to a female poet.' Feminism does not mean much to McDonald either: 'I've never had any problem with this feminist issue. ... In the area I belong to in Dundee, women have always been very strong.' Blackhall, however, seems more aware of the obstacles faced by her generation: 'And people would say: "Why do you want to do this art-thing, you'll just get married and have kids?" ... In some ways you envy men, who aren't similarly encumbered' (*Monsters*, Blackhall, 188–90; McDonald, 143).

So far as her poetry in Scots is concerned, Blackhall unexpectedly talks of her interest in the surrealist paintings of René Magritte and of the 'power and mystery inherent in the image'. She thinks 'in images as opposed to words. There's very little dialogue in my mind' (*Monsters*, 185, 184). In poetry, then, it's the image, the 'colour' of words, their rhythms and onomatopoeic sounds which interest her, rather than the attempt to communicate ideas through language. We see this in the many 'praise poems' she has written for different areas of the north-east countryside, thus fulfilling a traditional poetic role. 'Allt Darrarie – Burn of the Stunning Noise, Glen Muick', for example, is a north-east companion to MacDiarmid's 'Water Music':

> Slaverin, slubberin, gibberin, gabberin,
> Roon wi a wallop, a sklyter, a sweel,
> Yonder's the burn – in its bairnhood, it's blabberin –
> Heich-lowpin puddock, wi virr in its heel![10]

Other poems such as 'Pastoral' and 'Land Hunger' re-create in poetry the struggle with the land given narrative form in Lewis Grassic Gibbon's *Sunset Song*: 'Oh lan – ye hae bled the reid frae his cheeks, / Ye've rypit his pooches o siller, / Ye've bladded his bride ...' (*Stagwyse*, 6). Some of her earliest poems draw on the ballad tradition; 'Lost Youth' in particular is evocative of Marion Angus's reworking of the ballads.

Although they share a tradition, Ellie McDonald's poetry has to my ears a more contemporary 'ring' than Blackhall's. She began writing poetry in the early 1970s during creative writing classes at Dundee University when poet-in-residence Anne Stevenson encouraged her to write in Scots and to read everything she could that was written in Scots. 'That was a revelation'. McDonald did not come from a well off background but 'there was always an interest in poetry in the house'. She is a cultural nationalist, well aware that she is writing in a threatened language: 'the more I can write, the more I can communicate this language to other people. I'm not just doing it for poetry, but doing something for my own language' (*Monsters*, 141, 143). Despite her identification with tradition and her dismissal of feminism, however, she is aware that she is what Jessie Kesson called an 'ootlin'[11]:

> I've always wanted to write a poem about being different from other people, because if you're creative you are different. One of the greatest things for me was when I met Anne [Stevenson] and moved in among people who were creative. For the first time in my life I felt I belonged. (*Monsters*, 142)

She is hesitant about the current fashion for poetry readings, believing that 'the real message' is 'on the page'. Yet her own poetry is full of musicality and the *sound* of the speaking voice.

MacDiarmid is both one of her heroes – 'MacDiarmid broke the biggest barrier ever for Scots, probably since Fergusson and Burns' (*Monsters*, 142, 143) – and a presence in her poetry, which, like his own poetry, seems able to move unforcedly between the everyday and the cosmic. 'Sang o Joy' with its repeated phrases and rhythmic intensity has resonances of 'In the Hedge-Back'; 'Wudden Dream', 'The Gangan Fuit' and 'Fairans' evoke the lyrical passages and ballad imitations of *A Drunk Man Looks at the Thistle*, although McDonald's speaker in the celebratory 'Fairans' seems less anguished by 'houghmagandie' than the Drunk Man appears to be. In a different mode, 'Soliloquy: eftir the suddron o Wm Shakespeare' is a fine rendering of Hamlet's 'To be or not to be' which has the strength of Alexander Scott's translations from Anglo-Saxon poetry, and her version of Act III, scene i of *A Midsummer Night's Dream* leaves one hungry for more of 'Birky Bottom'. *The Gangan Fuit* also includes ironic poems on environmental improvement[12] – 'Naethan for it but the demolition squad, / Hard hats an sledge hemmers'; and on the disappearance of Dundee's industrial heritage in 'Jute Mill Sang', where there is no nostalgia and not much that is positive in past or present:

> Naebody kens whit's tae be pitten in its place,
> naebody greets for its demise.
> An stour blaws frae the houkit out wame o't
> sclairtan the cars an buses that birl awa
> tae concrete fields o spacelessness.

'Renoir: Luncheon of the Boating Party' is a witty mixture of perspectives: on the one hand, the woman in the street's view, treating art as if it were life – 'Sic slaisters, yon table wi bottles / a glesses aa owre the place. / In the efternuin tae if ye plais. … An men in thir semmits …'; on the other hand, the sophisticated art watcher who is into 'conceptual art' and knows that painting *per se* is out of fashion: 'Guid joab for Renoir he dee'd whan he did. / They widnae tak thon for the Tate. / Nae chance' (*Gangan Fuit*, 37, 36, 15).

McDonald is an accomplished, versatile poet. Her problem is lack of productivity. Although she began writing in the 1970s, it was not until 1991
that a collection of her work was put together and her output is, as she herself
acknowledges, meagre: 'maybe 30 poems I've kept in fifteen years' (*Monsters*,
144). Yet, in regard to the need to transform Scots-language poetry to meet
the conditions of the modern world while keeping contact with the traditions
of the past, McDonald's poetry has much to offer.

Thirdly, there is the Gaelic tradition, represented here in translation by Catriona
Montgomery (Catriona NicGumaraid) and her 1994 collection *The Length of the
Night* (*Re Na H-Oidhche*).[13] Like the other poets in this section, Montgomery first
began publishing in the early 1970s. She is a language loyalist, aware of the
severe threat Gaelic is under and aware of the problems that being forcibly educated in English has brought for Gaelic speakers, as it has for Scots. Her poems
include love poems, poems about the natural world, about her concern for the
loss of language, about human suffering. These are strong poems, strong in their
musicality and human relevance. They are not nostalgic, although the legacy of
the islands is celebrated and there is anger at its loss. There is savage irony in her
presentation of a contemporary, impoverished Highland chieftain appealing to
the American descendants of crofters evicted by his ancestors in 'To the American MacDonalds', while 'Tigrean Woman's Prayer' is a powerful lament inspired
by newpaper reports of famine and war in Africa, its intensity coming from a
poet whose history includes the Clearances and the laments of mothers under a
more northerly sky. Her own personal sense of displacement is communicated in
the poem to her daughter Eilidh:

> I thought that I would have you
> midst rock, sea-wrack and glen
> and that you would learn Diarmid's language
> fluently from myself
> not here: in this east city
>
> (*Length*, 21)

But there's celebration in 'Spring 1980' where she reports Eilidh's progress:

> step
>   by
>   step
> and learning to speak.
>
> (*Length*, 21)

This is a modern woman's voice but, as with the Scots-language tradition,
there is no certainty that conditions will allow it to multiply.

'Writing Woman' in the 1980s

Despite the variety and quality of the poetry discussed above, younger women
have on the whole followed Lochhead's break with the male Scottish poetic

tradition. Lochhead has said of her early poetry: 'My country was woman'[14] and *Memo for Spring*, which pre-dates the feminist theorising of the later 1970s, is a collection distinguished by its focus on female experience. Her third collection, *The Grimm Sisters*, written after a period in Canada on a Scottish Arts Council Exchange Fellowship and in greater consciousness of feminist debates taking place in North America and Britain, operated through revisiting and refashioning of fairy-tales, myths and ballad stories in order to interrogate accepted social commonplaces with regard to female experience, a process continued in *Dreaming Frankenstein*.[15] Lochhead's poetry therefore offered a radical departure from the forms of previous Scottish poetry. In the early 1970s, however, she was on the whole a lone voice, although Catherine Lucy Czerkawska's 1976 collection *A Book of Men and Other Poems*[16] shows awareness of the need 'to coldly turn about and see inside me'. The poem 'Being Me' is the most radical in Czerkawska's collection, challenging through its imagery the accepted view that 'roughly once a month' a woman is not herself (*Men*, 5, 10).

It is, however, with the generation of writers born in the later 1950s and beginning to publish in the 1980s that we find a more sustained attempt to follow Lochhead by openly 'writing woman'. Much of this writing came from women gathering together in poetry workshops and was published in anthologies such as *Hens in the Hay* and *Fresh Oceans* by Stramullion and the Polygon series of *Original Prints*.[17] The 1980s was the decade of female anthologies, culminating in the publication of Catherine Kerrigan's important *Anthology of Scottish Women Poets* in 1991.[18]

Apart from Lochhead herself, the most sustained and successful attempts to 'write woman', thematically and formally, in this 1980s' period are by Elizabeth Burns and Carol Ann Duffy. Burns has said that she is 'interested in the question of an identity for women working in what has been the mainly male domain of Scottish poetry' and in 'the idea of an unwritten history, of trying to recover, or rediscover, things which have been lost or forgotten, perhaps because they've been seen as female and insignificant'. Linked to this is her interest in 'the unseen', the 'intuitive' ways that people communicate with one another.[19]

Burns's first solo collection *Ophelia and Other Poems* (written in the 1980s but published in 1991) opens with a poem about intuition.[20] 'Sisters' tells how 'even when she moved / five hundred miles away / telepathy was alive between them / and love as strong as ever'. The sisters send gifts which pattern and complement each other and 'even before the letter / saying, between the lines, "come", / she is on her way'. In the prose poem 'Untitled Love Poem', pauses and silences communicate that some things are directly unsayable while at the same time they speak of the difficulties involved in manipulating language itself, in writing poetry: 'words are such skimpy   scrawly creatures ... I'm left with   slippery abstracts   piling up / as far from what I want to say   as printed ovals / are from music ...' (7, 31).

The exclusion of women from public roles and records is taken up in poems such as 'Work and Art / We Are Building a Civilization' and 'The Oddity'.

The former proceeds through two companion sets of images: 'Backs aching from carrying stones / Eyes blind from straining at needles'. The speaker uses the Brechtian technique of interrogating history in order to bring out what lies hidden, unacknowledged. The construction of the buildings on the Acropolis and the flax-picking, spinning and embroidery work involved in making fine decorative cloth both involve hard, physical activity: 'Toe-bones crushed / Fingers arthritic'. Why should the one be celebrated and the other ignored, forgotten? Is it 'because white marble in sun / because hilltop / because visible / because men'? The poem questions conventional divisions between male 'art' and female 'folk art', the one preserved, the other allowed to disappear, unrecorded, 'locked away in labyrinth of backstreets'. It ends, however, with a positive image of continuity and strength, the 'skin-frail silk' of the embroidered poppies transformed to the poppies that 'every spring converge in crevices / to flower again in scarlet / through the stonework' (44–6). 'The Oddity' takes up the theme of woman as poet, 'a crooked planet [who] does not fit / in the thin universe of this house' (48). There are connections to be made here with Lochhead's 'Dreaming Frankenstein' and with the fate of Sylvia Plath who is remembered in 'At Plath's Grave': 'She the freak, the poet / buried on this moor-top / where a harsh wind scrapes the sky / cripples the trees' (53) – the wounding language emphasising her psychological wounding as well as her cruel death.

Formally, Elizabeth Burns's poetry might be seen to epitomise what has traditionally been considered *feminine*: its images are decorative, painterly; it is gently musical, its pauses and silences giving form to the intuitive connections she believes are important. Yet this is in no way conforming or self-effacing poetry. Its themes are *feminist*, although these are brought to the reader quietly and decoratively, and the strength of her message gives validation to an imagistic approach which recovers and re-presents 'femininity', a quality more often rejected in recent times as socially conditioned or domestic or dilettante, something apart from the professional world of public significance to which modern women aspire. Natural world imagery has also been regarded with some suspicion by radical feminists, concerned about implications of essentialism in regard to an association with Mother Nature; concerned too about the idea of Nature as Earth Goddess, the object of the male poet's worship. There is danger in this, certainly, although many women writers have found themselves drawn to natural world images and scenarios. In Burns's 'Going Back to Chapelton', the story of a ripening and then fading love is told through imagery of farm and kitchen garden. The love affair is beautifully caught in images of colour, sound and taste and through the flow of the lines: 'July, barefoot, she is running outside / for breathfuls of the clean breezy air that ruffles / the sycamore'; 'then there are bowlfuls of scarlet strawberries / unwashed, earthy, rough against the tongue ...They eat them by the crackle of the applewood fire / summer and winter jarring together' (12). What validates the natural world imagery in this poem is its freshness, the specific way in which delight in the garden's richness and the richness of love is communicated; and the way in which the traditional trope of summer delight and winter mourning is overturned, so that it is not the 'slack fecund laziness / of summer months' which marks the high point of the love affair, but a winter in which 'so covered by the snow of love were they ... that they never dreamt of passion's thaw' (13). In 'Mother and Child in the Botanic Gardens', the imagery of exotic plants and flowers and child reclaims the magic of the planthouses from the male public world of order and prohibition.

Carol Ann Duffy was born in Glasgow in 1955 but brought up from the age of six in England. Her poetry has had an uncompromisingly female perspective since her first collection *Standing Female Nude* of 1985 and although her work ranges more widely and is very different in character from that of Elizabeth Burns, in *Standing Female Nude* in particular, it too offers themes and forms of expression which record women's experiences from the inside, often speaking what previously has been unspeakable in poetry from a female point of view.[21] Duffy's narratives are ambiguous, elliptical, leaving the reader to piece together scraps of information, things left unsaid or not properly understood by their speakers. In 'Girl Talking', for example, the speaker is a young Muslim girl, telling of an accident to her girl cousin when sent to the miller with wheat in exchange for flour: 'Something happened. We think it was pain ... Afterwards it did not hurt, / so for a while she made chapatis'. As the poem tells of the girl's withdrawal from her friends, her sickness and bleeding beneath the mango tree, the 'something [that] was burning her stomach' (*Selected Poems*, 3), the reader suspects that the miller may have taken more than wheat from the young girl and this impression is confirmed obliquely by the washing and praying of the men, her death, the visit of the Holy Man and the warning to the other girls not to go out at noon. So economically yet intensely told, this is a powerful story of something *unspoken* by those most intimately concerned, what Elizabeth Burns called 'making what was invisible, visible through words and images' (*Dream State*, 40).

In a completely different mode, 'Standing Female Nude' is a witty debunking of the myth of the male artist and his muse, a recovery of female subjectivity, spoken by the cynical muse/model whose low register punctures the artist's pretensions: 'Six hours like this for a few francs. / Belly nipple arse in the window light, / he drains the colour from me ... The bourgeoisie will coo / at such an image of a river-whore. They call it Art'. Georges, the artist – 'They tell me he's a genius' – is not always content with Art – he 'stiffens for my warmth' and 'possesses me on canvas as he dips the brush repeatedly / into the paint'. The model, however, is quite cynical and materialistic: 'Little man, / you've not the money for the arts I sell'. And then, reclaiming her own image: 'It does not look like / me' (*Selected Poems*, 20–1).

In another variation of the 'woman writing woman' theme, 'A Clear Note' tells the story of the lives of three generations of women – mother, daughter, granddaughter – each life-story related by the woman concerned, but with daughter and granddaughter adding their comments. Two generations of unfulfilled lives are recorded here, with the granddaughter having the possibility of more personal freedom, but carrying the knowledge of her mother and grandmother's emptiness in her memory. The poem's power comes from the vitality of its contrasting images of the women, their brave, imaginative spirits and the brutishness and dullness which imprisons them. Agatha and Moll – mother and daughter – each in their own time long 'to swim in impossible seas / under the moon' but are trapped by childbearing and by the power of their insensitive husbands. All her life Agatha wanted 'the fields of Ireland only / and a man to delight in me / who'd never be finished with kisses'. Instead, she has a man who would 'come home from work and take me on the floor / with his boots on and his blue eyes shut'. The brutal, mechanical nature of the 'love' act and constant childbearing – 'Again and again throwing life from my loins / like a spider with enough rope / spinning and wringing its own neck' – breaks her spirit so that her final plea is 'don't bury him on top of me' – which, of course, the family eventually do. 'What does it matter, they said, now she's dead?' Agatha's daughter, Moll, in her turn tells her daughter: 'Never have kids. Give birth to yourself, / I wish I had', for though her husband is not brutish, he has no imagination, no conception of his wife's 'black hole of resources'. The third story is more optimistic. The granddaughter Bernadette has escaped. She has her Granny's long auburn hair and keeps her story alive in her memory. The poem ends with her sending in imagination the moon her Granny had longed for: 'For Agatha, from Bernadette, the moon' (Standing, 30, 27, 31, 29).

This poem is not overtly ideological, yet its storytelling methodology brings a powerful enactment of the political and intellectual battles of women in the past to obtain the right to live their own lives freely and to fulfil the potential within them. Bernadette's comment, 'placing her [Agatha] years away / from the things that seem natural to us' (Standing, 31), points up the fact that so much of the unhappiness in the lives of women has been caused not by something essential in the nature of women, but by the social and religious systems of a patriarchal society and also by the lack of information about contraception which has meant the inability to control fertility and so take charge of bodies and lives.

Janice Galloway has said that in The Trick Is to Keep Breathing she had to stop short Joy's exploration of her own body in the bath because she could not find words and imagery to describe the female body which had not been already compromised by male usage.[22] Duffy, on the other hand, experiments with language to express female eroticism and love-making in its own terms. In 'Till Our Face', for example: 'Whispers weave webs amongst thighs. I open / Like the reddest fruit ... Something inside me / steps on a highwire where you search crimson / for a silver thread ... Your mouth laps petals till our face / is a flower soaked in its own scent'. Here, fruit and flower imagery, colour, touch, scent, the pace of a line, the effect of a word-choice such as 'open' at the end of a line, unexpected collocations – 'whispers … webs … thighs' all combine to produce a non-explicit but highly erotic communication of a love relationship (*Standing*, 22). 'Girlfriends' (derived from Verlaine) similarly explores the creation of a sensuous, erotic imagery to express love between two women (*Selected Poems*, 85).

Carol Ann Duffy has published five solo collections and a *Selected Poems* in addition to *Standing Female Nude*. In *The Other Country* (1990) and *Mean Time* (1993),[23] she brings together mothers and daughters, childhood and the faculty of memory in an exploration of identity both personal and related to place. The theme of national identity is a commonplace of Scottish poetry, but Duffy, writing in the more mobile and culturally diverse society of the late twentieth century, shows that a satisfying sense of self and place is not easily achieved. Key poems here are 'Originally' and 'The Way My Mother Speaks'. In the former, a child's language communicates a child's confusion as the family 'came from our own country in a red room / which fell through the fields … My brothers cried, one of them bawling *Home, / Home* … I stared / at the eyes of a blind toy, holding its paw' (*Selected Poems*, 65).

As mentioned earlier, for Duffy, 'all childhood is an emigration' but, like Janet Caird in 'Red Tulips', she understands that for some this emigration can be too abrupt, too painful. Is a sense of self ever recovered? 'Do I only think / I lost a river, culture, speech, sense of first space / and the right place?' In 'The Way My Mother Speaks', the mother's voice and Scottish phraseology keep the adult woman in touch with that 'first space': '*The day and ever* [...] *What like is it?*' (*Selected Poems*, 66, 88). 'Never Go Back' shows how impossible a return to the past is: 'Never return / to the space where you left time pining till it died. [...] You shouldn't be here [...] Forget. Already / the fires and lights come on wherever you live' (*Mean Time*, 30–1). In these poems, Duffy transforms her own childhood emigration into words and images which speak more widely of the experience of displacement, chosen or forced. In showing how impossible it is to reconcile what is remembered with what now is, she also shows how fragile our personal memories of our past are, how difficult it is for *our* certainty of our childhood experience to be reconciled with what those who were then the adults tell us that experience was: 'Nobody hurt you [...] The whole thing is inside your / head / What you recall are impressions; we have the facts [...] There was none but yourself to blame if it ended in tears'. And then, 'What does it matter now?' (*Other Country*, 24). But it *does* matter. It matters that in 'A Clear Note' Agatha's brutish husband *was* buried on top of her, despite her pleas; and that, as with so many women in the past, her diary was burned after her death – 'a catalogue of hatred' – so that her question 'Who will remember me?' (*Standing*, 30, 31) might not have found an answer, had her granddaughter not listened to her mother's stories and so kept her grandmother alive in her memory. Duffy's training was in philosophy and her exploration of identity, of unrecorded lives, untrustworthy memories and lost places, with her starting point so often taken from the experience of the female child or adult, is more complex than can be discussed here. She has a deservedly high reputation in British poetry, but her success is also a marker of how far poetry by women has travelled since the early 1970s.

Looking Forward to the Millennium: The 1990s

In 'Alphabet for Auden', Duffy playfully warns: 'Verse can say *I told you so* / but cannot sway the status quo / one inch' (*Standing*, 10). Having some poetic sisters, however, can make one feel less of an oddity; and the public success of writers such as Lochhead and Duffy has encouraged others. In addition, the raising of awareness as to *why* it has been so difficult for women in the past to become poets and the changes in society which are allowing more women to assume public roles have contributed to the confidence of the 1990s. To be a woman and a poet is no longer to be an 'ootlin'.

This more positive environment is reflected by the number of new voices appearing in the 1990s. Jackie Kay, who has published several poetry collections since 1991, is one of these. Another is Kathleen Jamie, whose first collection appeared as early as 1981 when she was nineteen, but who has gained a wider reputation with *The Queen of Sheba* (1994).[24] Both writers are among the best of younger poets writing today, female or male.

Another is Angela McSeveney who came to prominence in 1992 with *Coming Out With It*.[25] In some respects McSeveney's poetry continues the 'writing woman' approach of the 1980s, but hers is a bleak view of womanhood and especially of the female body. Her poetry shows that the feminist revolution has still some way to travel. While young women can now expect to go to university, to have sexual relationships before marriage with partners of their choice, to have careers and money of their own to spend, the advertising industry and the fashion world have created images of new womanhood which, for those who do not fit the stereotype, can be as psychologically debilitating as the previous restrictions of a patriarchal society. Lochhead's speaker in 'Fat Girl's Confession' had sufficient confidence in herself to laugh off 'Fat is a Feminist Issue', as she 'ravished the refrigerator' even while huffing and puffing in her 'Stephanie Bowman Sweat-It-Off Slimmersuit',[26] but McSeveney's girls are more vulnerable. Poems such as 'My breasts / walk ahead of me', 'Stretch Marks', 'The Fat Nymphomaniac's Poem' all communicate the psychological distress of the fat girl in a slimness-obsessed society where the Hollywood big-breasted heroine is out of fashion. The speaker in 'An Ugly Lover' cannot believe it when a man 'claimed' to love her: 'always I am wondering / what blow are you softening me for − / where will it fall?' (*Coming Out*, 56). For this poet, 'writing the body' also means writing about illnesses or bodily functions which are specific to women, and which, even though talked about more openly in contemporary society, still arouse fear: the 15-year-old's discovery of a lump in her breast in 'The Lump' – 'My life rose up in my throat / and threatened to stifle me'; the monthly ritual in 'Breast Exam' which all women are now encouraged to carry out, but which leaves one permanently with a latent fear of discovery – 'It can't always happen to other people'. Pregnancy is not the idealised mother and child of the advertising world but 'a maze of scars / on my mother's belly ... Three years gave back only corpses / for her trauchle' (*Coming Out*, 23, 60, 26).

McSeveney's writing style is bleak, like much of her content. She has said that this 'bare' style was developed during her university years when she was psychologically ill and trying to get to grips with her problem 'on the page'. Just as Lochhead said that she would not have needed to write some of her poems had she been able to read the feminist writings of the later 1970s, so McSeveney says that if she had had a psychiatrist in time, she 'wouldn't have been writing' her poems.[27] This might suggest that McSeveney's poetry is 'therapy', not poetry proper, but such a view would ignore the gap between, to rephrase Eliot, the woman who suffers and the mind which creates, the transforming which happens in poetry.[28] McSeveney acknowledges that many of her readers assume that 'the person in the poem is me always', but she herself is insistent that there must be an imaginative input, that a poem has not 'landed flat on the page ready made' (*Talking Verse*, 131). When one examines her poems closely they are carefully and imaginatively constructed. In 'I'm Unemployed', for example, the prosaic two-line stanzas pattern the emptiness of the speaker's situation just as the choice of the word 'erased' is exactly right for what unemployment has done to her. The incongruity of her comparison to 'a bluebottle in the ointment' communicates the otherness of her situation as seen by the public official, the nasty 'stickiness' of the problem she represents. There are no 'prearranged pigeonholes' in which her 'wavering outline' can fit (*Coming Out*, 38). Another kind of erasing is documented in 'Janey'. In contrast to Duffy's poem 'Girl Talking' where the child abuse is communicated obliquely, here it is stated abruptly at the outset of the poem: 'She was raped when she was seven'. The absence of rhythmic flow in the stanzas patterns the cutting-off of Janey's life – 'After that she didn't grow' – which is emphasised also through the only simile: 'sitting quiet / like a wee doll'. She is no longer a person. The poem is a complex of contradictory responses: the mother's self-defensive laughter; the unspoken worry about what can be done with her; the undisguised relief when she dies at sixteen of Spanish flu and the doctor's pragmatic comment – 'It's a happy release for her ... He should have murdered her too' (*Coming Out*, 53). One is horrified by the way, as in Duffy's poem, the adults further the abuse by trying to push it and the girl out of their lives. Who cares about Janey? Only the poet, it would appear, who uses her name five times in this short poem, thus giving her back her human identity.

There is also an awareness of dislocation between memories of childhood and the reality of the adult world in McSeveney's scenarios. For her speakers, too, childhood has been a painful emigration, as in the poem 'Gone Wrong':

> But in the back of my mind
> a child persists.
> 'Don't blame me', she says
> [...]
> What are you doing Woman?
> I've been a disappointment in you.
>
> (*Coming Out*, 77)

In a more positive poem, 'The Freedom', that disappointing woman recovers some equilibrium as, taking off her glasses before going into the swimming pool, she 'sashay[s] from the shower room', enjoying her body like the 'fat black woman' in the poems of Grace Nichols, one of McSeveney's heroines (*Coming Out*, 65).

Angela McSeveney contributes a strong new voice to English-language poetry in the 1990s, as does Kate Clanchy, whose *Slattern* was published to much acclaim in 1995 – a young woman's book about relationships where women call the tune: 'I put them all at sea'.[29] This is witty, clever poetry, turning the historical tables. Clanchy expands her theme register in *Samarkand* (1999), although the 'men' poems are there also. In both collections she writes with elegance and with a teasing, often complex imagery which is very much of the contemporary world.

The situation of poetry in Scots and Gaelic is less assured. There would appear to be few younger writers following after Blackhall and McDonald or, in the Gaelic context, Catriona Montgomery. In the 1980s Meg Bateman wrote some fine poetry in Gaelic but has temporarily stopped writing. A younger Gaelic writer is Anne Frater, whose poems are included in the Polygon *Dream State* anthology. Frater's love of her language and the wish to see it survive is a strong motivation behind her poetry. It is not certain, however, how many new poets will join her. Two newcomers in Scots are Alison Kermack from Frater's generation and Christine de Luca who belongs with the middle group of writers discussed, but whose poems in Shetland dialect and English were collected in 1994 and 1997.[30] Her Shetland Scots is dense and richly onomatopoeic, pulling the reader or listener into stories of Viking landfalls and everyday expeditions such as 'Gyaain fur da mylk' and 'Paet Wark'. The poems of ideas and the contemporary world are, however, in *English*. For all its interest, this is a poetry of 'idder times' (*Valkyries*, 41).

In contrast, Alison Kermack's demotic Scots poetry is contemporary and ideological, following Tom Leonard's *Intimate Voices* in breaking down 'thi langwij hyrarky' and showing 'how itz dafty say wun wurdz mare impoartint thin anuthir wurd ur wun way i speekinz mare impoartint thin anuther wy' (*Dream State*, 192).[31] Her poems are clever and often amusing in the way demotic phonetic spellings throw up new relationships between words, new implications. There are serious political points to be made in poems such as 'Saltire', 'The Shadow Minister' and the feminist 'Askinfurrit'. Ultimately, however, there is a danger that Kermack's approach remains restrictive.

Scottish women, young and older, now use a new-found confidence in their gender to produce mature poetry which is diverse in theme and style. It is not the 'informationist' poetry of the younger male poets, nor poetry which plays intellectually with language registers. It does not fight over old battle-grounds of religion and national identity, although it has concern for personal identity and sense of place and the natural world is among its imagery. This new poetry, in its variety, is socially grounded in that it is concerned with the conditions under which people live their lives and with the qualities which make us human. It also provides a narrative of the changes which have taken place in women's lives during this century. Literary traditions, at least, have been permanently transformed.

Notes

1. Margaret Elphinstone, 'To My Friend who Is a Woman and a Poet, Like Me', *Fresh Oceans* (Edinburgh: Stramullion, 1989), p. 29.
2. Liz Lochhead, *Memo for Spring* (Edinburgh: Reprographia, 1972); reprinted in Lochhead, *Dreaming Frankenstein and Collected Poems* (Edinburgh: Polygon, 1984). Kate Clanchy, *Samarkand* (London: Picador, 1999).
3. Janet Caird, *John Donne You Were Wrong* (Edinburgh: Ramsay Head Press, 1988), p. 27.
4. Carol Ann Duffy, *Selected Poems* (Harmondsworth: Penguin, 1994), p. 65.
5. Janet Caird, *Some Walk a Narrow Path* (Edinburgh: Ramsay Head Press, 1977), p. 42.
6. Tessa Ransford in Gillean Somerville-Arjat and Rebecca E. Wilson (eds), *Sleeping with Monsters* (Edinburgh: Polygon, 1990), pp. 193–200.
7. Tessa Ransford, *Medusa Dozen and Other Poems* (Edinburgh: Ramsay Head Press, 1994); *When It Works It Feels Like Play* (Edinburgh: Ramsay Head Press, 1998).
8. Valerie Gillies, *Each Bright Eye*; *Selected Poems 1971–1976* (Edinburgh: Canongate, 1977).
9. Valerie Gillies, *The Ringing Rock* (Aberdeen: Scottish Cultural Press, 1995).
10. Sheena Blackhall, *Stagwyse: Selected Poems by Sheena Blackhall* (Aberdeen: Charles Murray Memorial Trust, 1995), p. 15.
11. Jessie Kesson in interview with Isobel Murray and Bob Tait, in Isobel Murray (ed.), *Scottish Writers Talking* (East Linton: Tuckwell Press, 1996), p. 74.
12. Ellie McDonald, *The Gangan Fuit* (Edinburgh: Chapman, 1991); H. MacDiarmid, 'In the Hedge-Back', in M. Grieve and W. R. Aitken (eds), *The Complete Poems of Hugh MacDiarmid* (Harmondsworth: Penguin, 1985), vol. 1, pp. 25–6; H. MacDiarmid, *A Drunk Man Looks at the Thistle*, ibid., vol. 1, pp. 81–167.
13. Catriona Montgomery (Catriona NicGumaraid), *The Length of the Night (Re Na H-Oidhche)* (Edinburgh: Canongate, 1994).
14. Colin Nicholson, 'Knucklebones of Irony Liz Lochhead', in his *Poem, Purpose and Place Shaping Identity in Contemporary Scottish Verse* (Edinburgh: Polygon, 1992), p. 223.

15. Liz Lochhead, *Grimm Sisters* (London: New Editions in Association with Faber, 1981); reprinted in *Dreaming Frankenstein*.
16. Catherine Lucy Czerkawska, *A Book of Men and Other Poems* (Preston: Akros, 1976).
17. Chris Cherry, Ellen Galford, Joy Pitman, Lorna Mitchell and Stephanie Markman, *Hens in the Hay* (Edinburgh: Stramullion, 1980); *Original Prints: New Writing from Scottish Women* (Edinburgh: Polygon, 1985, 1987, 1989; 1992 edn edited by Elizabeth Burns, Sara Evans, Thelma Good and Barbara Simmons).
18. Catherine Kerrigan (ed.), *An Anthology of Scottish Women Poets* (Edinburgh: Edinburgh University Press, 1991).
19. Daniel O'Rourke (ed.), *Dream State: The New Scottish Poets* (Edinburgh: Polygon, 1994), p. 40.
20. Elizabeth Burns, *Ophelia and Other Poems* (Edinburgh: Polygon, 1991).
21. Carol Ann Duffy, *Standing Female Nude* (London: Anvil Press Poetry, 1985).
22. Janice Galloway talking to students at Glasgow University, Department of Adult and Continuing Education, October 1990.
23. Carol Ann Duffy, *Mean Time* (London: Anvil Press Poetry, 1993) and *The Other Country* (London: Anvil Press Poetry, 1990). Her most recent collection is *The World's Wife* (London: Picador, 1999).
24. Kathleen Jamie, *The Queen of Sheba* (Newcastle-upon-Tyne: Bloodaxe, 1994).
25. Angela McSeveney, *Coming Out With It* (Edinburgh: Polygon, 1992).
26. Liz Lochhead, *True Confessions* (Edinburgh: Polygon, 1985), pp. 12–13.
27. Robert Crawford, Henry Hart, David Kinloch and Richard Price (eds), *Talking Verse* (St Andrews and Williamsburg, VA: Verse, 1995), pp. 130, 131, 134, 117.
28. See T. S. Eliot, 'Tradition and the Individual Talent', in Eliot, *Selected Essays*, 3rd enlarged edn (London: Faber & Faber, 1951), p. 18.
29. Kate Clanchy, *Slattern* (London: Chatto & Windus, 1995), p. 1.
30. Christine de Luca, *Voes & Sounds* (Lerwick: The Shetland Library, 1994) and *Wast wi da Valkyries* (Lerwick: The Shetland Library, 1997).
31. Tom Leonard, *Intimate Voices: Selected Work 1965–1983* (Newcastle-upon-Tyne: Galloping Dog, 1984).

CHAPTER TWO

Kathleen Jamie's Semiotic of Scotlands

Helen Boden

Towards the end of her travels in Baltistan described in *The Golden Peak*,[1] Kathleen Jamie encounters three Westerners running a medical practice. One of them, the Irishwoman Alison, is active in supporting women's rights, but as a missionary is also imperialistically and inflexibly anti-Islam. This is one of a number of ontologically ambiguous cameos in Jamie's travelogue, and her decision to include it suggests an acknowledgement that gender and national identities, if no longer mutually exclusive, still do not always co-exist unproblematically.

On a more abstract level, a logical conclusion to current work being undertaken on nationality in cultural and sociological studies is either to reject the very concept of national identity, or to see it as a construct, entirely dependent on how it is represented and interpreted. As Stuart Hall puts it, 'national identities are not things we are born with, but are formed and transformed within and in relation to representation'.[2] Paraphrasing Hall's following comment on 'Englishness', Alice Brown, David McCrone and Lindsay Paterson point out that 'we only know what it is to be Scottish because of the way Scottishness has come to be represented'.[3] This parallels a similar conceptual shift which has taken place in feminist theory: the deconstruction and later rejection of the binary opposition between 'masculine' and 'feminine' in favour of a perpetual freeplay of *différance*, along with an increasing acceptance of gender as a social construct. So in their 'postmodern' phase, gender and national identity are linked by a common resistance to confining boundaries and limiting definitions: as Susanne Hagemann has put it, 'like genders, nations are constructs'.[4] The significance of Jamie's work lies in its skilful renegotiation with the ways the nation is and has been represented; with the past and its stereotypes.

In an essay on twentieth-century Scottish drama, Adrienne Scullion has asked what both negative and positive versions of Scottish national identity, as formulated variously by Colin McArthur, Tom Nairn, Beveridge and Turnbull, and David McCrone, can offer the literary critic.[5] A study of Kathleen Jamie's writings in prose and poetry offers some answers to this question. Her collection of poems *The Queen of Sheba* offers a creative counterpart to the work in other disciplines which is currently mounting a successful challenge to the 'inferiorist' approach to Scottish culture (for example, Beveridge and Turnbull),[6] often suggesting that women will play a significant role in further developments and changes. Read in the light of the above-named scholars and critics, as well as cultural theorists such as Homi Bhabha and Slavoj Žižek, who have undertaken important work on national identity without making specific reference to Scotland, Jamie's work offers a particularly pertinent example of how the new versions of the feminine in contemporary women's writing parallel altered approaches to identity as described by sociologists and political scientists.

An important conceptual parallel between work on women's writing and feminist theory and that on national identity is an interest in multiplicity and pluralism rather than dualism (and this of course has very special ramifications for Scottish writing). Criticism now sometimes suggests that the Caledonian antisyzygy has been cured, released into a healthier, multiple personality, one finally free from pejorative clinical vocabulary. The rebirth of the female hysteric (formerly incarnated and incarcerated as the madwoman in the attic), as the subversive bearer of *jouissance* and multiplicity, has no doubt been instructive here.[7] Although I agree with Berthold Schoene-Harwood that the Caledonian antisyzygy is 'a stereotyping, detrimentally restrictive mode of representation in great need of further specification or deconstructive dismantlement',[8] to reject dualism entirely is to erase the traces of a dominant trope in post-Enlightenment Scottish writing. It is still problematically present in Jamie's work; however, her use of dualist motifs can also be read as a key feature in a renegotiation of what 'Scottishness' means.

This is perhaps at its most evident when she tests ideas about national identity from a distance in *The Golden Peak*. She writes of Pakistani women: 'what they enjoy is being Muslim. What we enjoy is risk ... I look at them and see the optical illusion of protection and oppression. They look at me and see the illusion of freedom, the terrible freedom of the lost soul' (37–8). At the close of her account, she returns to this idea: 'everything presents itself to our Western minds as choice ... I wanted to explain the notions of choice and risk, and how we embraced both' (177). In the first quotation at least, Jamie tries to avoid taking an orientalist stance in her unhierarchised representation of contrasting subject-positions and her highlighting of the contradictions inherent in both of these positions. And in equating freedom, choice and risk, she is able to write herself out of a Calvinist mindset, resisting containment in a divided and determined subjectivity. But her self-definitions, serially articulated in difference from a whole range of Others, often serve only to reinscribe a binary logic. Unfortunately this all means that, as a traveller/tourist, sometimes the only subject-position available to Jamie in Pakistan is that of re-coloniser; and for most of 'the folks at home', the dedicatees of *The Queen of Sheba*, there are scant opportunities for the exercising of freedom and its concomitants, choice and risk. The subjects of 'Child with Pillar Box and Bin Bags' and of 'School Reunion' (15, 20), the child's mother, and Jamie's former schoolmates respectively, are objectified, allowing freedom of movement and choice only to the writing subject. However, Jamie is never arrogantly unaware of her cultural privilege: the complexity of *The Golden Peak* lies in her very alertness to the problems involved in representing the interconnected matrices of national and sexual difference. If the parallels repeatedly drawn between the two 'Northern territories', Scotland and Pakistan, seem overdetermined, and sometimes fail to rework the crude binarisms of orientalism (her interest in the magic and mysticism of pre-Islamic culture, which in the final sections of the book replaces the persistent cultural analogies, can be seen to posit a universal narrative of origins that once again equates Scotland with Pakistan), they do so because the writer is engaged in an experimental exploration of what it means to be Scottish, as well as of the foreign culture she is visiting. (And, lest the control of institutionalised religion be evaded entirely, the freedom she experiences is only that of the 'lost soul'.) In *The Golden Peak*, Jamie's investigation of how Pakistan represents itself to others, and how they (not only she, but a range of other Westerners: Alison, Ken, Jungly John) interpret it, anticipates more concentrated work on subjectivity and representation in later poems.

Nor does Jamie maintain a position of superiority in relation to her contemporary Scotswomen whom she has left behind even when physically returned from afar: she ironises her (educated, pretentious) stance by introducing the voice of the 'granny', who closes 'Arraheids' with the rebuke '*ye arenae here tae wonder / whae dae ye think ye ur?*' (*Sheba*, 40). The final line echoes the heckler 'from the back of the crowd' who disrupts the speaker's fantasy in the titular poem of the collection, 'The Queen of Sheba'. Here, the (anonymous, but probably male) questioner ostensibly addresses the newly arrived Queen, but the cry results in 'a thousand laughing girls and she' uniting in a closing chorus. The opening poem thus signals a collection comprising multiple voices, in which it is sometimes impossible to determine exactly who is speaking what, and to whom. Granny, the benign matriarch of a deil speaking in Jamie's head, is also present in an interview conducted by post between Jamie and Richard Price in 1992. Her maternal grandmother is introduced, at the beginning of the interview, as 'the part of me which is working class Scotland ... the source of my Scots language'.[9] 'Granny's' voice then proceeds to punctuate Jamie's intelligent, considered – but themselves divided – answers with sobering, deflating asides of 'pretentious, ken':

> You get people saying 'what are you running away from?' I think, 'small-minded rats like you'. I say, 'you're missing the point, we can be many things, we can be multi-faceted people. I can be Scottish, and go other places. *Bas!* It's Urdu, means 'enough'. Pretentious, ken? (104)

This tension, between dualism and multiplicity, colonial binarism and postcolonial contrapuntalism, persists; it pervades *The Golden Peak* and *The Queen of Sheba*, as well as Jamie's poetical, fantastical travelogue, *The Autonomous*

Region.[10] It becomes a trademark of her writing in the 1990s, representing a development from her first full collection, *The Way We Live*,[11] which often involved direct confrontation and opposition between masculine and feminine.

... But first

> she wants to strip the willow
> she desires the keys
>   to the National Library.
>   (*Sheba*, 10)

The Queen of Sheba is here shown to possess a desire for a *bona fide* Scottish identity; as an incomer, she needs to experience 'authentic' Scottish culture and to possess knowledge of Scotland. Much of Jamie's work deals with the stereotypes surrounding national identity: the material and abstract signifiers of Scottishness that have helped to define or obscure it, depending on the standpoint taken. As Hall has argued, 'national cultures are composed not only of cultural institutions, but of symbols and representations. A national culture is a *discourse*' (Hall, 292). 'The way Scottishness has come to be represented' (Brown et al., 207) has dictated the ways in which it has come to be popularly known and understood. Rather than rejecting the stereotypes, Jamie recycles them (as Scullion does (202)), implying that they are not invalid or inappropriate just because they have been previously *mis*appropriated, and proving the sociologists' thesis that such signifiers have no essential meaning: context and usage determine their interpretation. Jamie rewrites the narrative of the nation,[12] both by recontextualising and hence reinterpreting specific images and icons, giving them a new lease of life in an altered semantic and cultural environment; and by reworking established patterns and paradigms. In 'One of Us' (*Sheba*, 43), for example, the traditional direction of travel and colonial exploitation is reversed when a group of Hebrideans invade the central belt.

In 'The Other Question' Homi Bhabha focuses on the stereotype as a distinct and distinguishing feature of colonial writing, 'an arrested, fetishistic mode of representation' which admits only 'a limited form of otherness'.[13] But by acknowledging its ambivalence and complexity, the very fact that it is both 'always "in place"' and always 'anxiously repeated' (66), Bhabha allows for a reinterpretation of the stereotype, which would permit the very difference it ostensibly prohibits: 'my reading of colonial discourse suggests that the point of intervention should shift from the ready recognition of images as positive or negative, to an understanding of the *processes of subjectification* made possible (and plausible) through stereotypical discourse' (67). However, he proceeds cautiously, problematising further the crucial ambivalence of the stereotype by discussing it in relation to the fetish ('the disavowal of difference', 74) and the Lacanian imaginary:

> The fetish or stereotype gives access to an 'identity' which is predicated as much
> on mastery and pleasure as it is on anxiety and defence, for it is a form of multiple

and contradictory belief in its recognition of difference and disavowal of it ...
The stereotype ... is a simplification because it is an arrested, fixated mode of
representation that, in denying the play of difference (which the negation through
the Other permits), constitutes a problem for the *representation* of the subject in
significations of psychic and social relations. (74–5)

If the stereotype has a fixed meaning, it is meaning*less* once the cultural
specificities that supported the colonial situation are altered or removed. However, if its ambivalence is allowed, then it can be repeated, or reclaimed, by
those against whom it was originally used. Jamie's work seems to suggest this
possibility: the stereotype can always be modified with time. The 'arraheids'
of the poem can therefore represent the weaponry of the ancient past, and the
more recently historical, textually rather than physically lethal 'show o' grannies'
tongues' (*Sheba*, 40). That no one version has a claim to authority in itself
suggests a need for a creative and tolerant plurality or multiplicity. Indeed,
such labels are not limiting, precisely because of their potential alterability,
unlike, say, the universalising symbol, which because it masks difference can
serve to legitimate and consolidate an imperialist ideology. A useful analogy
can be made between Jamie's positive recontextualisation of the stereotype,
and the reclamation of myths and stories which were previously regarded as
recalcitrantly patriarchal and conservative by feminist writers (for example,
Margaret Atwood and Angela Carter). Lacking any essential meaning, re-read
or rewritten against the grain they show up new subtleties and possible interpretations.

Scottish identity is often defined in terms of the country's pasts (of romance,
defeat, industrialisation).[14] A new present does not, however, need to reject
older definitions entirely: to do so would mean a loss of defining continuity
with the past that has shaped this present. The title of another poem in *The
Queen of Sheba* signals that 'Mr and Mrs Scotland are dead'; but the poem itself
allows for the possibility that their possessions should be preserved – 'Do we
save this toolbox, these old-fashioned views / addressed, after all, to Mr and
Mrs Scotland? / Should we reach and take them?' (*Sheba*, 37). What is important, is that they (definitions, and postcards from the past) should enter the
public sphere, to be re-read, rewritten; recycled rather than binned. A defining
characteristic of Benedict Anderson's 'imagined communities' is, after all, their
communion with their pasts, and Jamie repeatedly shows the importance of
connectedness to spatial *and* temporal others.[15]

'One of Us' is one of her most politically significant poems and most astute
statements on the supposed fixity, and actual portability, of cultural meaning.
It deals with how the past is used to define present national identity, and
illustrates how the discourse of national culture 'constructs identities which
are ambiguously placed between past and future', and 'straddles the temptation
to return to former glories and the drive to go forwards ever deeper into
modernity' (Hall, 295). The poem tests Hall's concept of the 'foundational

myth', or story 'which locates the origins of the nation, the people and their
national character ... which predates the ruptures of colonization' (Hall, 294–
5), by positing the return of the repressed Highlander. The first stanza shows
the available natural resources being utilised by a group of 'native' (but temporally unidentified) Hebrideans:

> Our sealskin cloaks are clasped
> by a fist-sized penannular brooch,
> our slippers are feathery
> gugas' necks.
>
> (*Sheba*, 43)

These same raw materials-cum-cultural symbols are to be equated later in
the poem with 'tat: the / golden horn of righteousness, / the justice harp; what
folks expect'. In a different system of representation, their meaning is derived
jointly from their new contextual environment, and the ideological positioning
of those who interpret them. The protagonists on whom the backward-looking
stereotype has been conferred, cloaked in the mists of Romanticism as much as
the sealskin, are not content to remain disenfranchised and bereft of autonomy
in their own territory; their aim is to seize power and go on the offensive.
Empowered with what has come to be regarded as the 'silly magic' of Celtic
spirituality, they turn the stereotype on those who first used it against them:
'We took swans' shape / to cross the Minch'.

In the process of evading the 'civilised' mainland of the information society
(though 'a distant / Telecom van' is tellingly situated in their homeland too),
they encounter 'a forester making aeolian flutes / from plastic tubes': creating
a simulacrum of a 'natural' artefact from modern waste, in contrast to their
deployment of indigenous materials for practical purposes (or is it just for
show and as political statement?). Nonetheless, the kindly forester shares his
pay and offers advice on avoiding the media and other versions of polis: 'Avoid
/ the A9. For God's sake, / get some proper clothes'. As in this sense he too is
'one of us', identified by his allegiance, distinctions between real and simulacrum
are minimised. So, the magic that prevailed over the Minch failing in the face of
mainland economic and cultural forces, 'we ditched the cloaks', and purchased
the ultimate signifier of authentic Scottishness for the affluent tourist in the
central Highlands: 'yellow / Pringle sweaters in Spean Bridge' – but only as a
temporary measure. Thus disguised:

> house by safe house
> arrived in Edinburgh. So far so
> tedious: we all hold
> minor government jobs, lay plans, and bide our time.
>
> (43)

This ostensibly simple, tongue-in-cheek (but whose? and why, exactly?)
poem provides multiple examples of pluralism: the cultural signifiers and

commodities shift from the sealskin cloaks, through the 'tat' dignified – or ridiculed? – with the moral attributes of 'righteousness' and 'justice'; the aeolian flutes and plastic tubes, to the Pringle sweaters. Topographically, the customary Highland/Lowland, or west coast/east coast binaries are deconstructed in favour of a tripartite, linear model of Hebrides/central Highlands/Edinburgh. It is a geographical and economic fact that you cannot get from Lewis to Edinburgh by sea and land without also negotiating the central Highlands and all they have come to symbolise – which means navigating the past and how it has come to be represented. *The Queen of Sheba* as a whole interrogates the cultural stereotypes surrounding the constructs of both past/Highlands and modernity/ urban central belt, showing how temporal and regional boundaries are not co-extensive with those of any particular ethnic group, nor the stereotypes of Scottishness their exclusive property.

The stereotype still, however, refuses to become an unproblematic trope for creative textual play. A major problem is that stereotypic images some- times tend to be regarded as a specifically masculine way of labelling, and therefore to be associated with male usage. This is consistent with the gen- eral suspicion that 'national identities are strongly gendered' (Hall, 297). But instead of presenting a constraint to women writers, the stereotype, like the fairy-tale, can become a source of agency. A feminine historical lineage (where 'historical' is of course no longer synonymous with 'factual') can be established as an alternative to the more customary (masculine) versions of national identity derived from the post-1745 appropriations of Highland culture. It is with this different and older (prior to the 'fixing' as stereotypes of certain 'national' characteristics) tradition in mind that Scullion calls for a revalorisation of the imaginary, in distinction to Nairn's view that a predi- lection for such non-realist or non-rational cultural practice evidences a schizoid state. She argues:

> the imaginary has the potential to liberate and to allow the artist and critic to be creative in their engagement with the discourses of Scottishness. To use the fantastic infrastructure of the collective unconscious in a creative and abstract manner may also result in a vision of culture where meanings are open for reinterpretation and narrative closure is a practical as well as a psychological impossibility. (Scullion, 202)

Jamie works against both masculine/working-class/urban *and* Romantic- derived stereotypes, to produce a new non-urban verse, in which nature is no longer reductively troped as female; as well as a new urban realism, which renegotiates a space for an imaginative optimism amongst postmodernism's trademark-commodified surfaces, empty signifiers and parodic reappropriations of earlier cultural environments. The best example of this is 'Fountain', about a shopping mall (*Sheba*, 17). Jamie demonstrates that, against the odds, the signifiers can and do refer to something prior to their hijacking by the capitalist state, and permit a connectedness to be established with classical and native cultural traditions:

> ... bags printed
> Athena, Argos, Olympus; thinking: now
> *in Arcadia est* I'll besport myself
> at the water's edge with kids,
> coffee in a polystyrene cup.
> We know it's all false: no artesian well
> really leaps through strata
> fathoms under *Man at C&A* but
> [...]
> ... Who says
> we can't respond; don't still feel,
> as it were, the dowser's twitch
> up through the twin handles of the buggy.
>
> (*Sheba*, 17)

Jamie has spoken of the importance to her of various 'touchstones' – bicycle, typewriter, plane ticket (*Verse*, 103) – that represent for her the means for freedom. She is reluctant entirely to let go of the material anchors that connect her to home – hence the conclusion of 'Mr and Mrs Scotland are dead'. These pervade her work, and are the means by which she measures her own and others' identities. The Islamic shawl, for example, serves as a kind of ambivalent talisman: 'I began to think of the Islamic shawl as a symbol for the entire culture; one I would on occasion wish to draw around me, and on others simply want to tear off and stamp underfoot' (*Golden Peak*, 140–1). Similar 'touchstones' appear throughout her poetry, either as material signifiers reclaimed from postmodernism and the heritage industry, or as immaterial cultural practices, in her gestures to myth and folklore. Here Žižek's *Tarrying with the Negative* stands as a useful supplement to Bhabha's and Scullion's work, considering such cultural activity as a '*real* nondiscursive kernel of enjoyment' rather than a metaphysical abstraction:

> A nation *exists* only so long as its specific *enjoyment* continues to be materialized in a set of social practices and transmitted through national myths that structure these practices. To emphasise in a 'deconstructionist' mode that Nation is not a biological or transhistorical fact but a contingent discursive construction, an overdetermined result of textual practices, is thus misleading: such an emphasis overlooks the remainder of some *real*, nondiscursive kernel of enjoyment which must be present for the Nation qua discursive entity-effect to achieve its ontological consistency ... The national Cause is ultimately nothing but the way subjects of a given ethnic community organise their enjoyment through national myths.[16]

Žižek's larger argument that, paraphrasing Freud, '*the hatred of the Other is the hatred of our own excess of enjoyment*' (206) has obvious applicability to Scottish

culture because of the Calvinist ideology that was in part responsible for the
'fixing' of the stereotypes. Jamie exposes repression and reinscribes enjoyment,
through repeatedly and playfully testing and reworking old truisms. This can
be related to Brown, McCrone and Paterson's view that, following the Union
of 1707, 'the Scottishness that could be safely developed was precisely those
areas of life that were not political, such as the family, language or folk song',
resulting in 'a consigning of Scottish culture to the realm of the private and
therefore the non-political' (7). Cultural praxis, the organisation of enjoyment,
was thus relegated to – and yet preserved in – what was traditionally a feminine
sphere. In the act of publication Jamie returns physical and ritual markers of
national identity to the public sphere, and more importantly allows the two
spheres to coalesce, erasing in the process the boundary, and hence the means
of segregation. By suggesting some enabling possibilities for connections
between private and public, Jamie's work perhaps also helps to minimise old
distinctions between masculine and feminine.

In a 1992 interview, Jamie appears to evade a question on the importance of
having access to the work of other female poets, and whether the lack of this is
a problem specific to Scottish women writers (*Verse*, 104). She turns instead to
the importance to her of Scots and Scottishness:

> The volume of debate about things Scottish has increased ... but I still see a
> definite poverty of imagination ... we feel threatened and therefore hang on to
> anything and everything Scottish, even the bad old junk that should have been
> ditched years ago. Change would mean chaos and we're feart of chaos, we don't
> know it can be glorious ... There are more ways of being Scottish than writing
> in Scots about Scottish things (O heresy!) I mean, what is a 'real Scot' for God's
> sake, what is 'a sense of Scottishness'? Whether or not a sense of Scottishness
> pervades my work should be a matter of fact, not of worth. (106)

This simultaneous attraction to and repulsion from 'things Scottish' informs
poems like 'Mr and Mrs Scotland Are Dead', poems in which, according to
Raymond Friel, 'difficult questions are asked about the past and what we should
do with it'. Friel argues that Jamie avoids sentimentality by 'travelling lightly':
'it's as if she doesn't want to be weighted down by the clutter of the past', so
the poem stands as 'a sobering antidote to a national tendency for nostalgia
and inertia'.[17] But Jamie could equally be challenging the way the Scots have
been represented as nostalgic and inert, by redefining their cultural signifiers
for a modern world; these 'touchstones' appear too often in her poetry (and are
recalled too often in her travel writing where they *could* legitimately be forgotten and left behind) to be considered insignificant or as having been rejected.
After all, it is not that she conclusively decides *not* to preserve for a future
posterity Mr and Mrs Scotland's memorabilia (which is not *necessarily* 'bad old
junk'): the final six lines of the poem allow for what would happen if the
objects were later to be rediscovered in 'our silent house' – the 'our' suggestive
of an unspecified pair bond, but not the conventional 'Mr and Mrs'. They

would then be open to yet more, and further ironising interpretations, such as the speaker of the poem has imposed on the original objects/texts, thereby establishing a temporal continuum, an imagined community of readers stretching from Mrs Scotland into the future. (This would also involve further deconstruction of the private/public boundary, with the private memorabilia bequeathed into public ownership.) But if the rhetorical question 'do we take them?' were to be answered in the negative, future hermeneutic communities would be denied the possibility of self-definition and reinvention by teasing out new meanings for the personal and topographical signatures of 'Mr Scotland's John Bull Puncture Repair Kit' and 'his last few joiners' tools, / SCOTLAND, SCOTLAND, stamped on their tired handles' (*Sheba*, 37). Friel gives one possible, and plausible, reading of the poem, but it is also open to others that bring gender into the equation, and which allow it an intertextual relationship with Jamie's travel writing. Here we can glimpse an imaginative experimentalism growing out of variations on known and established cultural themes.

In 'Jocky in the Wilderness' the stereotypes of masculinity and nationality coalesce. Friel implies that Jamie's stance in this poem ('Jock: enough's enough! awa / and reconstruct yourself / in your various dens' (*Sheba*, 42)) is unsympathetic: 'how easy is it to re-invent yourself when you have no job and no sense of personal worth and no prospect of ever again working in the trade which has been an integral part of your maleness?' (45–6) – to which the least subtle answer would be that it isn't easy, but (as the female protagonist of *The Autonomous Region* demonstrates) women have always reinvented themselves, adapted to changed circumstances. James Kelman has given the Jockys in the wilderness their voice; Jamie's project is to articulate a response to this, and as the subject-positions in the poem shift between fly-on-the-wall narrator ('Jock's a-bawling on the Aberdeen train. / I'll punch your heid! he says to his weans / I'll punch *your* heid! repeat the weans'), the second person ('Jock-in-the-ditch are you no feart / they'll concrete over your redundant limbs?') and a commentary of women's voices ('come hame / when ye've learned / to unclench your fists and heart'), her stance is too indeterminate to be labelled unfairly harsh. Even 'Jocky' himself is unlikely to signify a single unified subject: he represents instead the collective stereotype of Scottish masculinity. But though large and containing multitudes, at the end of the poem 'Jocky's in the wilderness / Jocky all alane', and he will not survive as a signifier of Scottishness because he lacks the imagination and initiative to redeploy his resources in the manner of the narrator's gloriously parodic 'the [industrial] plant / is wede awa' (*Sheba*, 42).

It is Jamie's use of Scots that signals to the reader most directly her engagement with issues of national identity. The way the use of Scots in twentieth-century poetry has since MacDiarmid largely been associated with a masculine tradition has perhaps prohibited (or at least prolonged) for poetry a return, with a feminine inflection, to the imaginative and subversive uses of the language that have already revitalised drama and the novel. By making reference to the 'deep ear' of the oral tradition, crucially often a matrilinear tradition,

Jamie is able to reinvent a feminine Scots poetic, and subvert the legacy of MacDiarmid. In a radio interview Jamie has argued that 'we shift ... registers without realising. We must have more languages within us than we realise', and claimed that she reads her work with more emphasis on the Scots than exists in the written versions of her poems.[18] Jamie's poems exemplify Robert Crawford's beliefs that 'language is normally made up of languages ... discourse is always a blend of discourses' and 'Scots is in the ascendent, not because it is fixed but because it is fluid':[19] Scots is no more 'fixed' than the stereotypes. In the 1992 interview where she advocated change and chaos as glorious, Jamie dwells on the issue of the heterogeneity of language:

> I moved to Sheffield, and there I discovered I spoke Scots and English both, so then I got into a linguistic fankle, and couldn't write, couldn't find a voice, a language. (I'm beginning to understand that it's ok to have several, Scots do have several, and people are beginning to talk about this, this babel, the Scots polyphony). (*Verse*, 106)

In contrast to this fluid sense of national and linguistic identity, she rarely moves beyond fixed, binary gender positions and oppositions. In this final section I want to explore how the 'feminine principle' in her work comes as much from her linguistic and stylistic experimentalism as from her conscious selection of a female speaking voice or subject-matter.

The semiotic as defined by Kristeva in *Revolution in Poetic Language* is associated with the pre-Oedipal. Although this offers a potentially useful model for a reading of Scottish literature not predicated on dualism (because it occurs prior to the splitting of the subject), the semiotic's specific association with psychotics and young children could equally constrain it to serving the same purpose as the stereotypes that fix Scotland as divided, or primitive and unimproved. Kristeva's summary in the more aesthetically preoccupied *Desire in Language* is less problematic:

> This heterogeneousness to signification operates through, despite and in excess of it and produces in poetic language 'musical' but also nonsense effects that destroy not only accepted beliefs and significations, but, in radical experiments, syntax itself ... we shall call this [signifying] disposition *semiotic* (*le semiotique*), meaning ... a distinctive mark, a trace, index, the premonitory sign, the proof, engraved mark, imprint – in short, a *distinctiveness* admitting of an uncertain and indeterminate articulation because it does not yet refer (for young children) or no longer refers (in psychotic discourse) to a signified object for a thetic consciousness ... a disposition that is definitely heterogeneous to meaning but always in sight of it or in either a negative or surplus relationship to it.[20]

The refusal of physical and textual containment in poems such as 'Bairns of Suzie' and 'School Reunion' (*Sheba*, 25, 20) can be read as examples of the heterogeneous, surplus or negative relationships to meaning. Furthermore, the 'touchstone' and the stereotype can usefully be considered as 'distinctive marks', which, because they do not refer to an absolute signified, remain open for reappropriation.

In *The Autonomous Region*: *Poems and Photographs from Tibet*, however, Jamie moves forward into a completely new form of experimentalism. This sequence (it is neither 'poem' nor 'poems' and cannot properly be considered separately from Sean Mayne Smith's photographs) best illustrates what I would call the 'semiotic of Scotlands'. It features multiple subjectivities that move fluidly through time and space. Ostensibly structured around the two characters of Fa-hsien and Wen Cheng, the poems to some extent centre upon two material signifiers (touchstones?) associated with them at various points in the sequence: Fa-hsien's vessel and Wen Cheng's sun/moon mirror. Here, political and personal autonomy, jointly under threat, serve as interchangeable metaphors for each other. This echoes the way Mayne Smith combines landscape and human subjects, and operates on a linguistic level in individual poems when what is literal and figurative – what image and what abstract representation – becomes unclear and unimportant:

> Fa-hsien in the city. He says:
>   '*Need all situations be resolvable/resolved?*'
> or
>   '*Is* there a high pass over the mountains?'
> and hopes/hopes not. Rumour flits the city
> like bats, flits the city like bats by night,
> rumours on the lips of running tea-boys,
> delivered on the hour, on trays like tea.
>   And the rumours say yes, the rumours say no.
>
>   (13)

Such ontological ambiguity and imagistic density become distinctive markers of a Kristevan 'heterogeneousness to signification'. In this narrative Jamie also establishes herself in a tradition of, and in intertextual relationship with, earlier travellers. Nor – to an even greater extent than in *The Queen of Sheba* – are demarcations between different speakers always readily discernible, as a secondary narrator ('the maid into her dictaphone', reporting Wen Cheng's actions and speech, for example (34–6)) sometimes takes over, causing identities to merge. This holds true for the larger pattern of interchange between the stories of Wen Cheng and Fa-hsien, both of whom are also propelled temporally into a modern commodified environment (the vessel serves at one point as a thermos flask), as Jamie travels backwards into theirs. Her subject-position thus becomes enmeshed with theirs as she becomes their fellow traveller. Structurally, too, there are strange modulations: section titles do not necessarily correspond to, and are not co-extensive with, the narrative of events to which they apparently allude. A scientifically rigid demarcation of subsections is thus resisted: some sections are untitled, and the two 'characters' not contained solely within the section-headings that bear their names.

If *The Autonomous Region* is ostensibly structured around a masculine/feminine binary, this is deconstructed by the use of connecting images and phrases, common to both Wen Cheng and Fa-hsien, and the way each confronts potential divisions within themselves, resisting the constraint of sharp dualities, in the same way as their respective totems, mirror and vessel, resist confinement in a fixed, stereotypic meaning by remaining open to recontextualisation and reinterpretation. Towards the end of the sequence, Fa-hsien becomes partially identified with a Scots speech-zone when he develops 'a hanker for his ain folk, / [and] his auld hert follows suit' (51), and advises the narrator, '*set a stout hert tae a stey brae*' (57). Three of the final four lyrics, which seem semantically detached from the rest of the sequence, are entirely in Scots, and are associated with a crisis point: 'For Paula' alludes to the Tiananmen Square massacre, which took place when Jamie and Mayne Smith were on the border of the region; and in 'Sang o the blin beggar' the representative of the most politically disempowered stratum of society assumes the voice of his traditional literary *alter ego*, the bardic sage ('the stars grow dangerous; they ken the script / o constellation's no thir ain'). This attribution of Scots to the victims of an Eastern political attrocity serves to contribute to the debate about what an autonomous region is: the sequence seems to support the reading that if autonomy is always under threat, it can, paradoxically, always be reinforced by a sense of connectedness with other cultures. In this instance at least, it seems that universalisation can work alongside a prioritising of local cultural specificities, rather than erasing or homogenising them. Finally in the sequence, sexual and national differences are distilled into sounds and rhythms (Kristeva's 'musical' and 'nonsense effects') and semiotic marks prioritised over meanings:

> Xiahe. Wave droonin wave
> on a pebbly shore,
> the *ahe* o machair, o slammach.
>
> (78)

Notes

With thanks to Kathleen Jamie and Bloodaxe for permission to quote from Jamie's works.

1. Kathleen Jamie, *The Golden Peak: Travels in Northern Pakistan* (London: Virago, 1992).
2. Stuart Hall, 'The Question of Cultural Identity', in Stuart Hall, David Held and Tony McGrew (eds), *Modernity and Its Futures* (Cambridge: Polity, 1992), pp. 273–325 (292).
3. Alice Brown, David McCrone and Lindsay Paterson, *Politics and Society in Scotland* (Basingstoke: Macmillan, 1996), pp. 207–8. See also pp. 195, 197; and David McCrone, *Understanding Scotland* (London: Routledge, 1992), pp. 16–21 (28).

4. Susanne Hagemann, 'Women and Nation', in Douglas Gifford and Dorothy McMillan (eds), *A History of Scottish Women's Writing* (Edinburgh: Edinburgh University Press, 1997), pp. 316–28 (317).

5. Adrienne Scullion, 'Feminine Pleasures and Masculine Indignities: Gender and Community in Scottish Drama', in Christopher Whyte (ed.), *Gendering the Nation* (Edinburgh: Edinburgh University Press, 1995), pp. 169–204 (200).

6. Kathleen Jamie, *The Queen of Sheba* (Newcastle-upon-Tyne: Bloodaxe, 1994). Craig Beveridge and Ronald Turnbull, *The Eclipse of Scottish Culture Inferiorism and the Intellectuals* (Edinburgh: Polygon, 1989).

7. See also Scullion, 'Feminine Pleasures', p. 201.

8. Berthold Schoene-Harwood, '"Emerging as the Others of Our Selves": Scottish Multiculturalism and the Challenge of the Body in Postcolonial Representation', *Scottish Literary Journal*, 25:1 (1998), pp. 54–72 (54).

9. Kathleen Jamie interviewed by Richard Price, *Verse*, 8:3 / 9:1 (1992), pp. 103–6 (103); reprinted in R. Crawford et al. (eds), *Talking Verse* (St Andrews and Williamsburg, VA: Verse, 1995), pp. 99–102.

10. Kathleen Jamie, *The Autonomous Region* (Newcastle-upon-Tyne: Bloodaxe, 1993).

11. Kathleen Jamie, *The Way We Live* (Newcastle-upon-Tyne: Bloodaxe, 1987).

12. See John R. Gold and Margaret M. Gold, *Imagining Scotland : Tradition, Representation and the Promotion of Scottish Tourism since 1750* (Aldershot: Scolar Press, 1995), p. 201; and Homi K. Bhabha, 'Introduction: Narrating the Nation', in Bhabha (ed.), *Nation and Narration* (London: Routledge, 1990), pp. 1–7.

13. Homi K. Bhabha, *The Location of Culture* (London: Routledge, 1994), pp. 66–84 (76; 77–8).

14. For example, McCrone, *Understanding Scotland*, pp. 198–9.

15. Benedict Anderson, *Imagined Communities* (1983; London: Routledge, 1994); see also Bhabha on 'the essential question of the representation of the nation as a temporal process', in his *The Location of Culture*, p. 142.

16. Slavoj Žižek, *Tarrying with the Negative: Kant, Hegel and the Critique of Ideology* (Durham, NC: Duke University Press, 1993), pp. 201–2; with thanks to Ian Duncan for drawing my attention to this passage.

17. Raymond Friel, 'Women Beware Gravity: Kathleen Jamie's Poetry', *Southfields*, 1 (1995), pp. 29–48 (46–7).

18. 'Poet to Poet', BBC Radio Scotland, 13 April 1997.

19. Robert Crawford, *Identifying Poets: Self and Territory in Twentieth-Century Poetry* (Edinburgh: Edinburgh University Press), pp. 7, 163.

20. Julia Kristeva, *Desire in Language; A Semiotic Approach to Literature and Art*, ed. Leon S. Roudiez, trans. Thomas Gora, Alice Jardine and Leon. S. Roudiez (Oxford: Basil Blackwell, 1980), p. 133. See also Julia Kristeva, *Revolution in Poetic Language*, introd. Leon S. Roudiez, trans. Margaret Waller (New York: Columbia University Press, 1984), p. 25ff.

CHAPTER THREE

Liz Lochhead's Poetry and Drama: Forging Ironies

Aileen Christianson

Liz Lochhead (b. 1947) has been a presence in Scottish writing since 1972 when her first collection, *Memo for Spring*, was published.[1] There may, initially, have been an element of patronising tokenism in the response to Lochhead, publishing her first collection comparatively young. In the 1970s in particular, but also in the 1980s, Lochhead was in danger of being everybody's token Scottish woman writer who could be cited against the 'absence' of women writers in Scotland – in a way that Spark, absent from Scotland and so much more senior and 'international' in reputation, could not. But Lochhead, like her mermaid in 'Legendary I', set 'impossible tasks' by the North Knight, cheerfully 'refused to recognise the magnitude of her problems / ... inevitably' coming 'into her own' (*DF*, 62). Palmer McCulloch touches on her importance to other Scottish women poets who followed her (in Chapter 1) and Jackie Kay, in her poem 'Kail and Callaloo' acknowledging both sides of her cultural heritage, writes:

> Liz was my teenage hero
> OCH MEN and her stop and start rhythm
> I'd never heard of Audre Lord then.[2]

Both Lochhead's poetry and later her drama have been consistently interesting, allowing an assessment of more than a quarter of a century's work. It is work which itself shows an acute, critical awareness of being a woman and a Scot, these two roles providing many intersecting points in her work, both in tandem and separately, now one, now the other in the foreground of her preoccupations. This chapter cannot consider everything but will attempt something of an incorporating view of much of Lochhead's work, taking its tack from her own 1992 assessment of *Memo For Spring*, when she spoke of its function for her being 'the idea of forging-out a Scottish and female and working-class and contemporary identity as a writer'.[3] Developing this foursome reel of themes in relation to all her works, I would substitute language for 'contemporary identity', the latter being a given and silently implicit presence combining everything else.

Lochhead began in *Memo for Spring* with poems that seem personal and direct,[4] but which also show traces of the poet she was to become, moving from poetry which was 'all about grey streets and rain and here and now', not 'allusive in any way', to retelling in her third collection – *The Grimm Sisters* – 'familiar stories from another angle' with women the subject, not 'the object in the stories'.[5] She had given warning of her intentions at the end of an early 'here and now' poem about her home town, Motherwell:

> Oh, it's nice here, but
> slagheaps and steelworks / hem my horizon
> and something compels
> me forge my ironies from a steel town.
> ('On Midsummer Common', *DF*, 128)

Forging ironies becomes an integral part of Lochhead's poetic and dramatic identity, part of her 'voice and tone' (*Verse*, 87; see also 89).

The clarity of Lochhead's ironies and her voice mean that her poems are invaluable for critics to use to make specific points. 'Inter-City' (*DF*, 33–4), succinct expression of travelling across Scotland by train, following the line of the rift valley that runs from Helensburgh to Stonehaven splitting Highlands from Lowlands, is a poem much analysed. S. J. Boyd takes a Freudian approach, exercised by the 'penetration' of the train, symbolic masculine symbol, 'Hammered like a bolt' (Frankenstein's monster, put together awkwardly), and taking the penultimate line 'wide open' as hinting at female arousal. Cairns Craig, on the other hand, reads the poem as part of his narrative of the nation:

> the woman is *between* the 'artsyfartsy' portrait of absence and an all-too-insistent male language: she is *not* taking in the absence, but her 'own blurred/back to front face' superimposed on the 'small dark country'. By the identification of her own condition with the country's, she makes redemption of the feminine equivalent to redemption of the nation.[6]

Interesting as Craig's analysis of this (and other Lochhead poems) is, this approach carries the danger inherent in making female equivalent with nation, subsuming the female within the nation's narrative. He both invokes and continues the problematic dynamic of nation symbolised as female (as the poetic muse is traditionally symbolised as female), perpetuating the difficulties for female creativity that Lochhead is aware of: 'Being a feminist writer was stopping writing as if I might be a man' (*Monsters*, 10–11).

These two critics are representative of all of us who use Lochhead's poems (and drama). We raid her works to illustrate our arguments: sexuality (much of Lochhead's revue work in *True Confessions and New Clichés* provides very funny examples of ironic humour about the position of heterosexual feminists in 1970s and 1980s Britain,[7] caught between their sexuality and their politics) and its companion gender; class; nation. It is entirely legitimate to approach texts in this way. But what is equally or more important in Lochhead is a recognition of sequences within her work. Her poems should be relocated within these sequences, allowing them another layer of meaning, surely intended by Lochhead. Because she has been much anthologised (the only woman or one of few in several Scottish collections),[8] many of her poems are read out of sequence, details taken from individual poems, analysed to fit the argument, losing depth and resonance by being wrenched from context. Within context, however, they acquire different meanings. For example, 'Inter-City' is poem four in a sequence of five love poems: 'Sailing Past Liberty', 'Two Birds', 'My House', 'Inter-City' and 'In the Cutting Room' (DF, 30–5). Taken thus, the poet is returned to 'my / small dark country' from North America, and the last line, 'at a photograph called Portrait of Absence', refers to the absent lover. The whole sequence is about a relationship between two who are both together and apart, about the beginning and probable ending of that relationship:

> now I am here and
> you are there
> but that is neither here nor there
> as far as what we feel.
>   ('Sailing Past Liberty', DF, 31)

Proximity and distance are articulated as the poet writes: 'My House / is now also your house / ... / its walls have been printed / with your shadow' ('My House', 33); or, in 'In the Cutting Room', he edits his film and she '(beauty & the beast) at my business / of putting new twists / to old stories',

> Working together & we seem
> to love each other (but
> that too is an old story)
> yet not one of those fine few skills
> (loops of language
> spliced syllables of movement) we
> have learned to curse but labour at
> together   separate.
>   (DF, 35)

The poem and sequence conclude with Lochhead using the editing machine as metaphor for relationships: 'Ribbon of dreams, / have we put together too much / from scanty footage?' (35), hinting the probability of further endings and absence.

   The poem also uses one of Lochhead's characteristic techniques, the writing of the personal while simultaneously enacting the writing in the poem, 'loops of language / spliced syllables of movement' being the poet's stock in trade, particularly if, like Lochhead's, the poems deal in short run-on lines and meanings. In 'An Abortion', she witnesses the cow's painful birth of a deformed dead calf. This is the second poem in the Dreaming Frankenstein collection, immediately preceding a poem suggestive of Mary Shelley giving painful birth to monsters, 'Dreaming Frankenstein': 'he was inside her / and getting him out again / would be agony fit to quarter her / unstitching everything' (*DF*, 12). Lochhead had already begun her struggle with Mary Shelley and women's creativity in *Mary and the Monster* (1981), the first version of what became *Blood and Ice*.[9] But struggle with the anxiety and pain of creativity is also clearly signalled in 'An Abortion'; the 'emblem-bellow' of the cow drags the poet 'from my labour / at the barbed words on my desk top'. She may be 'shamed voyeur', but the cow's 'licking at those lollop limbs / which had not formed properly [...] as if she can not believe it will not / come alive, / not if she licks long enough' (*DF*, 9–11) becomes an emblem itself, the metaphor of birth pangs for something without life containing all the anxiety of the poet attempting the forming of poetry while fearing failure. In 'A Giveaway', Lochhead's poem about writing a poem about the end of a love affair, this becomes 'listen, you've got to be ruthless, / ... / you've got to cut and cut and cut. / Rewrite. [...] But finally I've scrubbed it, faced it, I know / the whole bloody stanza was wonky from the word go' (*DF*, 43). The idea of a poet's 'barbed words' ('An Abortion', 9) now clarified, this poem is a commentary on the lost lines and the lost affair, both cancelled out. Birth as metaphor for creativity might seem over-essentialised in its linking of blood and birth with woman's creativity, but Lochhead's sharp equivalence of feelings with writing reminds us of her view that 'a lot of women poets write as if ink were blood. But it's not. Ink is ink – and I would like to celebrate it for itself'.[10] Many of Lochhead's poems do just this, celebrating ink for itself: 'Poets don't bare their souls, they bare their skills' ('A Giveaway', 43).

Lochhead's range of language, 'female-coloured as well as Scottish-coloured' (*Monsters*, 11), is used to enact and satirise difference between men and women, or women and women, connecting with class, gender and individuals. She has many 'voices', constantly in dialogue within poems as well as her drama; for example, 'Kidspoem / Bairnsang' is a bilingual (and circular) poem, addressing directly the political issue of the subsuming of Scots by English in the educational process, ending with the oppressive power of the canonistic dead, white, English male:

> the first day I went to school
> [...]
> to the place I'd learn to forget to say
> 'It wis January
> and a gey dreich day
> [...]
> Oh,
> saying it was one thing
> but when it came to writing it
> in black and white
> the way it had to be said
> was as if
> you were grown up, posh, male, English and
>
> dead.[11]

Lochhead elaborates on linguistic diversity saying that:

> Scots is a fantastic language for multiplicity of register. There are all kinds of
> very, very local and particular class and almost gender and certainly geographical
> divisions which, you know, are mostly about class. Lots of Scots speakers, we
> have different ways of speaking.

She goes on to describe her variety of voices, to her sister, her grandmother, to
the interviewer, to the BBC. 'I'm not talking about putting on voices. I'm
talking about voices that are natural to you. I mean this is true of everybody.
It's truism' (*Verse*, 93). It was the availability of this variety of natural voices
that 'we use a lot in our ordinary, social discourse ... a wonderful method for
comedy' (94) that encouraged her to tackle her Scots version of Molière's *Tartuffe*
(1986). For this she used:

> a totally invented and, I hope, theatrical Scots, full of anachronisms, demotic
> speech from various eras and areas; it's proverbial, slangy, couthy, clichéd,
> catch-phrasey, and vulgar; it's based on Byron, Burns, Stanley Holloway, Ogden
> Nash and George Formby, as well as the sharp tongue of my granny; it's
> deliberately varied in register.[12]

Tartuffe is her most intensely 'Scots' work (in rhyming couplets), but this
description of variety of 'register' characterises all her writing, incorporating
English (and American in Nash) cultural stereotypes/archetypes, Holloway
(for Cockney wordplay), Nash (for epigrams and puns, rhyming and not-rhym-
ing verses), Formby (for Music Hall ditties), along with the anachronistic, the
'vulgar', the 'catch-phrasey'. Her chosen discourses clash and jangle, jolting
the reader or hearer's attention.

Lochhead has analysed her own use of cliché in terms of reader participation
in particular. Talking of irony, she says:

> it attempts to subvert ... from within. It relates to my attractions to cliché,
> which you cannot use without acknowledging it to be a cliché. You enter into a
> relationship with the reader whereby you have the reader join in the game with
> you, to complete the acknowledgement.[13]

This using of the everyday, the trite, is part of a kind of nod-and-wink school of
performance, consciously linking itself to an audience, part music-hall, part
postmodern (in the journalistic sense of the knowing 'ironic' use of the kitsch, the
clichéd, the stereotyped – 'it's alright, we *know* it's all these things, aren't we clever';
there is a temptation to pronounce it 'postmodren' as Norma Nimmo might have
said).[14] The humour as well as irony comes in her poetry from the clashing of the
everyday with the reader's expectations of the 'poetic', and in her drama from the
effect of 'complicity', a 'collective cocooning of stage and audience in a community
of speech which often includes, by implication, a sense of shared outlooks, values
and emotions'.[15] Lochhead has always exploited 'the stirring potential of cliché'.[16]

Lochhead's performance work, including her drama, is part of that music-hall tradition that survives in Scottish theatre as a living part of working-class culture, vigorously re-enacting itself each year at Christmas in the panto, contained by middle class sensibilities as 'ersatz', 'common', 'trite'. It is this mass popular culture, with Scottish actors 'rooted in music-hall and variety and with strong links to pantomime and TV sit-com',[17] which allowed the success of 7:84 Scotland productions, such as the first, John MacGrath's *The Cheviot, the Stag, and the Black, Black Oil* (1973), Wildcat productions, and Tony Roper's *The Steamie* (1987). In Femi Folorunso's view, either explicitly (in 'techniques of performance') or implicitly ('in dramatic consciousness'), in 'nearly every modern Scottish play, recognisable bits and pieces of music-hall aesthetics can be found', generating experience for audiences that is 'not private, but rather communal and consensual'.[18] Lochhead's performance pieces in *True Confessions and New Clichés* (also incorporating 'Sugar and Spite', 'Team Efforts and Assorted Revues'), and in *Bagpipe Muzac*, represent what she calls 'almost agitprop' or 'parodies' (*Verse*, 86). The pieces of 'True Confessions' eschew Scotland and language and concentrate on gender matters, making '*some* men (not *our* Real Pals) feel a bit got at' (*TC*, 2), and Lochhead writes her conflation of writing and relationship into a rap version of 'A Giveaway', 'Liz Lochhead's Lady Writer Talkin' Blues':

> So I dived out of bed to jot it down right
> Had too many good notions run off in the night
> […]
> He said Mah Work was a load a' drivel
> I called it detail, he called it trivial
> […]
> But someday soon I'll say enough is enough.
> And I'll set myself down to Write Him Off.
>   (*TC*, 37–9)

In *Bagpipe Muzak* Scotland and Glasgow are joined with gender relations as her targets: for example, 'Almost Miss Scotland' (3–6: 'Because the theory of feminism's aw very well / But yiv got tae see it fur yirsel', p. 6) and 'Bagpipe Muzak, Glasgow 1990' (24–6). In performance, these pieces are extremely funny (at least to women), but as with all sketches when read, as opposed to performed, they can feel one-dimensional even though their targets of pretentiousness (male or female) are often unchanged and still in existence years after they were first written. Lochhead herself acknowledges a danger in the music-hall tradition, of cosiness subverting irony: 'The subversive laughter of the music hall appeals to me a great deal. The trouble is that the folksy in this culture can become very cosy and self-congratulatory: hand-knitted instead of subversive' ('Knucklebones', 221). But she uses the 'cosy' of nursery rhymes in 'The Sins of the Fathers', a song from 'Same Difference' (written for Wildcat, 1983), to write of hidden male sexual abuse of children (at a time when adult incest survivors were first speaking out against what had been done to them as children):

> And the sins of the fathers
> Will visit the children
> Nightly in their heads.
> Men lie beside women
> Who are terrified children
> In the darkness of their beds.
> [...]
> Ask no questions, tell no lies,
> Keep your mouth shut
> Catch no flies.
> [...]
> Will visit the children
> Nightly in their beds.
>
> (*TC*, 101)

The use of nursery rhymes in circular repetition builds into a powerful expression of hidden incestuous rape. It is a precursor of the use that Lochhead makes of nursery rhymes and childish games to express violence and prejudice in the last scene of *Mary Queen of Scots Got Her Head Chopped Off*.[19]

Just as this chapter on Lochhead's work is the link between the chapters on poetry and those on drama in Part One of this book, so Lochhead's performance work in *True Confessions and New Clichés* can be seen as linking her poetry and plays, since most of her work in the second half of the 1980s and in the 1990s has been in drama. But there is a sense in which the two sides of her work are inextricably linked, dramatic poetry intersecting with poetic drama, common themes and style providing a homogeneity that is unexpected. I have already touched on Mary Shelley, her monster and creativity as a theme for Lochhead, both in her poetry and her drama. In the poetry it appears first in the sequence of three, 'Dreaming Frankenstein' itself (with its reference to Mary Shelley's nightmare dream of the story of Frankenstein and his monster), 'What the Creature Said' and 'Smirnoff for Karloff' (*DF*, 11–15), and then reappears in the later 'Lucy's Diary', 'despite myself, / the sea air is giving me an appetite', 'Renfield's Nurse' and 'The Bride' (linking the monster's movie bride with the ironic modern bride, superstitiously asserting the opposite to what she hopes: 'I lie beside you / utterly content that I know for sure / that this is never / ever going to / work', 70) (*BM*, 65–70). Like the lover in 'In the Cutting Room', Lochhead runs the theme 'over & over / forward back' (*DF*, 35) including in the several versions of *Blood and Ice*.[20]

Between *Blood and Ice*, *Dracula* and *Mary Queen of Scots Got Her Head Chopped Off* run other linking themes of sisterhood, class and blood. All three show both community and difference between women: the sisterhood (true and false) between women, blood, menstrual cycles, birth and bloodsucking, and the resistance and succumbing to victimhood. Mary's fugue, following mention of her mother's death in her birth, of 'Great … gouts and spatters … crimson trickle, tickling … a thin dark red line running … scribbling as if a quill was dipped in blood and scribbled … ' (ellipses in original, *Blood*, 12) connects explicitly woman's creativity and natural reproductivity. This passage points to the 'thick cloy, blood cloy … Two dents. Hard dents. Sharp teeth' of Jonathan's nightmare in Dracula's castle (*Dracula*, 128). In *Dracula*, Lucy's menstrual blood – 'My friend, my bloody friend'. MINA: 'The curse' … FLORRIE: '… it's many women are pleased to see such a friend' (105) – and Florrie's despairing 'Don't need to read. Telegram from the military … Dead, you bastard … Bloody generals! Bloody Empire! Dead and me three weeks late' (116) connect inexorably women's sexual desire for the dangerous (lived out by Lucy and Mina with Dracula) with the equal danger of procreation for the working-class Florrie.

In her 'historical' dramas, Lochhead makes clear both women's difference and their mutual position in the patriarchy. When Mina tries to be friendly with Florrie ('we'll have no more mistress and servants, I don't believe in them') and then immediately reverts to mistress/servant, and Lucy tries to placate Florrie ('I didn't think we'd find anyone else who'd do for us'), Florrie explicitly connects the hierarchical position of women with the position of servants: 'Oh, there's always someone who'll do. Your fine suitors'll find that out, Miss Lucy, never fear. You might even find yourself insulted how quick they forget you' (*Dracula*, 96–7).[21] The same dynamic is explicit in *Blood and Ice* between Mary and Elise:

> ELISE: Well I read the book too! You were always encouraging me to improve my mind were you not? Even although I was only a maidservant. Indeed I understand it very well. The Rights of Woman. The marvellous Mary Woolstonecraft [sic] was very keen on freedom for Woman. At least freedom for the Woman with six hundred a year and a mill-owning husband to support her – and a bevy of maidservants sweeping and starching and giving suck to her squalling infants – not to speak of her rutting husb——
> (MARY *slaps her hard. ELISE and MARY looking at each other, echoing the* CLAIRE/MARY [who are step-sisters] *mirror scene in Act I* [scene iv])
>   Don't you think we are sisters? Are we not somewhat alike? (*Blood*, 25)

In *Mary Queen of Scots Got Her Head Chopped Off*, the sisterhood across class lines is expressed by the dual roles of the actors playing Mary and Elizabeth, each playing the maid of the other, Bessie and Marian, and by the conflict that both Mary and Elizabeth feel between their roles as queen and as woman:

> LA CORBIE: Twa queens. Wan green island.
> […]
> LA CORBIE: … Ony queen has an army o' ladies and maids
> That she juist snaps her fingers tae summon.
> And yet … [ellipsis in original] I ask you, when's a queen a queen
> And when's a queen juist a wummin? (*Mary*, 12, 16)

The idea of woman as victim, implied in Claire's 'thin red choker' round her throat ('"à la Victime" … such a piquant bit of stylishness' (*Blood*, 11)) and in the stage direction of Lucy ('like all the perversely and against-every-last-odds-still beautiful big-eyed total victims' (*Dracula*, 114)), is enacted in *Mary Queen of Scots Got Her Head Chopped Off*. The blood of the 'victim' Mary is incorporated into the colour of her execution, a tableau of all executions:

> LA CORBIE: (*Very quietly*) Mary Queen of Scots got her head chopped off.
> Mary Queen of Scots got … head … chopped … off. [ellipses in original]
> (*And all around* MARIE/MARY *suddenly grab up at her throat in a tableau, just her head above their hands. Very still in the red light for a moment then black.*) (*Mary*, 67)

The complicated and problematic pairing for feminists of the terms 'woman' and 'victim' was articulated by Susan Brownmiller, the feminist who theorised the function of rape in patriarchal society in *Against Our Will*:

> I recall being puzzled and finally rebelling over the sympathy accorded to Mary Queen of Scots in her battle with Elizabeth in the tragic plays of Schiller and Maxwell Anderson. Mary was imprisoned in her tower and beheaded; Elizabeth won and survived. But it was haughty Mary, reduced in physical size and carefully feminized, who became the subject of romantic glorification, against the grain of history.[22]

Lochhead also problematises Mary Queen of Scots by pairing her with Elizabeth as well as by using her customary techniques of alienation and anachronism in the play. But she subscribes to the conventional twentieth-century view of the Reformation, represented by Edwin Muir's extremely negative view of Knox based on his belief that Calvinism was 'a peculiar religion – a religion which outraged the imagination', helping 'to produce that captivity of the imagination in Scotland which was only broken in the eighteenth century'.[23] Knox is presented as villain and Mary as martyr-victim in *Mary*, Lochhead offering 'not a re-vision of the historical Mary, but a re-vision of the myth that popular culture has built up around her'.[24] Her Knox is a variation of Muir's cultural destroyer of a golden pre-Reformation age, his religiosity expressed in that modern formulation of bigotry, the bowler-hatted bully of the Orange Walk (*Mary*, 47). Rather than Knox being seen as a radical challenge to the notions of kingship, he is Knox the oppressor, the international Protestant allied with English forces, opposed to the international Catholic allied with European Catholicism, who has torn out the Virgin Mary 'from oot the sky o' Scotland', leaving a 'black hole, a jaggit gash, *naethin*'' (23). This verdict is from La Corbie, the ironic commentator whose function, according to Harvie, is to problematise 'the neutrality of other tellings of history'.[25] But La Corbie's neutrality is in fact a disguise for a conventional position on Mary and a Knox whose villainy is compounded by the modern view of him as gender oppressor/abuser of women, his *The First Blast of the Trumpet against the Monstrous Regiment of Women*

(1588) read as a misogynistic document of hatred against women rather than a political anti-royalist text. Lochhead's presentation of Knox as pantomime villain undermines the central gender equality of the Mary/Elizabeth dynamic, ensuring that her Mary is also part of the nostalgic Mariolatry that La Corbie's opening speech satirises: 'National pastime: nostalgia' (11).

Lochhead's recent play, *Perfect Days*, satirises the 'fashionability' of the 'new' Glasgow, 'seeing as we're your regional style capital of Europe ... it's all a load of bollox'.[26] It is extremely funny about the dilemmas of the late thirty-something single-woman-with-no-partner-wanting-a-bairn but has a painful core dealing with death and unresolved pain between mother and daughter. This and its smart humour place it recognisably as part of Lochhead's overall work, despite its snappy prose dialogue and its apparent lack of poetic connection with Lochhead's earlier poetry and drama.[27] But *Mary* seems the most appropriate work to end on. It combines Lochhead's poetic drama and dramatic poetry in a powerful work (on stage or page), its dramatic sweep exemplifying her preoccupations with gender, class, nation and language. Lochhead is the writer (before writers such as Galloway and Kennedy in the 1990s) who was claimed for these intersections. Her articulacy of these elements in interview as well as writing, signposting the way for critics, leads us away from an overtly personal interpretation of her poetry in particular, refusing us the assumption that women's poetry is inherently 'autobiographical'. Like the lover posing for a drawing in her early 'Object', her work is 'capable of being looked at / from many different angles' (*DF*, 155). Her poetry and drama are works whose ironies forge intersections for our view of women, writing and Scotland.

Notes

With thanks to Liz Lochhead for permission to quote from her works.

1. (Edinburgh: Reprographia, 1972); reprinted in Liz Lochhead, *Dreaming Frankenstein and Collected Poems* (Edinburgh: Polygon, 1984), p. 123–59; hereafter *DF*. For a complete list of Lochhead's works in collections and anthologies, 1972–92, see Hamish Whyte, 'Liz Lochhead: A Checklist', in Robert Crawford and Anne Varty (eds), *Liz Lochhead's Voices* (Edinburgh: Edinburgh University Press, 1993), pp. 170–91; hereafter *Voices*.
2. Shabnam Grewal, Jackie Kay, Liliane Landor, Gail Lewis and Pratibha Parmar (eds), *Charting the Journey: Writings by Black and Third World Women* (London: Sheba Feminist Publishers, 1988), pp. 195–7 (196).
3. Interview with Emily Todd, *Verse* (Winter/Spring 1992), pp. 83–95 (89); republished in Robert Crawford, Henry Hart, David Kinloch and Richard Price (eds), *Talking Verse* (St Andrews and Williamsburg, VA: Verse, 1995), pp. 115–27.
4. But Lochhead even then was aware of 'consciously creating a sort of persona speaking these poems who was perhaps a younger, slightly more dewy-eyed and innocent than I was myself and it was a fairly conscious literary thing' (*Verse*, 88).
5. Interview with Rebecca Wilson in Gillean Somerville-Arjat and Rebecca E. Wilson

(eds), *Sleeping with Monsters: Conversations with Scottish and Irish Women Poets* (Edinburgh: Polygon, 1990), pp. 8–17 (9). *The Grimm Sisters* (London: Next Edition / Faber & Faber, 1981), reprinted in *DF*, pp. 69–104.

6. S. J. Boyd, 'The Voice of Revelation: Liz Lochhead and Monsters', *Voices*, pp. 38–56 (51–2). Cairns Craig, 'From the Lost Ground: Liz Lochhead, Douglas Dunn, and Contemporary Scottish Poetry', in James Acheson and Romana Huk (eds), *Contemporary British Poetry* (Albany, NY: State University of New York Press, 1996), pp. 343–72 (355).

7. *True Confessions and New Clichés* (Edinburgh: Polygon, 1985); hereafter *TC*.

8. For example, Roderick Watson (ed.), *The Poetry of Scotland* (Edinburgh: Edinburgh University Press, 1995) (the only contemporary woman poet); Roderick Watson (ed.), *MacCaig · Morgan · Lochhead Three Scottish Poets* (Edinburgh: Canongate, 1992). Douglas Dunn (ed.), *The Faber Book of Twentieth-Century Scottish Poetry* (London: Faber & Faber, 1992); Charles King and Iain Crichton Smith (eds), *Twelve More Modern Scottish Poets* (London: Hodder & Stoughton, 1986).

9. The first version *Mary and the Monster* is unpublished; two versions of *Blood and Ice* are published: (Edinburgh: Salamander Press, 1982), cited here, and Michelene Wandor (ed.) *Plays by Women Volume Four* (London: Methuen, 1985).

10. Interview with Peggy Reynolds, *Kaleidoscope*, BBC Radio 4, 30 May 1992; cited Varty, *Voices*, p. 152.

11. *Penguin Modern Poets*, Vol. 4: *Liz Lochhead Roger McGough Sharon Olds* (Harmondsworth: Penguin, 1995), pp. 61–2.

12. Liz Lochhead, 'Introduction', *Tartuffe: A Translation into Scots from the Original by Molière* (Edinburgh and Glasgow: Polygon and Third Eye Centre, 1986).

13. Colin Nicholson, 'Knucklebones of Irony Liz Lochhead', *Poem, Purpose and Place Shaping Identity in Contemporary Scottish Verse* (Edinburgh: Polygon, 1992), pp. 201–23 (216).

14. 'Meeting Norma Nimmo', *Bagpipe Muzak* (hereafter *BM*) (Harmondsworth: Penguin, 1991), pp. 34–5.

15. Randall Stevenson, 'Snakes and Ladders, Snakes and Owls: Charting Scottish Theatre', in R. Stevenson and Gavin Wallace (eds), *Scottish Theatre since the Seventies* (Edinburgh: Edinburgh University Press, 1996), pp. 1–20 (5).

16. Candia McWilliam, *A Case of Knives* (1988; London: Abacus, 1989), p. 112.

17. Roger Savage, 'A Scottish National Theatre?', in Stevenson and Wallace, *Scottish Theatre*, pp. 23–33 (29).

18. Femi Folorunso, 'Scottish Drama and the Popular Tradition', in Stevenson and Wallace, *Scottish Theatre*, pp. 176–85 (176, 178).

19. Another link is in Myra McFadyen, the actor who first performed 'Sins of the Fathers' and was then La Corbie. She was a member of Communicado, the company whose 'special and co-operative way of working … allowed *Mary* … to come into being'; Lochhead's acknowledgement, *Mary Queen of Scots Got Her Head Chopped Off and Dracula* (Harmondsworth: Penguin, 1989), p. 6.

20. For a full discussion of Lochhead's different versions of *Blood and Ice*, see Anne Varty, 'Scripts and Performances', *Voices*, pp. 148–69 (149–57). This essay and Varty, 'The Mirror and the Vamp: Liz Lochhead', in Douglas Gifford and Dorothy McMillan (eds), *A History of Scottish Women's Writing*, pp. 641–58, provide the most detailed discussions of Lochhead's theatre, radio and TV work, 1981–95.

21. See Jennifer Harvie, 'Desire and Difference in Liz Lochhead's *Dracula*', *Essays in Theatre / Etudes Théâtricales*, vol. 11, no. 2 (May 1993), pp. 133–43.

22. Susan Brownmiller, *Against Our Will Men, Women and Rape* (1975; New York: Simon & Schuster, Bantam Books, 1976), p. 374.

23. Edwin Muir, *John Knox: Portrait of a Calvinist* (London: Collins, 1930), p. 308; cited Cairns Craig, *The Modern Scottish Novel: Narrative and the National Imagination* (Edinburgh: Edinburgh University Press, 1999), p. 19; for further discussion, see pp. 18–22.

24. Jan McDonald, 'Revision: The Reconfiguration of Myths', in McDonald and Jennifer Harvie, 'New Twists to Old Stories', *Voices*, pp. 124–47 (134).

25. Jennifer Harvie, 'Metatextuality', ibid., p. 140.

26. *Perfect Days* (London: Nick Hern, 1998), p. 46.

27. *Britannia Rules* (1998), an extended two-act version of Lochhead's earlier *Shanghaied* (1983), seemed in performance thinner than *Perfect Days*, tipping from the 'subversive' into the 'cosy', although Joyce McMillan saw it as a 'gentle but powerful reminder of how complex identities are', 'Best of British', *The Scotsman*, 14 September 1998, p. 11.

CHAPTER FOUR

Sharman Macdonald:
The Generation of Identity

Susan C. Triesman

I don't want to be a bloody dragonfly when I die, Lily. They live for a day, dragonflies. That's all they have in the sunlight. I don't want my heaven to be a single day of bliss and then oblivion. I want more.

(The Winter Guest)[1]

I am suggesting that sexual difference is where we imagine, where we theorise; gender is where we live, our social address, although most of us, with an effort, are trying to leave home.[2]

Born in Glasgow in 1951, brought up and educated in Ayr and, from age fourteen, Edinburgh, Sharman Macdonald has spent most of her adult, and all of her writing, life in London. From her study window, beyond the large blank sheet of drawing paper which is the starting point and mind map for each project, she looks out into the garden – to her collection of significant stones from Scottish beaches.

Macdonald worked as an actress in the period before 1984, when innovation in British theatre was fuelled by the urgent need of dramatists, directors and designers to create theatre languages that could express the critiques and desires of a generation exploring new and desired modes of political and personal reality while the Thatcher government fought a fierce rearguard action against both history and the future. When she started writing plays, she was aware that 'the stage can stage anything'.[3] She writes to this possibility and this freedom, allowing a nexus of images and ideas to gather as she works, and leaving space for the audience to use its imagination.

If you laid Sharman Macdonald's stage-sets end to end, you would have a significant stretch of coastline – from Edinburgh's Portobello to Algeria. Sea; sand; rocks; archetypical nature defines the boundary of a country – its identity – nature in perpetual transition from one state to another. Slowly, rock is eroded to mundane grains of sand. Suddenly, the deep subterranean dynamic of tectonic shifts creates continents, the danger that produces the new. What else? The nuclear power station. Pollution from sewage. Fossils. A place of instability appearing as fixity. Holidays – time taken out of time. Macdonald's landscape is a place of liminality, where the sign systems of patriarchal discourse can be exploded and revealed as an arena of struggle in which there is space for change – the embrace of anomie for the sake of creativity.[4]

This landscape is crucial to the investigation of the construction and reclamation of identity which is at the heart of Macdonald's work. She highlights human relationships which are still largely marginalised in society and on stage, placing her characters at the edge of the elements to confront the trajectory of, in particular, women's rites of passage. She gives voices to those who are usually denied a voice, those defined by patriarchal society as Other: women – grandmothers, adolescents, children. And those other Others, adolescent boys and Scots, other disempowered people. Speech arising from repression and denial gives utterance to the taboo, the dangerous, the unutterable: their real feelings and desires. The revelation of their entitlement to their own subjectivity is often expressed in comedic or violent modes: Chloe and Lily, the old ladies who are the Vladimir and Estragon of *The Winter Guest* (1995), hold their own mortality at bay with a programme of attendance at, and comic reviews of, funerals.

This generation and gendering of identity, in local and national cultural contexts, is deeply affected by two aspects of the Scottish experience: the constraining Presbyterian culture and the wild Scotland of the edge of the sea – where nature offers a meeting place for new understanding. The edge of the sea is an important trope in women's writing and in feminist theory. For Toril Moi, Kristeva's emphasis on marginality 'allows us to view this repression of the feminine in terms of positionality rather than of essences'. If women occupy a marginal position in the patriarchal symbolic order, then they can be construed as 'the limit or borderline of that order' and as a 'necessary frontier between men and chaos'. In addition, because of their marginality, women will also merge with the chaos and thus 'share the disconcerting properties of *all* frontiers: they will be neither inside nor outside, neither known nor unknown'.[5] This is what gives rise to the double standard, and to the idea of Woman as the Dark Continent. But it also opens up other possibilities. Myra Jehlen suggests that 'the female territory might well be envisioned as one long border, and independence for women, not as a separate country, but as open access to the sea'.[6] In Freudian theory, to dream of being in and emerging from water, is to dream of rebirth: for the playwright and director Simone Benmussa, stage work is akin to dream work in that it is 'the reflecting surface of a ... deferred dream. It is the meeting place of the desires'.[7]

It is not surprising that rites of passage on the edge of the sea have a privileged place in Macdonald's œuvre: plays, films and novels. Liminality is the stage at which the person taking part in a ritual is on the threshold, significantly in no-man's-land, where taboos are broken in order to release a rich range of social possibilities expressed as multi-vocal symbols. This is where the raw and the cooked are differentiated and controlled, the dynamic process in which desire and culture are negotiated and society emerges. Interestingly,

Sharman Macdonald describes the Scottish voice that 'entrances' her as raw, full of energy, as if it were sited in the pre-symbolic order, and available for anything, not bound by rules. There is a great sense of freedom in her use of the spoken voice, moving freely from one register to another: tragic, comic, ironic, sarcastic, lyrical, furious. As with the construction of the plays, which undermine linear expectation, there is deliberate genre strain. She works with rhythms, humour and lyricism from Scottish song, nursery rhyme, the Bible (King James), her Welsh Catholic father's stories, the storyteller grandmother who ran away from Skye to become a Tiller Girl, the strong women in her family. The raw energy of the voice also relates to the way Glasgow demotic is received outside Glasgow – as uneducated, inarticulate, falling off the edges of society, the voice of the underclass. Macdonald's orchestration of everyday language opens depths of meaning in an unexpected manner – this heightening of the mundane is an important strategy in redefining the relative importance of events in her characters' lives. Morag's attack on her daughter over the questions of love and sanitary towels (*When I Was a Girl*, 40) is a fine example.

The liminal's deconstruction of boundaries and the confinement of norms is reflected in Macdonald's strategies as a writer. These strategies are familiar to both feminist and post-structuralist theory and practice, and refusal of boundaries and play of signifiers are deeply linked to the question of national culture. Scottish women's playwriting is characterised by the transformative and the transgressive, presenting 'the classic experience of the Other, where otherness becomes a multiple oppression crucial to character structure' and where the poetic and the comedic engage with the underlying structures of the dominant culture in order to deconstruct them.[8] It is especially important that, since they inhabit the structures they are destabilising, women dramatists render the familiar unfamiliar. The movement of feminist artwork in every medium has been away from the logocentricity of patriarchal discourse towards demystifying structures of authority in representation, and confronting received wisdom about aesthetic experience.

Brechtian historicisation of the text, fragmentation of the whole, disconnections, overlappings and variations, metonymy, privileging of the domestic arena which is seen as women's place, use of the mundane to reach deeper structures, and the foregrounding of non-verbal determinants of meaning from music to kinesics: all are in the playwright's arsenal. The potency of this derives from the fact that theatre is 'a sort of cybernetic machine ... a genuinely polyphonic system of information, which is theatrical; a density of signs'.[9] Since the relationship of these signs works across time during performance, other considerations come into play: the audience engages with changing meanings which are not clear until the play is over, and the facility for the theatre space to act as a metaphor for mythic journeys is enhanced by complexity. The play does not need to be mythic with a capital M for the audience to experience the way values, in crossing borders, can transcend the established order. The play of signifiers across both text and performance opens the space of interpretation to the audience. Macdonald's rich vein of theatre languages and symbols encourages engagement, as the audience deals with the tensions between them. After all, the power of symbolic life lies in the fact that it cannot wholly 'tame and domesticate the abyss of pure, unframed experience and potentiality ... At best, in Ricoeur's terms, it transforms the ambiguity of being into a multiplicity of meaning'.[10]

Time has a key presence in Macdonald's work. Diachronic and synchronic time may be juxtaposed: history cannot simply be read as destiny. Both *When I Was a Girl, I Used to Scream and Shout* (1984) and *When We Were Women* (1988) explore non-chronological, fragmented time. *When I Was a Girl* finds Vari on holiday, spending the day on the beach with her mother, Morag, and her friend, Fiona, in the present in 1983, while the past returns to the repressed (Vari's inscription into society as feminine) in its own chronological order, through a series of increasingly extraordinary flashbacks. The movement of time during the Second World War in *When We Were Women* swings violently between 1944 and 1943, interpellating the dance of love, death and betrayal in their own chronological order: the rhythm of the scenes is like a series of blows. In *All Things Nice* (1991), *The Winter Guest* (1995), *Borders of Paradise* (1995), the radio play *Sea Urchins* (1997) and the opera *Hey, Persephone!* (1998), simultaneous chronological time produces sardonic and ironic juxtapositions. With the exception of *All Things Nice*, they are framed within one day. The character of experienced time – both for the characters and for the audience – is symbiotically connected to the rhythm and pace of the changes.

Where Macdonald keeps a chronological time frame as such, in *The Brave* (1988) and *Shades* (1992), she explodes the convention by presenting Woman and her actions and desires as Excess. The excess in *After Juliet* (1999) is rooted in the strong doggerel that is the basis of the script. Excess brings its own problems of critical reception: its very success produces discomfort – it is a way of presenting character through a particular deconstruction of character and situation. Peter Nicholls, writing about early Expressionist performance, quotes from Jacques Derrida's *Writing and Difference*: 'In this new theatre we find that narrative indeterminacy and the hyperbolic pitch of emotion conspire to unsettle and exceed representation.' Nicholls adds:

> Restored to its absolute and terrifying proximity, the stage of cruelty will thus return me to the autarchic immediacy of my birth, my body, and my speech ... the dream of Expressionist drama purges the self of any contact with the past/the father.[11]

The novels *The Beast* (1986) and *Night, Night* (1988) share all the same time frames as the play, although chronologically mapped;[12] simultaneous time and flashback, memory and fantasy, present shared and developing views from multiple viewpoints which are equally strong even when a neighbour has a few moments centre stage. Through the course of a day in *The Beast*, we see the binary oppositions presented by the two couples who meet for a picnic on Hampstead Heath unpeeled with barbed wit to expose the artifice of the cocooned city life which denatures humanity, while those who are in touch with their humanity can still participate in the fairy-tale or even touch the Dionysian. The book, which was shortlisted for the Booker Prize, is a sharp and hilarious adult fairy-tale of transformations. *Night, Night*, another adult fairy-tale, starts with Frances's dream of herself as Cinderella giving her breast milk to guests, and over several years juxtaposes the warmth of children's inner lives and the solidity of the local angel with the domestic terrorism of the banal in the husband, Joe, who will not allow his wife love (the law of the father which also finds expression in the terrifying bombing of Libya).

We do not see the whole through Frances's eyes. It is very important that we enter the minds of others and the constructs they are building. This is also true for the plays: nobody stays still within time, but creates or re-creates structures from memory and fantasy, from taking action and making decisions – or refusing to do so. The time frames have a key role in enabling the break-down of the privilege of the protagonist as the sole interpreter and focus. Moira's getting of wisdom in *All Things Nice* is played in counterpoint to her mother's transgressions and disillusion, her grandmother's cynicism and the rare lyricism of the old Captain.

Historicisation – using time zones to make the family unfamiliar and intercut with the present – reminds us that the people we were, are still part of us. The dismantling of textual authority precludes the conventional pleasure of narrativity which colludes in gender differentiation and the concept of destiny. The interruption of the action produces shocks of recognition which remind the audience that history *is* narrative, by disturbing diachronic time. As Elin Diamond says, when considering Caryl Churchill's *Cloud 9*:

> By disturbing diachronic time Churchill lays bare the problematic of history and female identity ... Churchill thus succeeds in semiotising, making readable, the narrative of history in which the parts for women are written by patriarchal law.[13]

There are other signifiers of time: the paradoxes of fossils and sand in *Borders of Paradise*; the surf the boys ride so beautifully is eroding the cliff to sand and bringing down the skeletons of fish a million years dead; the graceful boys, the rigid bones, the threat that the wrong choice for the future, after this holiday from real life, will be the prison of adulthood. Cot has to liberate himself from the carapace he has built by using the pain of self-mutilation to circumvent the pain of racism, another ideology of difference, of the macho and hierarchical.

The weather of each play, unusually, is given in great detail – it is the passing of time and it is the weather in the psyche. The frozen wastes of *The Winter Guest* and the deceptive and treacherous sea beneath them, are present almost as a character both in the play and the film, bodying forth the loss that Frances feels after the death of the husband, with whom she had had such an intense relationship that there was no space in it for her son, Alex. For the same reason it is cold indoors (the heating has broken down). Everyone is outside time and normality: the sea is frozen as far as can be seen, and it is dangerous to walk outside. Nita dares Alex to walk on the ice, and he crashes through it. As Alex is brought closer to humanity by Nita, she cuts her foot on the broken glass of a photograph of his father. The only warmth is that of humanity and its capacity to love. Frances's thaw begins to start with the gesture of rubbing her mother's face against the collar of her fur coat. The boys on the beach, with all their thoughts of the future fuelled by castration fears and the reality of unemployment and other tragedies of adult life, stick a penis on that anomalous figure, the snowman, only to see it knocked off again. In an attempt to help with Tom's problem, Sam offers him a tube of Deep Heat to aid him in getting an erection, with agonising results. Underneath the humour of the boys' exchanges, and the tenderness of their handling of some abandoned kittens, there is a thread of despair as thick as the haar (sea mist) that drifts in over the now thawing ice floe, and into which Tom vanishes as he walks out to 'fresh land … To nothing. And all the time in the world for it' (241).

In *Shades*, rain and thunder act as prophet of doom. The hothouse atmosphere of the pre-Oedipal womb of a flat is quite overpowering as Pearl gets ready for the evening on which she hopes she will receive a proposal. Her son Alan alternately helps her to dress, brushes her hair, is forced to dance with her, and is a small boy who still wets the bed – he keeps dreaming of water, and when Pearl asks why he can't dream of rugby, he says he plays it by day, so he doesn't need to. As she dances with Callum in Act II, the wind blows through the empty ballroom. The violence and savagery of the dance itself, which Callum forces on her, breaks down her resistance until he forces her to tell him about her husband whom she has not forgiven for dying so young: in conjuring him up, she loses Callum, but meets herself, and is able to release her son to be himself, finally opening the window to let in fresh air.

The generations of the family signify the contradiction of time passing, but also being fixed, through inheritance, memory, or family myth; the arbitrary in love, as falling in love and marrying literally means living with a stranger: contiguity as relationship. The rite of passage is a removal from normal time and its constraint. As the participant moves to a new era and role in life, structures of power in society and the family change. The intersticial is the mode of transport: contiguity – working in the inbetween. These are moves and choices predicated on changing sexuality and desire.

Sexual identity in a gendered society is destructive. Based on the concept of difference, it is reductive, refusing people the multiplicity of possibilities they might have, making them withdraw from their own potential, and giving authority to discrimination. The ideology of femininity is replicated through the family, as well as institutions such as education, the law and the communications industry. The hard thing to deal with is the way in which the ideology works, the way the concept is interiorised and made to seem a truth about the human condition. And women are taught to police and further this project themselves. This is a major reason for women artists' insistence on breaking up the apparently seamless surface and story of women's lives. If you cannot reach the depths of character structure, and address its production and reproduction, there is little hope for change. Of course, as Jacqueline Rose points out, Freud recognised this, and Lacan puts this recognition at the centre of his work:

> Our sexual identities as male or female, our confidence in language as true or false, and our security in the image we judge as perfect, or flawed, are fantasies … Hence one of the chief drives of an art which today addresses the presence of the sexual in representation – to expose the fixed nature of sexual identity as a fantasy and, in the same gesture, to trouble, break up, or rupture the visual field before our eyes.[14]

For Macdonald, the rupture of this seamless surface is critical to the structure and language of the work. From Vari and Fiona in *When I Was a Girl* enacting their genital explorations and Morag's denunciation of 'jigging', the horrors of the misinformation and terrors inflicted on the very idea of sexuality produce a child who finds it hard to separate and become a woman. Morag's view of love is dour and severely restricted (its sources are explored later in *When We Were Women*) to the point where she can declare smugly, 'We never had a symphony in the house. There was no need' (80).

In seeking to avenge herself on her mother, who finds a man and has decided to live abroad with him, Vari gets herself pregnant in a wonderfully transgressive scene – the act takes place in full view, but completely undercuts the voyeuristic by the provision of a running commentary and suggestions from Fiona. The light touch of the play exposes the ideological work without beating a drum about it. Indeed, the play was intended to be mischievous, partly inspired by Macdonald's annoyance with the more puritanical self-congratulation of some feminists who could never see that women might need to look more closely at themselves.

Her second play, *The Brave*, had a very downbeat reception, and I feel that some of the critical cavilling was actually a response to Macdonald not behaving as a nice little woman this time, but creating a big, noisy and difficult play. It opens by plunging us in deep water: Ferlie, who has come to Algeria for a holiday and to visit her sister Susan who is a terrorist in exile, has just felled a local man who saw her as a sexual object. She is discovered standing over his body at the edge of the sea. The play is an assault on the male gaze and all it implies, and particularly on the codes of behaviour by which women are expected to live. At the heart of them is the instruction to smile, regardless of what you are feeling. Being polite and obeying implanted patriarchal edicts, Ferlie had smiled at the man, though he was annoying her, and had been assaulted. Her self-defence classes meant that she landed him on the floor.

Ironically, here he is the Dark Continent, the unknown Other. Because Susan cannot be exposed, they haul him to Ferlie's room in the hotel, where he eventually dies.

They are being watched by some expatriate Scots engineers, Jamie and his sidekick Robert, from whom they have to accept help, secretly removing the body to bury it. The burial ground Susan has chosen is the original but decaying Hollywood set for Samson and Delilah in the desert. In order to get there, Jamie prostitutes Ferlie to a policeman. Ferlie becomes more dissociated from herself as the play goes on, but ironically this allows her to express herself, rather as Elspeth's incipient Alzheimer's allows her to work through streams of consciousness in *The Winter Guest*. Eventually Ferlie achieves a freedom she had not expected from the holiday, after outbursts trying to sum up the banality of her marrriage and to assess her left-wing solidarity (sleeping with striking miners): 'Look at me. I'm the same. (*She isn't smiling*)' (181). She gambles with her own life before returning to Scotland, standing at the edge of the sea where the deadly snakes like to cool themselves. *The Brave* is uncompromising although there are some very funny lines in it. Jamie is obnoxious, racist, nostalgic and patronising; the only Algerians are compromised by their own positions; Susan had fled from her own fears of jail. It is a deliberately skewed mix of romantic visions of Casablanca and the downmarket packet holiday, a place where there is no escape from yourself, and knights on white chargers turn out to be seedy, misplaced patriots.

If excess is the key to dealing with sexual identity in *The Brave*, *When We Were Women* takes another step towards deconstruction: of images of war and of happy family life, through the struggle for life during the war, and in terms of what ordinary life is seen to be. The play is part detective *film noir*, with Mac being watched by the mysterious woman who is later revealed as his wife, Cathleen, and part war movie, as bombs rain down and illegal hints of light escaping the blackout, together with moments of radio music, provide the meeting place for Isla and Mac. We first see Mac crawling on his stomach on the road, to avoid the bombs. Isla's parents, much as they love her, care more for what the neighbours will say than for Isla's feelings, when they think of her future without Mac, who has bigamously married her, forcing her to give up the baby. And Isla gives no credit to her mother's problems about the bills: there is a shocking mime sequence when her father, Alec, beats Maggie up.

The mime sequences, and the wedding dance which starts in the house and then takes in even the mysterious woman, together with the jagged interrupted sounds and lights, are a very important element in the creation of meaning in the performance. The discourse between movement and the apparently settled state of things inside the parental home shows up the instability, and emphasises that the struggle for survival in war is an extension of the struggle in daily life, with its hidden domestic violence.

All Things Nice takes up the idea of the male gaze, both ironically and seriously, as two adolescents may or may not have seen a flasher opposite the school. This is one of the most complex of the plays, spatio-temporally and morally, with Moira's mother, Rose, away in the Trucial States (now the United Arab Emirates) writing letters and rehearsing for Anouilh's sexual comedy *The Rehearsal*. Moira is staying with her Granny in Glasgow – and the leering Sea Captain – and being bullied by her friend, Linda, a plain girl who sings Purcell and launches into the melodrama of the death of Dido while Moira is suffering and being denied any respite by her grandmother. The play is a forensic drama, with a twist, but the real hermeneutics concern the creation of the Presbyterian consciousness and its relationship to voyeurism and sexuality.

Non-verbal determinants of meaning play a very large part in Macdonald's work. The surfing of the boys in *Borders*, the swimming race in *When I Was a Girl*, the menacing clapping rhythms in *Shades*, the banging of the window shades in *The Brave*, the children's games in *Hey, Persephone!*, the sound of the sea and the air breathing in *Sea Urchins*, the fencing match in *After Juliet*: movement, dance, sound, music, rhythm, pace. This is a polysemic stage space, with multi-layered sets, ensuring that even the fine scripts are only one of many languages creating the meaning. The complexity of the total stage world jars you out of complicity: there are too many things to observe. *Persephone* took this to a particular extreme, as extraordinary noises and a collage of random objects cut across the reworking of the myth's narrative.

Woman's body is the major sign:

'The body is the inscribed surface of events (traced by language and dissolved by ideas), the locus of a dissociated self (adopting the illusion of a substantial unity) …' Foucault's perspective helps identify the body as a site of ongoing power relations which are often disguised (and traced) by language as the body is manipulated and re-presented (dissolved) through various discourses.[15]

The arena of gender discourse itself, the history of what happened to it, attacks the iconicity of Woman as body and reveals the need to release the play of significers on every level. In this way, Macdonald re-appropriates the sign as we see the potential in the interstice between one inscription and the next.

This appropriation operates in both the plays and the novels. Frances (*Night, Night*) acquires a tattoo as actual, painful and permanent writing on the body (an artistic if painful choice) as she starts to reclaim her identity through representation, deconstructing the male gaze through parodic action. The whole sequence alienates iconicity by disrupting the concept of fixity in representation, and exploring the arbitrary relationship between image and concept. Frances intended to have a dove of peace tattooed on her bottom. The young tattooist persuades her to have Masaccio's Eve instead: the writhing face mourning for humanity. Juxtaposed with the tattoo parlour, Joe, going mad, rides home from Coventry on the train and sees Frances's face in a Renaissance picture in someone else's book, and a newspaper picture of a small dead girl. When Joe sees the *Eve*, he goes 'down on his knees' 'crying tears of blood for the death of the world' (125–6, 134). This ability to mix the local and the universal through a central ironic image defamiliarises Woman as icon. The body is the site of fantasy and of representation, and also of power.

Macdonald employs comedy as a major tactic, a strategy of survival: comical juxtaposition, inappropriate verbal language, inappropriate behaviour and the use of the obscene. As Kristeva says, the obscene can mobilise the signifying resources of the subject.[16] The comedic and parodic ranges from creating a mundane domestic world for the Demeter/Persephone myth as the score for an opera, to the horror of some opera patrons who expect their fictive heroines to inhabit a more salubrious space, to the one-liners which spring up throughout her work, very often as a swift judgement on what has happened. Comedy as a method brings the disorder and the unpleasant of the subconscious, as well as the conscious and political, to judgement. Freud sees the joke as a judgement, part of a playful aesthetic attitude which might produce a freedom from which another sort of judging would be released, since it abnegates the usual rules and regulations. He distinguishes between jokes and the comic: 'The joke, it may be said, is the contribution made to the comic from the realm of the unconscious.'[17] Montrelay takes the idea further – the pleasure of the joke does not just lie in the return of the repressed. 'Does it not, rather, lie in putting the dimension of repression into play on the level of the text itself?'[18] As women are taught to withhold themselves from the male world of moral decision and judgement and responsibility, it is particularly shocking to recognise judgement through pleasure. This is an area of transgression which Macdonald opens, allowing the signifiers free play through metaphor and metonymy, and through the mundane, enabling us to witness pain and the ability to change. It is part of the psychosemiotic deconstruction which is a crucial part of reinventing and reclaiming oneself – one of the strategies for achieving one's own desire in life, or at least recognising what you need in order to do this. The rise of female stand-up comics also emphasises that telling jokes is a way of asserting subjectivity.[19] *The Beast* relies on a central pun: the beast in man, which civilisation seeks to tame, has vanished, and Roger no longer recognises himself. His sexuality has been trained into a mild performing trick by a wife who cannot have an orgasm. Jade has been given a yeast culture by a woman in her charity shop: 'The beast came from Russia. Really. A dissident got out. Some such thing. He brought the beast with him ... Do you realise it's always been alive? I can't bear the thought of it' (68). It is ironic that the story, taking place during the Thatcher years, undoes Thatcher's project to commercialise and dehumanise society. By the end of the book, Roger has reclaimed himself, Jade has allowed her real self to come through orgasmically. Live culture wins in the end.

None of Sharman Macdonald's plays have been premièred in Scotland. Most of them are unknown on the Scottish stage. Reviewers consistently refer back to her award-winning first play, *When I Was a Girl*, which is frequently revived, as if she had written nothing since. Irina Brown, then Artistic Director at The Tron in Glasgow, chose to put the radio play *Sea Urchins* on stage.

Unfortunately, this underlined the reviewers' feeling that the work had not moved on, since it revisits much of the ground of the earlier play, and the stage robbed it of its freedom of movement and its atmosphere. Macdonald was widely praised for the maturity and depth, the Chekhovian quality, of *The Winter Guest*. Its polyphonic structure, the four concurrent journeys through the implacable presence of existence, was recognised. However, I believe that the whole range of her dramatic work needs to be seen in Scotland. Placing the voice at the heart of much of her work in front of an audience which shares that voice would be immensely productive, allowing value to the hard things she says and having a strong effect on both audience and author.

Sharman Macdonald has been supported and nurtured by London writers' theatres, The Bush and The Royal Court. In Scotland, the emphasis is on new writing by Scottish writers living in Scotland. And the unfortunate reappearance of compulsory macho Scottish plays, often adaptations of cult novels rather than original playscripts, from the sordid underbelly of life, the *Trainspotting* stable, suggests that only male working-class experience is authentic. At the end of the century there were almost no theatres with women as artistic directors in Scotland, a major change during recent years. Stellar Quines is the only touring company specialising in women's work, with Focus only occasionally doing projects. While some women's plays are being presented, there is still the tendency to see them as a minority interest. The complexity and difference of Macdonald's work should be but is not represented.

Notes

With thanks to Sharman Macdonald, Richard Downes at BBC Scotland and Patricia MacNaughton.

1. Sharman Macdonald, *The Winter Guest, Sharman Macdonald: Plays 1* (Faber & Faber: London, 1995), p. 252. *When I Was a Girl, I Used to Scream and Shout*; *When We Were Women*; and *Borders of Paradise* also appear in this collection. *The Brave* appears in *When I Was a Girl, I Used to Scream and Shout*; *When We Were Women*; *The Brave* (London: Faber & Faber, 1990). Macdonald's other published plays are *All Things Nice* (London: Faber & Faber, 1991), *Shades* (London: Faber & Faber, 1992) and *After Juliet* (London: Faber & Faber, 1999). *The Winter Guest* has been filmed (1997).
2. Elin Diamond, 'Brechtian Theory/Feminist Theory', *TDR*, Spring 1988, p. 7.
3. Conversation with Sharman Macdonald, April 1998.
4. See Bernice Martin, *A Sociology of Contemporary Cultural Change* (Oxford: Basil Blackwell, 1981), pp. 49–51.
5. Toril Moi, *Sexual/Textual Politics: Feminist Literary Theory* (London: Methuen, 1985), p. 166.
6. Myra Jehlen, 'Archimedes and the Paradox of Feminist Criticism', *Signs* 6, Fall 1981, p. 582.
7. *Benmussa Directs* (London: John Calder, 1979), p. 9.
8. Susan C. Triesman, 'Transformations and Transgressions: Women's Discourse on the Scottish Stage', in Trevor Griffiths and Margaret Llewellyn-Jones (eds), *British*

and Irish Women Dramatists since 1958 (Buckingham: Open University Press, 1993), pp. 124–5.

9. Roland Barthes, 'Barthes on Theatre', trans. Peter Mathers, *NTQ*, IX:33 (1979), pp. 25–30.

10. Martin, *A Sociology*, p. 30.

11. Peter Nicholls, 'Sexuality and Structure: Tensions in Early Expressionist Drama', *NTQ*, VII:26 (May 1991), pp. 160–70.

12. Sharman Macdonald, *The Beast* (London: William Collins, 1986). *Night, Night* (London: William Collins, 1988).

13. Elin Diamond, 'Refusing the Romanticism of Identity: Narrative Interventions in Churchill, Benmussa, Duras', *Theatre Journal*, 37:3 (October 1985), p. 178.

14. Jacqueline Rose, *Sexuality in the Field of Vision* (London: Verso, 1986), pp. 227–8.

15. Anna Cutler, 'Abstract Body Language: Documenting Women's Bodies in Theatre', *NTQ*, XIV(2):54 (May 1998), pp. 113–14.

16. Julia Kristeva, *Desire in Language* (Oxford: Basil Blackwell, 1984), p. 142.

17. Sigmund Freud, *Jokes and Their Relation to the Unconscious*, trans. James Strachey (London: Penguin Books, 1976), p. 270.

18. Michèle Montrelay, 'Inquiry into Femininity', *m/f*, no. 1 (1978), p. 96.

19. See Lizbeth Goodman, 'Gender and Humour', in Frances Bonner, Lizbeth Goodman, Richard Allen, Linda Janes and Catherine King (eds), *Imagining Women: Cultural Representations and Gender* (Cambridge and Oxford: Polity Press in association with Blackwell Publishers and the Open University, 1992), p. 28.

CHAPTER FIVE

Sue Glover, Rona Munro, Lara Jane Bunting: Echoes and Open Spaces

Ksenija Horvat and Barbara Bell

This chapter considers the dramatic work of three playwrights: Sue Glover, Rona Munro and Lara Jane Bunting, representatives of different generations, sensibilities, class and geographic denominations. We also consider their creative role in the larger framework of the contemporary Scottish theatrical tradition from which they have arisen and the way concepts of dislocation and space occur in their work.

Sue Glover, born in 1943 in Edinburgh, has lived most of her life on the east coast of Scotland, apart from two years in London and a year in France. She began writing professionally in the 1970s, mostly for radio. In 1980 the Little Lyceum, Edinburgh, commissioned her first full-length play, *The Seal Wife*. Her theatre output includes *The Bubble Boy* (1981), *An Island in Largo* (1981), *The Straw Chair* (1988), *Bondagers* (1991), *Sacred Hearts* (1994) and *Artist Unknown* (1995). Her radio plays (all for the BBC) include *The Watchie* (1976), *Shift Work* (1979), *The Benjamin* (1983), *The Wish House* (1984), *Mademoiselle Perle* (1986) and *The Child and the Journey* (1994); and her television scripts, *Home Front* (STV, 1980), *The Spaver Connection* (STV, 1982), *The Bubble Boy* (STV, 1983), *Dear Life* (BBC, 1992), two episodes of *Strathblair* (BBC, 1992) and fifty episodes of *Take the High Road* (STV).

Rona Munro, born in Aberdeen in 1959, is one of the younger generation of Scottish playwrights who began writing professionally in the early 1980s. Her first play, *Fugue*, was commissioned by the Traverse Theatre, Edinburgh, in 1983. Writer-in-residence (1985–6), with Paines Plough Theatre Company, London, since 1985 she has given workshops in drama and writing for community groups, women's groups, schools and universities. Munro's work includes *Piper's Cave* (1985), *The Way to Go Home* (1987), *Saturday at the Commodore* (1989), *Bold Girls* (1990), *Your Turn to Clean the Stairs* (1992) and *The Maiden Stone* (1994).

Lara Jane Bunting, born in Catrine, Ayrshire, in 1969, works there as a teacher. She began her professional writing career after winning the Scottish Young Playwright award in 1987 and 1988. Her plays include *Vodka and Daisies* (1989), *Love but Her* (1990), *The Grave of Every Hope* (devised piece, Scottish Youth Theatre and the Royal Shakespeare Co., 1992), *Alfreda Abbot's*

Lost Voice (Visible Fictions, 1993), *Cumnock Chronicles* (7:84 Scotland, 1994), *John Paul Jones* (with Stuart Thomas, 1995), *It's not Enough* (7:84 Scotland, 1996), *My Piece of Foreign Sky* (1996), *Whispers of Waters and Yarns* (devised piece, 7:84 Scotland, 1997) and *Louis* (1999).

Audrey Bain considers the 1970s as 'a good point to begin investigating the emergence of a women's tradition in playwriting' because of three major women playwrights,[1] Ena Lamont Stewart, A. J. Stewart and Joan Ure, who wrote and were instrumental in establishing the Scottish Society of Playwrights in 1973. All three had variously been writing for the professional stage during the 1940s–1960s.

Developments in the 1980s in Scottish theatre, including the Traverse initiative for new writing and playwriting workshops for women, facilitated the emergence of playwrights such as Sue Glover, Marcella Evaristi, Liz Lochhead, Rona Munro, Catherine Lucy Czerkawska, Anne Downie and Sharman Macdonald. At the same time, theatre critics like Joyce McMillan began to question the policies of artistic directors in major Scottish theatres. She speculated that 'a certain orthodoxy in taste created by the great male-dominated plays of the 1970s was preventing women playwrights from receiving commissions at the major theatres' to the extent that a number, Evaristi and Czerkawska amongst others, turned away from stage production and towards radio and television.[2]

The number of drama productions by women playwrights is fewer than those by men and this might indicate that problems encountered by women playwrights – lack of funding or commissioning, difficulties over access for research, distortion of plays' themes in the production process – are exclusive to them. But the 1998 Staging the Nation conference found that this argument is limiting since similar problems are encountered by female and male playwrights.[3] In a recent interview with the authors, Sue Glover spoke of difficulties over funding and access to research, particularly in regard to her most recent project, *Klondykers*, about the fishing industry, but did not see them as exclusive to female writing. Rather, the problems come from general economic difficulties and marketing policies which encumber Scottish and British theatre production; problems which have made theatres somewhat cautious.

Through the chill of expediency, Scotland's playwrights, and particularly its female playwrights, have sought to find imaginative ways to carry on their craft. The 'female' artistic structure of collaboration has been explored fruitfully by a number of women, notably Marcella Evaristi, Liz Lochhead and Lara Jane Bunting; a recent successful working relationship between Irina Brown, then Artistic Director at the Tron Theatre in Glasgow, and Zinnie Harris resulted in Harris's *Further than the Furthest Thing* (1999). Sue Glover has made clear the value she sets on opportunities to build up working relationships with particular directors or companies. However, this type of developmental cooperation is increasingly rare. When interviewed, Sue Glover commented ruefully that any urban/rural divide is as nothing to the perennial Scottish east/west divide, adding that no-one in the west of Scotland knows who she, for example, is. This situation may be linked to the perennial debate surrounding the (non)possibility of a Scottish National Theatre, regional differences and agendas superseding national loyalties.

Unsurprisingly of all the women playwrights who appeared on the theatre scene between the early 1980s and 1990s, those who have gained the largest international reputation are expatriates. Sharman Macdonald and Rona Munro moved to London early in their careers, and although their plays generally have a Scottish theme, they are written from the perspective of an outsider looking in. Those who have remained, such as Liz Lochhead, Sue Glover, Anne Marie di Mambro and Lara Jane Bunting, explore, in their distinctive styles, the immediate issues that shape and affect contemporary Scottish society, with particular attention to women's position and a redefinition of gender roles. Their writing challenges the traditional orthodoxy of the inferiorising of the domestic (female) sphere in relation to the workplace (male) sphere.[4] Earlier plays such as Ena Lamont Stewart's *Men Should Weep* (1947) and *Business in Edinburgh* (1970) had subverted the notion that the domestic milieu is depoliticised and dominated by private discourse. Plays by a newer generation of women playwrights utilise domestic drama to undermine the dichotomy between public and private spheres; some use a domestic milieu to show how the former affects women's lives, while others remove female protagonists from the domestic milieu altogether, interrogating women's sense of dislocation in a male-dominated world.

Sue Glover deals with issues of dislocation and space. She sees *Bondagers* (1991) as the beginning, in modern Scottish theatre, of the removal of dramatic action from the enclosed areas of tenements, workplaces, the kitchens of kitchen-sink drama into the open spaces of the beach, sea, fields and woods. This removal is also evident in her early plays which have a strong sense of the visual; she has always wanted but never had her plays produced on a raked stage. Yet the productions still exemplify the movement and excitement of her visual sense. Her conjuring with open spaces is representative of the way in which a female force can transgress beyond the constrictions of a patriarchal norm. In her first full-length play, *The Seal Wife* (1980), the character Rona is a representation of a woman dislocated in the man's world, and alienated in her destructive domestic milieu. Sue Glover found inspiration for *The Seal Wife* on the beaches near where she lived:

> The beaches are always attractive. And yet now there is the oil rig that wasn't always there. And there is still coal on the beach, it is not actually coal from the mines, it's just the coal in the ground that comes with the sea which pushes it onto the shore ... [A] friend of mine knows about them because she lives in the area, so we went down to her cottage between the road and the beach, and I remember thinking 'How wonderful'. So we went for a walk down the beach and as we came down ... there it was, just a little baby seal lying on the sand and it looked at us and off it went into the sea. And we went further ... and

passed by a rock and there was another one and again ... it went to the sea ...
And I think it was after that I went to the Isle of May ... When we were coming
back, the boat made a round so that you see [sic] the whole island ... It was a
huge big cliff and it was stoned with seals ... There also was a man ... and his
wife, they had a cottage near the sea and they hunted seals ... I went and talked
to him once. I suppose it was all about the woman having a baby.[5]

In *The Seal Wife*, Rona comes from the sea, which becomes a symbol of aggressive female sexuality, 'her dark place'.[6] When pregnant, she spends most of her
time on the beach and pier, places representative of that hidden part of a woman's
mind where she escapes from her traditional responsibilities into a creative
and personal space. Lara Jane Bunting uses the dark in a similar way in *My
Piece of Foreign Sky*.

Glover further explores women's position in the microcosm of the family
and the macrocosm of society. *The Straw Chair* is the story of Rachel, Lady
Grange, infamous wife of the Lord Justice Clerk, who, having discovered he
was a Jacobite conspirator, was forcibly abducted by her husband and
imprisoned on St Kilda for seven years. In creating the character of the
'uncomfortable' wife, a drinker and a loudmouth, Glover gives voice to the
tale of a silenced woman, whose sanity and existence were threatened by the
expectations of a patriarchal society. Like *The Seal Wife*, much of *The Straw
Chair*'s action is located against the background of a bare landscape in proximity to the sea, representing both the landscape of a woman's mind and the
vastness of her imagination and fecundity. Initially Glover thought she was
writing a radio play, but then thought 'it has to be bigger than that; it has to
be like a soap opera, radio is just not big enough',[7] and her sense of visuality
and vitality of language found a better outlet in the concrete staging of her
play. The setting also represents Rachel's dislocation from the patriarchal
world of Edinburgh, economically and sexually exploitative of women, and
childbride Isabel's separation from her family and the father who shaped her
destiny.

Adrienne Scullion has established two significant points about rites of passage in workplace dramas. First:

[g]enerally these dramas are about rites of passage or turn on a series of ceremonies
or rituals of initiation. Such plays are often exceedingly formal, even classical,
in construction with a clear semiotics of gender being referenced and repeated:
a 'new boy' enters a pre-established community of adult men, his 'masculinity'
is tested, and he is either accepted by or expelled from the group.[8]

Glover uses this 'masculine' structure in *The Straw Chair* to show the transformation of Isabel from a shy and timid young girl into a fully grown,
sexually aware and empowered woman, under the influence of Rachel and
Oona, two other female characters. In these characters, Glover re-creates the
three types of the feminine which comprise the separate spheres model, virgin,

strumpet and old hag, and then proceeds to deconstruct these types through their interaction with each other and with Aneas, the only male character who appears on stage.

Secondly, Scullion suggests that workplace dramas 'traditionally [emphasise] communities of men – groups of male workers wherein women are totally absent or, at best, marginal players – and tend, therefore, to concentrate on the prevalent Scottish myth of an aggressively dominant masculinity' (179). In *The Straw Chair*, Glover inverts this by portraying a community of women. The only male character seen on stage is marginalised, to the extent that he becomes a puppet both of outside social forces and of his own false ideologies. However, the community of women is one in discord, because all three characters belong to very different social and linguistic strata, Isabel's rigid middle-class discourse sharply contrasted with Rachel's eccentric, rude, upper-class linguistic behaviour and with Oona's rural Gaelic. These three represent different Scottish social classes; they are forced together through no choice of their own, Rachel brought to the island of Hirta as a prisoner by her husband's men and Isabel brought there to accompany her parishless, middle-aged minister husband. Only Oona is indigenous to the island, and completely at ease with its mystic earthy atmosphere.

All three characters are enclosed by the vast sea around them. Rachel hates the sea because it divides her from her rightful place in aristocratic circles of Edinburgh, and from the social prestige she believes belongs to her by birth. On another level, her hatred of the sea might be interpreted as her rejection of her aggressive female sexuality which was unacceptable to the society of the time and which was the reason for her downfall. At first the sea makes Isabel sick, but eventually she is both drawn to and fascinated by it. Once again, the sea represents the powerful force of female sexuality, but this time with positive connotations, Glover's metaphors of sea and snakes showing Isabel's fresh interest in her body:

> I could glide over rocks ... and slither in the sea. Would you love me, dressed in scales? ... Aneas? Would you hold me closer if we were both created new and innocent with scales? ... Would you slither in the sea ... around me ... with me? (I. iv)

For Oona, the sea represents the unity of an old pre-Christian spirituality and nature, which is at the core of the Gaelic world of Hirta. As the play develops, differences between the three women diminish and what remains is the overwhelming sense of mutual acceptance and cooperation. There is also a visible shift in the power-structure: Rachel's authority wanes as her spirit crumbles, while Isabel is increasingly empowered by her acceptance of her sensuous nature and of the island's overwhelming spirituality, symbolised by her learning to speak Gaelic and by her trip to Borarae with the local women.[9]

In *Bondagers*, Glover explores in depth the issues of economic and sexual exploitation of women, and further concentrates on the 'phenomenon of

gender-specific communities' (Scullion, 179) by portraying the lives and rela-
tionships of six women at a nineteenth-century Borders farm. Using Nina
Auerbach's hypothesis that 'sisterhood ... looks often like a blank exclusion',[10]
Scullion argues:

> Contemporary Scottish drama's marked interest in the depiction of communities
> of women has ... found moments of exclusion, disillusionment and
> disenfranchisement. However, and perhaps in reaction to the determinedly
> formulaic drama around communities of men, and developing from the drama's
> engagement with the idea of family, Scottish playwrights have found and
> described moments of celebration and release in their engagement with female
> communities. (192)

In *Bondagers*, Glover diverges from the naturalistic structure of the earlier
plays. Although it retains a two-act structure, they are construed as independent entities, each beginning with carefully choreographed song sequences
which symbolise the two differing cycles of nature and those within wom-
en's bodies. Glover juxtaposes the domestic sphere of Maggie's kitchen with
the space of the fields, representing the life-giving force of both nature and
woman. Taking her explorations of women's experience and the plurality of
female discourses one step further, Glover removes male characters from the
stage. This does not remove the influence of male-dominated culture on
these women though, for it is reinforced by the constant mention in their
conversation of three male characters who figure strongly in their everyday
life; maister Elliot, his hind Andra, and a young ploughman Kello. Glover
suggested in interview that giving the men a space on the stage would have
clouded the main focus of the play: the presenting of the consequences of
economic and sexual exploitation of women's labour in the mid-nineteenth-
century Borders from a specifically female perspective. What Glover lays in
front of her audience is a different kind of history, a hidden herstory of women
behind the traditional history prescribed by men. The use of space also refers
to female identity as well as to procreative power. Sara talks of her man,
Paddie, leaving for Canada:

> He wanted – something, adventure, Canada. It was me said no, I wouldn't go.
> This parish was my calf-ground: Langriggs, Blackshiels, Billieslaw; the fields,
> the river, the moor up yonder with the lang syne rigs. Patie loved the land.
> 'Her'. But maybe I loved her more. (I. ix)[11]

The language and dramatic context of Sara's monologue carry undertones of
folk-tale. The listing of the names of different places and locations has a dream-
like mantric quality, very similar to Brian Friel's opening scene in *The Faith
Healer* (1979), while the dramatic context of the scene – with Maggie, Liza
and Jenny surrounding Sara and listening to her – evokes the traditional position of the storyteller encircled by her listeners. In *Bondagers*, scenes of
storytelling, song and dance are used to invoke the idea of unity amongst
women.

This use of folk elements is common in a number of plays by Scottish women playwrights, from Glover and Lochhead to Munro and Bunting. Furthermore, Glover in *The Seal Wife* and *Bondagers*, Munro in *Fugue* and *The Maiden Stone* and Bunting in *My Piece of Foreign Sky* use these elements and those of dream and hallucination to explore concepts of female sexuality and procreative force. These are seen as transgressing the patriarchal codes and as needing to be silenced by the unified endeavours of male-dominated social, historical and religious systems. In *The Straw Chair* the female characters are in conflict with religious norms which glorify the bourgeois image of the feminine as silent and obedient, the Madonna-like image of woman. Glover explores this conflict further in *Sacred Hearts* (1994). The schism, between the expected societal gender roles and women's existences, is emphasised in this play through the story of a group of prostitutes who hide in a Lyons church from a Jack-the-Ripper type of murderer. *Sacred Hearts* is not a murder mystery; Glover is not interested in speculating about the identity of the murderer. Rather, she uses historical events to develop a subtle and detailed analysis of the contradictory ways in which women are seen by men, particularly men in power, and the ways in which they perceive themselves. To show the claustrophobic state of the female protagonists' minds, Glover sets the play in the confined space of a church. The church building, traditionally seen as the space where spiritual peace and a feeling of safety are provided, becomes suppressive and unsafe. When men invade it and force the 'unclean' women out, the local priest – the man who should protect them – chooses not to act. In this sense, the very pillars upon which a patriarchal society is built are shown as hostile to women.

In *Fugue* (1983) Rona Munro experiments with the notion of plural female identities by splitting her protagonist into several facets. On one level, the play can be analysed as an interplay of different aspects of the protagonist's conscious and subconscious mind. On another, it is a devastatingly honest analysis of the ways in which a patriarchy suppresses female needs and desires to the point where they are seen as monstrous. Female sexuality and imagination are symbolised by the woods:

> KAY 1: Drenched four warm limbs in cold air. A small wood. It was my forest ... dead leaves, black, damp, halfway to earth, smell like spice ...
> KAY 2: This is where I was an outlaw ... this is where I was an Indian with a twisted bow ... this is where I was a tiger...[12]

In Munro's play femaleness is represented as a liberating force, and the animal imagery that Munro uses is reminiscent of the image of the 'Wild Woman' of Clarissa Pinkola Estés's *Women who Run with the Wolves*, who comes to us through the sounds of nature.[13] In Munro's work, female sexuality is often seen as predatory, linked with images of the woods, the cave and the land, and with rich visual and olfactory properties. For example, in *Piper's Cave* (1985), the cave represents the wild female imagination, while the beach symbolises 'a liminal symbolic space at the edge of the known, a place where things might be remade',[14] the space of a woman's unconscious. *Piper's Cave* is a play about male violence, and the incapacity of male imagination to overcome pre-set ideas of gender roles and inability to accept the equality of the feminine principle.

Munro sets the action of *Bold Girls* (1990) in two different environments, Marie's kitchen and a local club. This shift between locations enables Munro to explore changes in the roles and behaviour of her female protagonists. The initial setting of the first part, Marie's kitchen, is shown as her private space, 'stuffed with human bits and pieces, all the clutter of housework and life'.[15] The setting is dominated by two pictures – the Virgin and Marie's late husband Michael – defining the two forces dominating her life, religion and family. The sudden appearance of a strange girl, Deirdre, brings disruption into Marie's world; her values and beliefs are put to the test and found wanting. Munro places her female characters in the traditional domestic setting only to show the falsity of the traditional model of separate spheres (domestic/private/female versus workplace/public/male). As in Glover's *Bondagers*, men are absent – both Nora's and Marie's husbands are dead and Cassie's is in prison – and the ways in which the women have been affected by this absence are explored. The spaces used, kitchen and club, are depicted as cramped and claustrophobic, embodying the women's struggle with the bleak reality of war-torn Belfast around them.

The link between female sexuality and space is also explored in Munro's *The Maiden Stone* (1994). As in *Piper's Cave*, in which the fable of the mythical piper is used, Munro uses various elements of folk storytelling to weave a tale about four very different women in mid-nineteenth-century Scotland. Here, Munro explores the choices available to women in a patriarchal society and their implicatons, as well as the possibilities for a woman to express her identity through artistic rather than biological creation, a theme also explored in Glover's *Artist Unknown* (1992). *The Maiden Stone* portrays the relationship of two female protagonists – a middle-aged English actress Harriet and Scottish wet-nurse and wanderer Bidie – and the influence that their words and actions have on Harriet's young daughter Miriam and a local girl Mary. Harriet and Bidie are both foreigners in rural Auchnibeck, but while Harriet feels exiled from wealthy artistic circles in Edinburgh, Bidie, like Sara in *Bondagers*, is represented as an Earth Mother at one with the land.

For Harriet, procreation is neither essential nor a natural function of womanhood. She tells the 16-year-old Mary about her own children's births:

> I bore two children at the back of a stage with only the company to help me when they were not required in their parts. Each time, Mary, each time I rose from my child bed, put that new thing in a basket and walked out on stage to say my lines, to dazzle them and the pain was nothing, the fear and the blood were nothing because they saw me and I was transformed.
> BIDIE: Noo if that's true mistress you must be awfy lucky wi your labour, but you've the hips fir it, it could be so.

HARRIET: There is nothing, nothing you cannot be when their eyes are on you.
Nothing. (I. vi)[16]

This emphasises the dichotomy between artistic and biological creation in
terms of the fulfilment of women's aspirations and needs. Harriet seeks her
fulfilment in acting rather than motherhood although acting is a profession
based on pretence and imagining; Harriet's account of her elopement with her
first husband is counterpointed by Bidie's acerbic comment implying that
Harriet's story is a figment of her romantic imagination, the truth being perhaps
more mundane:

> I got behind him on his horse. I held him tight. I closed my eyes. We left my
> house, my family, my name, my fortune, everything. We galloped past the fields
> and streams of all my nursery games and I saw nothing but the dark, felt nothing
> but his back against my cheek, heard nothing but the hooves and the wind. I
> was seventeen when I first played Juliet, new to my art and new to my love. I
> looked down at him, throwing his words out into the smoky dark for me to
> catch. He came and called for me under my father's window and I climbed
> down to him.
> (BIDIE *laughs*.)
> Are you wed at all, mistress? (38)

Bidie is the complete opposite to Harriet, her image that of the archetypal
mother figure. In Act I, scene i, she walks centre stage with a baby on her hip;
in scene ii, she arrives on stage on a cart pushed by her children, 'her brood',
invoking Brecht's Mother Courage, archetypal mother figure of twentieth-
century theatre:

> (BIDIE *is enthroned on a handcart, surrounded by bags and bundles. Her brood are
> pushing her, pretending to be horses, snorting and stamping and neighing. They push her
> faster. BIDIE roars with laughter.*)
> BIDIE: Mind! You'll tip me oot!
> (*They wheel her to a stop facing the startled* HARRIET. BIDIE *lies at her ease amongst the
> bundles and smiles at the other woman.*) (6)

Bidie is dominated by her sense of belonging to the land, and her need to
protect her children (she assaults the sergeant who attempts to rape her teen-
age daughter). The procreative power of nature's cycle is seen as a female
force, echoing the link between woman and land in *Bondagers*; but the cycle
is also shown as a potentially life-taking force with the power to destroy the
life-giver, symbolised in the folk-tale of the maiden stone of the play's title. By
representing two completely different but equally strong female characters,
Munro shows how in the past century a woman had two choices: either facing the consequences of her sexuality (Harriet almost dies in childbirth, Act
II) or giving up her sexual needs altogether (Miriam rejects her sexuality in
favour of social respectability, becoming a teacher, then an occupation of

unmarried women). The play constitutes a powerful criticism of patriarchal hypocrisy which has confined female sexuality and imagination throughout history.

However, the end of *The Maiden Stone* suggests that women and men depend upon each other for comfort and survival, overriding gender differences:

NICK: Aye. So you thocht I was deid.
BIDIE: It's been ten years. But I never saw your soul pass me on the road.
NICK: An you ken fit soul looks like dee you?
BIDIE: Oh aye.
NICK: Fit's that then?
BIDIE: Like a wee girl. A bonny wee girl. Jist big enough tae tie bows in her hair.
(*Mimes doing it.*)
Pause.
NICK(*grins*): Havers.
BIDIE: Mebbe. Have you drink on you?
NICK: Aye.
BIDIE: Come intae the shelter then pet.
NICK: I'll be on my road the morn.
BIDIE: That's aye been the way wi' baith o' us. Come in or this wild nicht may kill us baith. (85)

Here Munro also offers us a potentially different reading of the concept of masculinities in drama, her male characters far removed from the macho representations of the Scottish male workplace. Harriet's husband Archie is dominated by her, and Bidie comments on Nick's soul being 'like a wee girl', indicating the feminine side of his character.

Lara Jane Bunting also explores women's choices in modern society. Her play *Vodka and Daisies* (1989)[17] is reminiscent of Marcella Evaristi's *Wedding Belles and Green Grasses* (1981) and deals with the hopes and expectations of five girls growing up in a small west coast town. Bunting employs a similar structure to Evaristi, the action jumping from past to present, and back, to show the protagonists' expectations, realised or otherwise. Unlike Glover and Munro, Bunting uses naturalism in her presentation of provincial Scottish life. The complexity and honesty of the depiction of adolescence, friendship, love, machismo, homosexuality, provincial closeness and bigotry prevent the play falling into melodrama. Two of the girls leave: Anna to continue her education at art college, and the 'bastard' Leeny to escape local prejudice. In doing so, Leeny rejects her mother, the only character to oppose the patriarchal norms of their society. Bunting shows that leaving is not necessarily the best choice, but is still a choice. In interview, she comments '*Vodka and Daisies* was a celebration of women from my area who [stayed] there, who [resisted] the move towards escaping'.[18]

Bunting's interest in showing slice-of-local-life stories is further explored in her play *My Piece of Foreign Sky* (1996).[19] The play deals with the life of a miner's family in Catrine, Ayrshire, and in particular with the effects of redundancy on relationships. Central to it are Nell's relationships with her son Lex and husband Sanny. Nell's early marriage and pregnancy have made it impossible for her to pursue her dreams, so she lives them through her son, wishing him to have a different, better future, away from the uncertainty of mining life. This is represented in the play's title, which comes from a poem Nell recited to Lex as a child, and which he repeats in the play:

> LEX: Och. Ma mither. When Ah wis wee. She yised tae tell me this poem.
> ELLEN: Poem?
> LEX: Aye. She yist tae waish ma face, then comb ma hair, then kiss the tap o ma heid, an tell me the poem. To my child. You are the trip I did not take. You are the pearls I did not buy. You are my blue Italian lake. You are my piece of foreign sky.

When reciting the poem, Lex speaks in standard English, depicting Nell's belief that the better life she dreams of is completely separate from her own environment. Furthermore, the image of the vastness of sky represents one woman's aspirations and hopes for a space which is truly her own where she does not have to fulfil the expectations of others. Woman's inner space is also represented by images of the dark. Nell's husband Sanny, a former miner, yet afraid of the dark, makes Nell leave the light on in their bedroom until he falls asleep and this is seen as typical of the constant demands and pressures made upon Nell by him. While Sanny is at work Nell sleeps with the lights off in a space where she can enjoy solitude. Once Sanny is out of work and at home all the time, Nell feels both her outer and inner space threatened. Sanny feels her act of switching off the light is an act of spite, failing to understand Nell's need to assert her own identity independent of her function as mother and wife:

> NELL: Dae it tae you? Ah don't sleep wi the licht oaf tae get ait you! cun ye no see that? Ah dae it fur me. Ye hear me? Fur me. Me. Nell. A wumman thit's goat a life wi meenits in it thit you Sanny cannae share. Meenits thit ur mine. Jist mine. Hinkin an dain hings thit only Ah ken aboot. An they meenits keep me sane. Lyin in the daurk. Just the daurk an me. Ah oun be whauever Ah waint. (20)

Bunting subverts the domestic sphere by having men invade it, echoing Ena Lamont Stewart's *Men Should Weep* where the Morrisons' relationship deteriorates once John is out of work and, in a gender reversal, Maggie becomes the sole breadwinner.

Opposed to Nell is Ellen, Lex's fiancée, whose dreams of the future are focused on familiar community and marriage, an example of a woman of a younger generation who chooses to stay in her home town and make a go of what is available, when the choice to leave is an obvious and easier one. Unlike

Nell whose unfulfilled dreams have left her bitter, Ellen seems to have no expectations other than the welfare of her family and everyday survival:

> NELL: Aye. A joab everyboady thocht wid last furever.
> ELLEN: It's no like that oany mair Nell. Ah cunnae expect oanything fae Lex ur ma weans. Acause aa we'll huv tae dae is get oan wi nuthin hope thit it'll get better. An ma luv fur him is the stroangest hope we've goat. That an his luv fur me. Too bloody richt Ah'll mairry'im, lie aside 'im ait nicht fae noo oan.
> NELL: An never dream? Never waint mair?
> ELLEN: Aye that's richt. Never. (29)

Her refusal to believe in anything beyond an everyday reality, which sees a woman as a reflection of her domestic responsibilities, may be a weak attempt to convince herself that she does not want anything more out of life, similar to the female characters in *Vodka and Daisies* who claim they have made the right choice by staying at home. Bunting's writing is ambiguous; Ellen's attitude may be interpreted as that of a young generation who have either learnt from Nell's generation, or have not. This ambiguity can be seen as a sign of maturity in Bunting's writing. She herself is representative of this new generation of women who may believe that they live in a world where the feminist battles have already been fought and won.

In her play *Love But Her* (1993),[20] Bunting sets out to explore woman's invisibility in a man's world. The play deals with the life of Jean Armour, Robert Burns's wife, whose talents and individuality have been hidden from the world, buried by accounts of her husband's pursuits. In writing this play Bunting gives Armour a voice, letting her speak for herself. In a review of the first production, Joyce McMillan drew attention to this:

> Bunting's play ... makes a neat, skilful job of presenting the story from Jean's point of view. Burns ... is a peripheral figure, and not a particularly attractive one. In the foreground sits ... Jean, ... her friend Nance, and ... Burns' daughter Jessie, raised by Jean as her own ... [T]he play ... conveys a powerful sense of the women's hard, physical lives, and of the extent to which Burns' work as a poet and collector was influenced by their singing of traditional songs.[21]

Again, the emphasis is on depicting women's communities, with their sense of solidarity, and giving voice to women silenced in a world where honour and status are measured by men's rules. The musical sequences suggest a perception of the women's community based on a creative, storytelling tradition; excluded from public life by gender and class, the women stay at home, do domestic chores, rear children, accompanying their tasks with conversation and song. To emphasise the folkloric, communal spirit, Bunting wrote this play in tableaux form, using her own Ayrshire dialect, local folk songs and fiddle music. Again, the setting is the domestic environment of the kitchen; however, in Bunting's play it becomes the place of creativity, the inner space of woman's mind where imagination can run wild, unshackled by the oppressive outside world.

With Glover, Munro and Bunting, storytelling and singing are passed from artist to artist, much as they used to be passed from one generation of women's communities to another, giving them voice. These three women playwrights use the images of open, empty space to depict woman's inner world of imagination and desire. In this way, they give outlet to the unheard voices, suppressed dreams and hidden communities of women. This breaking of silence can be seen as a communal act which gives courage to the voices of individual women. In their writing, they provide a means for a rebalancing of gender roles.

Notes

1. Audrey Bain, 'Loose Canons: Identifying a Women's Tradition in Playwriting', in Randall Stevenson and Gavin Wallace (eds), *Scottish Theatre since the Seventies* (Edinburgh: Edinburgh University Press, 1996), p. 138.
2. Cited Bain, 'Loose Canons', p. 139; Joyce McMillan, 'Women Playwrights in Scottish Theatre', *Chapman*, 43–4 (Spring 1986), pp. 72–3.
3. March 1999, Drama Department, Queen Margaret University College, Edinburgh.
4. The basis of the oppositional model is that in which women's place is in a private, domestic domain inferior to men's public, workplace domain of authority, making women's position in society silent and powerless. See, for example, Dale Spender, *Man-Made Language* (London: Routledge & Kegan Paul, 1985).
5. Interview, November 1996, by Ksenija Horvat, p. 8.
6. Penelope Shuttle and Peter Redgrave, *The Wise Wound: Menstruation and Everywoman* (London: Victor Gollancz, 1978), p. 266.
7. Interview, November 1996, by Ksenija Horvat, p. 1.
8. Adrienne Scullion, 'Feminine Pleasures and Masculine Indignities: Gender and Community in Scottish Drama', in Christopher Whyte (ed.), *Gendering the Nation: Studies in Modern Scottish Literature* (Edinburgh: Edinburgh University Press, 1995), pp. 169–204 (179).
9. See also Ksenija Horvat, 'Plurality of Female Discourse in Three Plays by Sue Glover', in *Cats on a Cold Tin Roof: Female Identity and Language in Plays of Five Contemporary Scottish Women Playwrights* (unpublished Ph.D.; Edinburgh: Queen Margaret University College, 1999), pp. 24–86.
10. Nina Auerbach, *Communities of Women An Idea in Fiction* (Cambridge, MA, and London: Harvard University Press, 1978), p. 3.
11. Sue Glover, *Bondagers*, in *Made in Scotland: An Anthology of New Scottish Plays*, selected and introduced by Ian Brown and Mark Fisher (London: Methuen Drama, 1995), p. 140.
12. Ellipses in original. Rona Munro, *Your Turn to Clean the Stair & Fugue* (London: Nick Hern, 1995), p. 80.
13. Clarissa Pinkola Estés, *Women who Run with the Wolves: Contacting the Power of the Wild Woman* (London: Rider, 1992).
14. Susan C. Triesman, 'Transformations and Transgressions: Women's Discourse on the Scottish Stage', in Randall Stevenson and Gavin Wallace (eds), *Scottish Theatre since the Seventies* (Edinburgh: Edinburgh University Press, 1996), p. 131.

15. Rona Munro, *Bold Girls* in *First Run 3: New Plays by New Writers*, selected and introduced by Matthew Lloyd (London: Nick Hern Books, 1991), p. 3.
16. Rona Munro, *The Maiden Stone* (London: Nick Hern Books, 1995), p. 39.
17. First performed: Annex Theatre Company.
18. Sarah Villiers, 'From Strong Roots Do Fine Plays Grow', untraced newspaper article.
19. Lara Jane Bunting, *My Piece of Foreign Sky* (1996, manuscript), p. 11; first performed at the Link Theatre, London.
20. Revised for the Brunton Theatre, Musselburgh, 1999.
21. *The Guardian*, 26 January 1993.

CHAPTER SIX

Jackie Kay's Poetry and Prose: Constructing Identity

Alison Lumsden

Recently, Jackie Kay (b. 1961) wrote: 'I think I will always be interested in identity, how fluid it is, how people can invent themselves, how it can never be fixed or frozen.'[1] Kay's concern with identity is hardly surprising; as a black woman adopted and brought up in Glasgow by white Scottish parents she is uniquely placed to comment on the interface between personal and cultural identity. As a lesbian and single mother, her sexuality also provides her with an interesting starting point from which to consider the relationship between identity and gender through the medium of the text. Kay's almost Lacanian concern with the fluidity of identity and language is also reflected in her choice of genres; she is a writer of poetry for both adults and children, a novelist and a playwright. Her positioning in this book, at the close of the section on poetry and drama but providing a bridge into the next on prose fiction, reflects this generic flexibility.

Identity and the construction of subjectivity are prominent themes in Kay's first collection of poetry *The Adoption Papers* (1991) which itself demonstrates the difficulties of describing Kay's work in terms of genre, since its opening sequence, 'The Adoption Papers', was originally broadcast on radio.[2] It also encapsulates a desire to disrupt any straightforwardly monolithic construction of self in its formal concerns, since it is printed in three typefaces, each representing a different 'voice' by which identity is explored; that of the daughter, the adoptive mother and the birth mother. This immediately implies a fragmented, elusive subjectivity, as each persona is given space to voice her own particular desires and fears which between them contribute to the adult whom the adopted daughter will become.

Thematically 'The Adoption Papers' also offers a study of the linguistic and cultural parameters of identity. Revisiting concerns which have informed postmodern feminist thinking since at least the mid-1970s, and which have been significantly elaborated upon in post-colonial critical discourses, Kay explores both genetically inherited, teleologically inscribed, essentialist models of self, and those which posit the subject as a social and familial construct, interrogating the tensions which sit between these apparent binary oppositions. Here, identity is, at times, constructed through a common language, a shared past and common memories ('the mother who stole my milk teeth / ate the digestive left for Santa' (20)), a position which the adoptive mother reiterates reminding the reader that identity is as much about this shared experience as it is about biological inheritance (a form of teleological determinism):

> she's my child, I have told her stories
> wept at her losses, laughed at her pleasures,
> she is mine.
> [...]
> I listened to hear her talk,
> and when she did I heard my voice under hers
> and now some of her mannerisms crack me up
>
>   (23)

However, simultaneously, the poems also assert the desire to locate oneself within the perceived certainties of a biological past – a desire reinforced by the photograph 'Human chromosomes' on the collection's cover. The daughter, for example, wants to uncover the details of her own moment of birth – 'I was pulled out with forceps' (28) – and while she may acknowledge the limits of a biologically grounded notion of self, she also recognises that, in her desire to recover and inscribe her fractured identity, it is inescapably seductive. In the poem 'Generations' she voices this ontological contradiction:

> I have my parents who are not of the same tree
> and you keep trying to make it matter,
> the blood, the tie, the passing down
> generations.
> We all have our contradictions,
> the ones with the mother's nose and father's eyes
> have them;
> the blood does not bind confusion,
> yet I confess to my contradiction
> I want to know my blood.
>
>   (29)

The longing expressed here cuts across constructions of the self as only familially constructed, so that the poems offer no solution to the questions of identity which they have raised but simply give voice to the tensions inherent within the familiar parameters in which feminist postmodernity has conducted the negotiation of female subjectivity. 'The Meeting Dream' with which the sequence ends is, tellingly, not an actual conclusion to the narrative which the poems have told, but only the daughter's imagined resolution, a provisional location of self in relation to lost/longed-for otherness:

> *If I picture it like this it hurts less*
>
> One dream cuts another open like a gutted fish
>   nothing is what it was;

> she is too many imaginings to be flesh and blood.
> There is nothing left to say.
> Neither of us mentions meeting again.
>
> (33)

Repeatedly Kay resolves the questions of identity raised in her work via such imagined possibilities; hypothetical constructions which are both open-ended and provisional, suggesting that subjectivity is not fixed into any one position, but is, rather, multiplistic, *elusive* and flexible.

While 'The Adoption Papers' deals mainly with the personal parameters by which the self may be defined, it also explores subjectivity as it is socially constructed through race and gender. While questions of gender may not be particularly foregrounded in this sequence, they are present and are again expressed in terms of a binary tension between essentialist and socially constructed notions of femininity. 'I want to stand in front of the mirror / swollen bellied so swollen bellied', 'I want my waters to break / like Noah's flood' (11) states the adoptive mother, seemingly positing a connection between 'natural' femininity and a woman's biological potential for reproduction. A similar connection is reiterated in the birth mother's sense of loss and her inability to suppress the bond which she has with her child: 'I cannot pretend she's never been / my stitches pull and threaten to snap / my own body a witness / leaking blood to sheets, milk to shirts' (13). Similarly, whatever other parameters may shape the daughter's adult self, she also realises that she is a woman shaped by a biological imperative:

> I know my blood.
> It is dark ruby red and comes
> regular and I use Lillets.
> I know my blood when I cut my finger.
> I know what my blood looks like.
>
> It is the well, the womb, the fucking seed.
>
> (29)

However, this passage also throws us back to the larger debate in the poems between biological (blood) inheritance and familial construction, simultaneously contextualising any model of femininity based only on a biological 'telos'.

The passage also links us as readers to the other main ontological negotiation at work in Kay's poetry: the interrogation of her own blackness. Post-colonial discourse argues that 'in the language of colonialism, non-Europeans occupy the same symbolic space as women'.[3] While this is problematic, here Kay explores the ways in which, in a white, Scottish society, blackness, like femininity, may be a form of negation; 'Just as we were going out the door / I said oh you know we don't mind the colour' (14) states the adoptive mother, 'to think she wasn't even thought of as a baby, / my baby, my baby' (24). As the daughter grows, however, the issue of her blackness also emerges as a site in which further to explore the tension between essential and constructed models of identity. Her blackness is both something imposed upon her by society – the boy's taunting of her as 'Sambo' (24), the teacher who 'shouts from the bottom / of the class Come on, show / us what you can do I thought / you people had it in your blood' (25) – and a marker of an apparently essential aspect of self which cuts through simple social factors. 'Maybe that's why I don't like / all this talk about her being black' states the mother in 'Black Bottom':

> I brought her up as my own
> as I would any other child
> colour matters to the nutters;
> but she says my daughter says
> it matters to her.
>
> (24)

Frantz Fanon describes the particular needs of Negroes living within a white culture (his example is the United States) to attach themselves to a cultural 'matrix'.[4] In Kay's work colour, like gender, may be in part a social construction, but it is also a vital aspect of subjectivity which the individual must acknowledge and interrogate in order to come to terms with her self.

As Gabriele Griffin reminds us, however, 'The Adoption Papers' sequence of poems is only part of Kay's first collection; the second half, 'Severe Gale 8', further de-stabilises any straightforward and stable notion of self, by setting personal identity within a wider ideological context.[5] The adoptive parents in 'The Adoption Papers' are clearly shown to have political affiliations – 'I put Marx Engels Lenin (no Trotsky) / in the airing cupboard ... All the copies of the *Daily Worker* / I shoved under the sofa' (14–15) – but 'Severe Gale 8' offers a more overtly political series of poems which explore the absurdities of Thatcherite Britain – 'NHS' and '££££' for example (36) – alongside poems on those who apparently stand outside its 'norms'. The experiences of a lesbian couple are presented in 'Pounding Rain' – 'News of us spreads like a storm' (44) – while the paranoia and fear of a couple with AIDS are explored in 'Dance of the Cherry Blossom' (50). A sense in which such identities may be particularly alienating when seen from a Scottish perspective is explored in 'Dressing Up' where a transvestite suggests the irony by which his own life is regarded as 'odd' while the dysfunctionality of his family is seen as part of the accepted 'norm'. While his family is 'all so squalid / ... / real typical working class / Scottish: Da beats Ma drinks it off' (57), it is his transvestism which is seen as unacceptable: 'Ma ma didn't touch her turkey / ... / She had a black eye, a navy dress' (57). 'Severe Gale 8' provides a counterpoint to 'The Adoption Papers' suggesting that however much identity may be familially (or genetically) constructed, the individual must exist outside the family in an often hostile society which sets its own parameters for the ways in which we are defined.

The positioning of the subject within wider ideological structures is more overtly explored in Kay's subsequent collections of adult poems *Other Lovers* (1993) and *Off Colour* (1998).[6] *Other Lovers* opens with the poem 'Even the Trees', which evokes a black history of injustice, suggesting that this must be reiterated so that black identity may know its own heritage for 'Everything that's happened once could happen again' (9). In *Other Lovers* the terms of this black identity are inscribed in a number of poems focusing on the blues singer Bessie Smith.

Toni Morrison suggests that 'for a long time, the art form that was healing for Black people was music',[7] and Kay articulates the significance of music to black culture in her long standing interest in jazz and blues. In a short biography of Smith she writes of this fascination:

> I will always associate the dawning of my own realization of being black with the blues, and particularly Bessie's blues ... Bessie's blues still fill me with a strange longing. I don't know exactly what for. Blackness? A culture that will wholly embrace me? Belonging? Who knows.[8]

Other Lovers explores some of these questions supporting Morrison's thesis that an awareness of one's cultural 'ancestors' is crucial in the construction of a black subjectivity: 'It was the absence of an ancestor that was frightening, that was threatening' Morrison writes (330), suggesting that awareness of one's shared past may lead to a knowledge of identity which stretches beyond simple familial ties. In 'The Red Graveyard' Kay writes:

> Why do I remember the blues?
> I am five or six or seven in the back garden;
> the window is wide open;
> her voice is slow motion through the heavy summer air.
> Jelly roll. Kitchen man. Sausage roll. Frying pan.
>
> Inside the house where I used to be myself,
> her voice claims the rooms. In the best room even,
> something has changed the shape of my silence.
> Why do I remember her voice and not my own mother's?
> Why do I remember the blues?

> (13)

The implication is that somehow, by an expression of her own blackness via the blues, the singer can offer an imaginative appropriation of subjectivity for the speaker unavailable to her (white) mother.

While this may imply that blackness may be a more important aspect of identity than any other for the poet of *Other Lovers*, as is so often the case in Kay's work this seeming ontological refuge is quickly de-stabilised, here by the fact that an overtly Scottish poem 'Watching People Sing' follows immediately after the Bessie Smith sequence. Kay has stated that she was 'steeped in Scottish culture',[9] and this poem evokes many instantly recognisable aspects of it, describing a family gathering which erupts into a ceilidh, encouraged by the 'Teacher's whisky' passed round by the poem's speaker. 'Ae Fond Kiss', 'A Man's a Man for a That' and, poignantly, 'John Anderson, My Jo' provide the singers with a link to 'The mouths of the people of the past' (16), who offer the speaker both a context in which she may belong, and the possibility of a future grounded in that context:

> Yet still, Anna's voice
> singing *John Anderson my Jo John*
> makes the song mine. I know him.
> I can see him coming down the hill.
> *Now we maun totter down John*
> *And hand in hand we'll go*
> *And sleep thegither at the foot.*
> Oh God, I think. Oh God, who will
> sleep at my foot, who will sing to me like that
> eyes brimming with love and change and spark.
> (17–18)

In this poem the Scottish dimension is also expressed through language, as a smattering of Scots dialect words both position the speakers as Scottish – '*Gie it laldy*', '*g'on yoursel hen*' (16) – and simultaneously suggest that the language may itself provide a bridge to 'the people of the past' – her Scottish 'ancestors' or the continuities so crucial to Benedict Anderson's 'imagined communities'[10] – emphasised here by the fact that the poem not only follows the sequence on the speaker's black heritage, but also precedes a series of poems on the relationship between language and identity. One of Kay's most concise statements on the ways in which language can be both alienating and inclusive is found in one of her children's poems, 'English Cousin Comes to Scotland'.[11] Cora Kaplan, following Freud and Lacan, argues that 'through the acquisition of language we become social and human beings: the words we speak situate us in our gender and our class. Through language we come to "know" who we are'.[12] Julia Kristeva, moreover, suggests that it is via language that we are positioned within the symbolic order.[13] Kay's poetry is resonant with such apprehensions and in *Other Lovers* she suggests the ways in which the deprivation of one's language may be seen as both a form of colonisation – '*distance* / between one language and another, one / culture and another; one religion / and another. The *little languages* / squashed, stamped upon, cleared out / to make way / for the big one, better tongue' (21) – and a means by which identity may be destroyed:

> The day they forced her to speak
> their tongue, she lost
> the black-eyed susan.
> She went back in
> time
>
>   (21)

Kay has written about her experiences of being black in Scotland; deprived
of her 'ancestors' she suggests that she 'never had any sense of Black culture at
all' and that she was always treated as an 'anomaly' (*Monsters*, 122). 'This irri-
tates me, a lot', she states, 'that people can't contain both things, being Black
and being Scottish, without thinking there is an inherent contradiction there'
(*Monsters*, 121). Not surprisingly, then, the ontology which her own poetry
describes is one which demands that her readers both acknowledge and
embrace difference:

> What we need is to be able to come together on the basis of our differences and
> not on the basis of our similarities; so that as people we ought to be able to
> embrace those differences and acknowledge them and not just sweep them under
> the carpet and pretend they're not there. (*Monsters*, 124)

It is these sentiments which are expressed in one of the shortest, but perhaps
most significant poems in *Other Lovers*, 'In my country'.[14] The speaker describes
a woman passing around her 'as if I were a superstition', demanding '*Where do
you come from?*'. The answer is succinct, offering no explanation beyond "Here.
These parts", seemingly demanding a recognition, without further justifica-
tion, of multiplicity (24). If, however, the country to which the speaker belongs
is Scotland, Kay herself seemed in 1990 to be far from optimistic about its
ability to embrace such multiplicity either in racial or sexual terms: 'I don't
know if I could actually read lesbian poems there' (*Monsters*, 127).

Scotland is one of the overt themes of Kay's most recent collections of poems
Off Colour. The title of the collection plays with questions of both sickness and
racial origin, exploring metaphorical inscriptions of illness, including the state
of Scotland itself. The opening poem 'Where It Hurts' is partly written in
Scots dialect and while Glenda Norquay argues convincingly that we must be
cautious about aligning speaker with nation,[15] this poem may easily be read as
a metaphor for Scotland's own particular ailments. The speaker claims to be
'Heavy, like the battle o' Culloden' and 'Sick to the back Scotch teeth' (9,10).
Much of this dis-ease arises out of a sense of alienation, a rupture from its own
communal past:

> How did I get like this? So far away from myself.
> I used to love ballads, folksongs.
> *I will go I will go when the fighting is over.*
> But the fighting of the body is never over.
>
> (11)

The prognosis for this ailing body, Kay concludes, is far from good. It is 'a big
bitter pill to swallow / – will it be red, will it be yellow? / After all I've been
through. A great thumping death' (12).

The particular forms of Scotland's sickness are explored elsewhere in *Off
Colour*. 'Christian Sanderson', for example, explores a history of Scottish racial

intolerance, describing the story of a woman transported to Australia after stealing sixteen shillings because her 'dochter wis starving' (28). The poem provides a double condemnation of Scotland, suggesting both a history of class injustice – 'They said I wis a thief by habit. / What kin o habit's hungry, bony?' (29) – and of gender discrimination – 'Women that suffer sullen poverty want tae forget things' (29). Written in Scots and in the first person it also offers an ironic comment on Scotland's failure to recognise those who do not fit easily into its own definitions of 'Scottishness', in spite of their carrying the linguistic markers of national identity: 'The Mulatto this, / the mulatto that. I felt like saying, / "My name is Christian Sanderson" ... / Whit's going tae happen tae my dochter?' (29).

Scotland's racial intolerance is also brought humorously up to date in the poem 'The Broons' Bairn's Black'. Here, those bastions of Scottish conservatism, that ideal 'kailyard' family the Broons, are used to express the collective intolerance of the Scottish nation; 'Scotland is having a heart attack / The Broons' Bairn's Black' (61). The Broons, in fact, also appear elsewhere in this collection suggesting that Scotland's racism is not its only sickness. The power relationships between men and women are also wittily dissected in 'Maw Broon Visits a Therapist' where Maw (who may provide a voice for many Scottish women) for once articulates the causes of her own discontent:

> A'm built like a bothy, hefty.
> A'm constantly wabbit and crabbit.
> Ma hale faimily taks me for grantit.
> A'll aye be the wan tae dae it
>
> whitever *it* is.
>
> (47)

Rather more sinisterly, in 'Paw Broon on the Starr Report' (57), the Scottish male's infamous reputation for insensitivity is ironically expressed.

In these poems, a cultural and ideological negation of marginal ontologies, concealed behind the naive societal discourses of Scotland's 'ideal family', is exposed. But the Scottish nation and its hypocrisies are not the only form of 'sickness' in this collection. In 'From Stranraer, South' Kay explores the 'illness' which exists within family ties, built, as they so often are, upon their own 'symbolic orders' of disappointed expectations and guilt, inscribed in recrimination and rebuke. The speaker describes how she has fallen in love with a girl round the corner causing a dis-ease which for her mother 'will never get better' since it violates what is 'natural'; 'for what is a life for but to be a good daughter' (42). However, in the poem that follows, 'Bed', this 'natural' order is subverted as Kay reveals the sicknesses which are in fact endemic within mother–daughter 'love': 'A'll be gone and how wull she feel? / No that Am saying A' want her guilty' (44). *Off Colour* is about many kinds of sickness; the sickness of Scotland's intolerance, of dysfunctional families who mask their dis-eases behind 'normality', the 'sickness' of racism. All embody an intolerance of the multivalent difference which Kay encourages her readers to embrace, suggesting that it is a failure to acknowledge multiplicity, either in our selves or in our society, which is in fact the real ailment.

Many of Kay's poems are written in sequences; 'The Adoption Papers', for example, 'Severe Gale 8' or 'Other Lovers'. Others contain common motifs or resonances; the 'Broons' poems, or those called 'Virus' in *Off Colour*. These aspects of Kay's poems encourage them to be read as narrative, and while this tendency is sometimes disrupted to ironic or dislocating effect, Kay has also said of 'The Adoption Papers' that 'it's also a story, so you could read the whole collection like a novel' (*Monsters*, 123). Prose fiction seems, therefore, a natural development for Kay.

Trumpet (1998) is in some ways the culmination of themes which have preoccupied Kay since the outset of her writing career.[16] Its main plot is in part a reworking of an early play, *Twice Over*, which tells the story of a grandmother whose family discover only after her death that she has been a lesbian.[17] Its concern with the ways in which the loss of a loved one unravels personality, deconstructs identity, is reminiscent of her exploration of this theme in the 'Other Lovers' poems. Its overarching ontological concern with the ways in which identity and subjectivity are constituted – in terms of the symbolic order as manifested in discourses of gender, Scottishness and colour – revisits Kay's early contemplation of these themes in *The Adoption Papers*. *Trumpet* is, however, far more than a reworking of old themes, since the discursive mode of the novel gives Kay the space to negotiate these problematics in more complexity.

The story of *Trumpet* is an extraordinary one. It is an account of a black male trumpet player, Joss Moody, who after his death is discovered to have been a woman. The novel presents the responses of his family – including the wife who obviously knew his secret and the son who did not – alongside those of several others, ranging from the venal reporter Sophie Stones, to the undertaker, and Joss's drummer Big Red. This method of narration allows Kay to enact in the story's telling the evasive fluidity of the inscribed subject, since the multiple narratives allow the reader no fixed position by which Joss's constructed identity may be contained; rather, the at times competing perspectives imply that his/her life and death can never be safely delimited through standard teleological narrative modes.

Thematically the novel also concerns itself with the ways in which the self is overtly constructed, primarily in its exploration of gender. Significantly, as Joss's story emerges it is clear that it is not simply an account of a transvestite or lesbian, but of a woman who has almost willed herself into being a man. The perplexed undertaker, for example, describes his discovery of a body which seems to shift gender by the simple matter of putting on, or taking off clothes.

'It had never happened to him before. He had never had a man turn into a woman before his very eyes' (111):

> All his working life he has assumed that what made a man a man and a woman a woman was the differing sexual organs. Yet today, he had a woman who persuaded him, even dead, that he was a man, once he had his clothes on. (115)

This apparent 'shifting' in gender is what is emphasised by several of the characters — Big Red, or the Moody's cleaner Maggie — who insist that Joss never seemed anything other than what he appeared. To all intents and purposes, Joss has been a man, a point made again, more subtly, by the fact that both Millie and Colman, those who knew him best, persist in referring to Joss as 'he' after his death. 'I am still holding out my hands when the first of his breasts reveals itself to me' (21), Millie states as she recounts her first discovery of Joss's gender, implying a sense of her own disorientation which is in turn conveyed to the reader. Later, as Colman becomes disenchanted with Sophie, he too lashes out with an assertion of his father's gender and the pronoun by which he should be defined: "Don't bother with this him/her bullshit. That's bollocks, man. Just say him" (142).

These accounts imply that gender is not a biological imperative, not an essential given, but a contingent ontology which we can constitute almost at will. This flexibility of subjectivity and identity is reinforced by the experiences of other characters in the novel. Big Red, for example, describes how his own sense of self has been modified by his shifting nick-names; 'Big Red's temper earned him his nickname. He was proud of it. Ever since he was a boy he's been graffitied with nicknames' (145). Colman, Joss's son, suggests that identity is constructed via the clothes we wear, describing the different responses he can provoke in others simply by putting on his biker's uniform; 'Everybody hates bikers. He could just put the gear on and join the clan and nod at other bikers on the road. When he stopped to get a bacon roll, people would instinctively let him go in front of them. It was quite a discovery' (138). These experiences suggest that Joss's life offers only an extreme example of the ways in which we all shape our selves, since all identity is fluid and contingent — a negotiation of a profusion of psychological, cultural and ideological discourses and their concomitant 'fantasy selves'.

If gender is something we can 'invent' for ourselves, however, the novel implies that race and nationhood may also be constructed imaginatively. Kay has said that because there were no other black people in Scotland, she began writing 'out of that sense of wanting to create some images for myself' (*Monsters*, 121). She explores this process in the poem 'Pride' (*Colour*, 62) where she describes a chance/imagined meeting on a train with an Ibo man who gives her, momentarily, a sense of a culture — black 'ancestors' or an 'imagined community' — to which she might belong. In *Trumpet*, Colman's experiences as a black person in Britain reiterate a sense of alienation, and Joss himself implies that black people growing up in such an alien culture must 'imagine' a heritage for themselves, a 'fantasy Africa' (34) in order to reinforce a sense of their black inheritance and its implications.

Yet, if *Trumpet* seems to posit the idea that subjectivity and identity are almost infinitely flexible, it does not suggest that they thus become void of meaning, or meaningless. In the novel, Joss describes his feelings as he plays the trumpet, suggesting that this is the one time when he can move outside his constructed selves to a Kristevan subliminal space beyond language and identity, seemingly escaping the 'symbolic order' and the inscriptions of race and gender by which it is constituted: 'All his self collapses – his idiosyncracies, his personality, his ego, his sexuality, even, finally, his memory. All of it falls away like layers of skin unwrapping. He unwraps himself with his trumpet … he is nobody' (135). However, this space beyond the liminal is by definition temporary, and the novel also implies that the fictional identities we assume like clothes may be 'necessary fictions' – essential if we are to conduct ourselves within society, itself inscribed within the symbolic order. The novel begins, after all, with both Millie and Colman brought to a point of disintegration by their grief to the extent that they no longer find it possible to negotiate their ways in the world: 'I look unreal', states Millie in the opening paragraph, 'I look unlike the memory of myself. I feel strange now. It used to be such a certain thing, just being myself. It was so easy, so painless' (1). Colman begins the novel with similar sentiments; 'It's a whole different ball game. Know what I mean. I haven't got the same life' (46). Thus *Trumpet* is not only Joss's story but also one of how Millie and Colman de- and re-construct themselves, finding ways to exist after his death. For Colman, this is a journey which takes him through a process of longing for that elusive other, the essential self, to a recognition that this desire itself may be a 'fantasy'. For Millie it involves the discovery that she can make decisions – still *he* – in Joss's absence:

> I got a lovely letter this morning, forwarded on by our secretary. A wonderful letter, from a group of women jazz musicians that want to form a band. They want to call it The Joss Moody Memorial Band. It has given me hope. I am not sure whether Joss would actually have liked the idea or not. But I like it. (268)

Trumpet is, finally, a narrative which in both its thematic and formal preoccupations suggests that identity and subjectivity are fluid and flexible; struggles and journeys of will or imagination as we construct for ourselves fantasy Africas, Scotlands or genders. However, it is also a novel in which the need for such 'necessary fictions' is implied, for we could not exist in a world without 'ancestors' or with no sense of 'sex … race … memory' (131) since, in such a subliminal space, beyond history, language and the symbolic order 'everything that's happened once could happen again' as the subject would, to use Millie's formulation, have lost the memory of itself. This is in fact, the significance of the legacy which Joss leaves to Colman. The story which he tells him in his posthumous letter may or may not be true, but it is, nevertheless, valuable, providing Colman with both a sense of a past and of an 'imagined community' to which he might belong: 'I am leaving myself to you. Everything I have got. All the letters I have kept hidden ... all of this is my past, this is the sum of my parts; you are my future' (277). Our identities may be fluid and flexible, acts of the imagination, but they are, in the end, the only way we can have of knowing ourselves.

Ultimately, Kay's work suggests the critical importance of recovering or imagining a multivalent subjectivity – whether in terms of biological inherit- ance, race or gender – in order to explore the full parameters of identity. However, it also implies that such an identity must be fluid rather than 'frozen', to use Kay's own terms, expressing a plurality within it which she invites her readers to embrace. Of course, any study which places 'Scottish' and 'women' together in its title must resist the temptation to describe these terms as if they can be defined unproblematically. Kay's work, by its formal polyphony and its thematic engagement with the vital potentialities of self and identity, reminds us that there can be no single agenda for women's writ- ing. It is, consequently, an important voice in the new Scotland, which must include such diversity within its own definition of itself.

Notes

With thanks to Jackie Kay and Bloodaxe for permission to quote from Kay's poetry.
  1. 'Jackie Kay', in Neil Astley (ed.), *New Blood* (Newcastle-upon-Tyne: Bloodaxe, 1999), pp. 73–80 (73).
  2. Jackie Kay, *The Adoption Papers* (Newcastle-upon-Tyne: Bloodaxe, 1991).
  3. Helen Carr, 'Woman/Indian: "The American" and His Others', in Francis Barker, Peter Hulme, Margaret Iversen and Diana Loxley (eds), *Europe and Its Others*, 2 vols (Colchester: University of Essex Press, 1985), vol. 2, pp. 46–60 (50).
  4. Frantz Fanon, 'On National Culture', in Dennis Walder (ed.), *Literature in the Modern World: Critical Essays and Documents* (Oxford: Oxford University Press, 1990), pp. 265– 271 (268).
  5. Gabriele Griffin, 'In/Corporation? Jackie Kay's *The Adoption Papers*', in Vicki Bertram (ed.), *Kicking Daffodils: Twentieth-Century Women Poets* (Edinburgh: Edinburgh University Press, 1997), pp. 169–77 (172). This volume also contains an essay dealing with language and polyphony in Kay's work: Paraskevi Papaleonida, '"holding my beads in my hand": Dialogue, Synthesis and Power in the Poetry of Jackie Kay and Grace Nichols', pp. 125–39.
  6. Jackie Kay, *Other Lovers* (Newcastle-upon-Tyne: Bloodaxe, 1993) and *Off Colour* (Newcastle-upon-Tyne: Bloodaxe, 1998).
  7. Toni Morrison, 'Rootedness: The Ancestor as Foundation', in Walder, *Literature in the Modern World*, pp. 326–32 (328).
  8. Jackie Kay, *Bessie Smith* (Bath: Absolute Press, 1997), pp. 138–9.
  9. 'Jackie Kay', in Gillean Somerville-Arjat and Rebecca E. Wilson (eds), *Sleeping with Monsters: Conversations with Scottish and Irish Women Poets* (Edinburgh: Polygon, 1990), pp. 120–30 (122).

10. See Benedict Anderson, *Imagined Communities* (1983; London: Verso, 1991).
11. Jackie Kay, 'English Cousin Comes to Scotland', in Kay, *Two's Company* (London: Blackie Children's Books, 1992), pp. 44–5.
12. Cora Kaplan, 'Language and Gender', in Walder, *Literature in the Modern World*, pp. 310–16 (312).
13. Julia Kristeva, *Revolution in Poetic Language*, trans. Margaret Waller (New York: Columbia University Press, 1984), p. 4ff.
14. This poem is in fact a reworking of Kay's earlier 'So You Think I'm a Mule', discussed in Susanne Hagemann, 'Women and Nation', in Douglas Gifford and Dorothy McMillan (eds), *A History of Scottish Women's Writing* (Edinburgh: Edinburgh University Press, 1997), pp. 316–28. McMillan also discusses this poem in another essay in this volume, 'Twentieth-century Poetry II: The Last Twenty-five Years', pp. 549–78.
15. See Glenda Norquay, 'Janice Galloway's Novels: Fraudulent Mooching', later in this book, p. 137.
16. Jackie Kay, *Trumpet* (London: Picador, 1998).
17. Jackie Kay, 'Twice Over', in Philip Osment (ed.), *Gay Sweatshop: Four Plays and a Company* (London: Methuen, 1989), pp. 121–46.

PART TWO

Contemporary Scottish Women's Prose Fiction

CHAPTER SEVEN

Muriel Spark and Candia McWilliam: Continuities

Aileen Christianson

Continuities in Muriel Spark's Later Work

Muriel Spark (b. 1918) is the oldest of the authors considered in this book. She has lived outwith Scotland since she left for Rhodesia (Zimbabwe) in 1938. Of her twenty novels published between 1957 and 1996, fifteen were published before 1980, the remaining five since 1981. For these reasons, in her case, there is, perhaps, a need to interrogate both 'Scottish' and 'contemporary'. She used to write cautiously of being 'a writer of Scottish formation' but now says 'I write as a Scot and I write as a Catholic... I don't even have to think about it', identifying herself in a relaxed fashion as a Scottish writer.[1] It has certainly always been the case that her relationship to parts of a Scottish tradition in literature has been clear in her writing. *The Prime of Miss Jean Brodie* (1961) has Miss Brodie explicitly link herself to William Brodie of the eighteenth century, respectable cabinet maker and councillor by day and burglar by night,[2] which in turn reminds the reader of the doubleness exemplified in R. L. Stevenson's *The Strange Case of Dr Jekyll and Mr Hyde* (1886). Dougal Douglas in *The Ballad of Peckham Rye* (1960) is a 1950s' version of Gilmartin in James Hogg's *Confessions of a Justified Sinner* (1824), ambiguous and dangerous.[3] And she acknowledges her reading of the Ballads at school which 'entered my literary bloodstream, never to depart',[4] their style and themes leaving their imprint on Spark's own: succinct and clear with repetitions, shifts in time, juxtapositions of the supernatural and the everyday, and sudden deaths. Janice Galloway sees Spark's early success as like 'a bolt from the blue' in a literary London reading Kingsley Amis and John Braine,

> then there she was, with her terrifying clarity of vision: lies, death, and 'the providence of God' ... Of course, the presence of the Infinite in the everyday, terse delivery and crowding epiphanies are part of Scottish writing's traditions, but Literary London, less well-read in these matters, was confounded.[5]

Spark is both an influence on contemporary Scottish writing and a writer within a separate strand of post-Second World War British literature, part of literary history rather than the present. Within Scotland, she was the writer who was there, a Scot, a woman (particularly important for aspiring Scottish women writers for whom there were not many apparent role models) and acknowledged as in the first rank of literature from early in her career. She has finished her twenty-first novel, and talks about writing a play and poems.[6] Still working, she is definable as a current writer. But is she 'contemporary'? Her works seem to exemplify a continuity of themes, style and plots. The most recent novels, as the earlier, are presented in a kind of separate and idiosyncratic perfection which may influence contemporary writers (for example, Shena Mackay, A. L. Kennedy, Candia McWilliam) rather than be itself contemporary. The earlier novels describe the worlds of the 1930s–1950s (for example, *The Prime of Miss Jean Brodie* (1961), *The Ballad of Peckham Rye* (1960)), the later take place in the early 1950s (*Loitering with Intent* (1981), *A Far Cry from Kensington* (1988)) or in an apparently contemporary but strangely disconnected world of the rich (*Symposium* (1990), *Reality and Dreams* (1996)). But in the end the question can only be evaded; Spark exists, she is outside of fashion (not 'timeless' in any bland way) and, still writing, is a force to be reckoned with.

In this chapter I will concentrate on Spark's five most recent novels, *Loitering with Intent*, *The Only Problem* (1984), *A Far Cry from Kensington*, *Symposium*, *Reality and Dreams* and her autobiography, *Curriculum Vitae*, with some reference to earlier novels, particularly *The Driver's Seat* (1970). Everything stems for Spark from a concern with fact and fiction, truth and lies, and for this reason it is useful to consider the metafictionality of her novels, linked with what might be called the metafactionality of her autobiography. Fictionality is interrogated in all her novels and in her commentaries on her work. In 1962 she said: 'Fiction is one aspect of the truth, perhaps, but in fact if we are going to live in the world as reasonable beings we must call it lies';[7] and, in 1999: 'Yes, lies do interest me because fiction is lies ... And in order to do this you have got to have a very good sense of what is the truth. You can't do the art of deception, of deceiving people so they suspend disbelief, without having that sense very strongly indeed' (Galloway, 8). In Spark's autobiography she foregrounds the non-fictionality of memoirs, drawing attention to the factual, 'truthful' nature of autobiography, corroborated at every turn:

> I felt it time to put the record straight. I determined to write nothing that cannot be supported by documentary evidence or by eyewitnesses; I have not relied on my memory alone, vivid though it is ... Truth by itself is neutral and has its own dear beauty; especially in a work of non-fiction it is to be cherished. (11)

She uses the legal terms 'corroboration' (the essential principle of Scots law) and 'hearsay' (26, 27) and tells us that she has 'all and everything ... conserved in a vast archive ... [T]he silent, objective evidence of truth, should I ever need it' (185). But this rejection of lies and emphasis on the factual nature of her memoirs serves only to draw attention to the possibility of fictional aspects of autobiography. She reminds us that in her own work for the Foreign Office's

disinformation unit, she 'took in a whole world of method and intrigue in the
dark field of Black Propaganda' where she learned to mix 'detailed truth with
believable lies' (147–8) and this returns us to the idea of fiction as 'some kind
of truth'.[8] As her war effort, Spark learned to deceive the enemy through fiction,
the method expressed in A Far Cry from Kensington as the author Emma Loy's
'style of ferreting out facts and juxtaposing them with inventions'.[9]

Curriculum Vitae might complicate our ideas of the fictionality of Spark's
novels: 'Miss Christina Kay, that character in search of an author ... Miss Kay
was not literally Miss Brodie, but I think Miss Kay had it in her, unrealized, to
be the character I invented' (56, 57). But the novels also cause us to question
the possibility of absolute truth in an autobiography. In the early novel The
Ballad of Peckham Rye, Spark had both drawn attention to the 'art' in autobiography and satirised the idea of fictionalising of autobiography in Dougal
Douglas's words, 'I thought it was a work of art you wanted to write ... If you
only wanted to write a straight autobiography you should have got a straight
ghost'.[10] Mrs Hawkins, at the beginning of A Far Cry, lies at night, 'prefiguring
the future, picking out of the past the scraps I had overlooked, those rejected
events which now came to the foreground, large and important' (5). The
insomniac narrator rearranges her past, forming the novel that contains a fictional representation of Derek Stanford, Spark's erstwhile collaborator on books,
the instigator of lies about her life (the 'false and erroneous statements ... that
well-meaning scholars tend to repeat ... like fleas hopping from here to there,
sucking the blood of the intellect' (Curriculum Vitae, 11)). The character Hector
Bartlett, 'urinator of journalistic copy ... "pisseur de copie"' (Far Cry, 45), who
attempts to destroy Nancy Hawkins, represents revenge embedded in Spark's
fiction. As Nancy 'settle[s] the bill' (189) at the end of the novel, so Spark also
settles her account with Stanford in this fictional representation, using fiction
to assert her truth, before publishing an explicit list of Stanford's inaccuracies
in Curriculum Vitae (191–2). Derek Stanford/Hector/'pisseur de copie' are forever
linked as examples of the unskilled, unoriginal and unsuccessful, Stanford's
work on Spark exposed as both fictional and unconvincing.[11]

The most explicit exploration of the ideas of autobiography and of fiction
comes in Loitering with Intent. Curriculum Vitae, with its emphasis on 'fact' and
Spark's records, has been pre-fictionalised in this novel, Spark transferring 'a
number of my experiences in the Poetry Society, as I usually do [my italics],
into a fictional background' (184). Fleur, like Caroline of The Comforters (1957),
is another protagonist close to Spark herself. In a precursor to Spark's own
'vast archive ... the silent, objective evidence of truth' (185), Fleur comments
on her store of letters, 'neatly bundled up in thin folders, tied with pink tape,
1949, 1950, 1951 and on and on'.[12] While writing her first novel, Fleur works
as a facilitator to Sir Quentin Oliver, the originator of the 'Autobiographical
Association'. Working with the members, she had 'set them on to writing fictions about themselves' (83). In this novel Spark foregrounds the way a writer
arranges facts, events, people, the way that 'autobiography' is indeed 'life writing'.

As Glenda Norquay has noted, Spark became 'increasingly adventurous in testing the boundaries of the fictional world, disrupting it by emphasising its own inherent contradictions and, at the same time, using the fictional paradigm to explore her own moral perspective'.[13] When everything can be read as text, divisions between fiction and non-fiction become debatable. Spark plays with these divisions throughout *Curriculum Vitae*, meticulously pointing out the sources in her life for particular novels or short stories. Her novels individually draw attention to their fictionality; taken together with her autobiography they constitute metafaction, an extension of her metafictionality, drawing attention to the interplay of fact and fiction.

Reviewers comment on the division of Spark's novels between those that 'are written around a single, organising consciousness' and those which deal in a more omniscient way with narrative, sometimes giving a 'first (misleading) impression ... of a disorienting randomness of focus'.[14] William Boyd, in his review of *Reality and Dreams*, finds that:

> her unique sensibility functions best when the voice is subjective, the point of view confined or in the first person, as in her two wonderful late novels *A Far Cry from Kensington* and *Loitering with Intent*. This method localises, and validates, that clear-eyed, unabashedly, brutally honest gaze on the world and its denizens. Omniscient narrative has the opposite effect. Perhaps in this elderly century (Spark toys with this notion) the predetermined, the ordered, is fundamentally inimical.[15]

The majority of her novels centre round the omniscient narrator.[16] Perhaps they are inimical to Boyd because they represent Spark's engagement with the problematics of Calvinism. Norquay has suggested that Calvinism creates a 'dichotomy between the need to act as if saved and simultaneously to acknowledge an implicit uncertainty as to salvation' (1985, 37). Educated in her Edinburgh girls' school with its official religion the Presbyterianism of the Church of Scotland, and an unofficial one of toleration 'always with a puritanical slant' (*CV*, 53), Spark is one of those artists writing from a Calvinist cast of mind or cultural context that Norquay suggests brings with it a predisposition for certain forms of response to the world in their art: that the world itself is a work of fiction, that with the fear of playing God the authors must find a way of acknowledging authorial fallibility, while working with a distrust of language and a sense that it always falls short of expressing God's meaning.[17] Further:

> The form of novel which she adopts, with its exposure of control and foreknowledge, is one which closely resembles a Calvinist view of the universe, the view that all is known to an omniscient God with absolute control of human lives through the framework of predestination. (Norquay 1985, 323)

Spark's fictional modes can also be connected to the medieval Catholic view of literature that the anagogical or highest level of interpretation can only be truly accessible to God. The roots of her fictional concerns are thus both Catholic and Calvinist, embodying, like Claire in *Reality and Dreams*, 'miraculous and contradictory qualities ... understanding and incomprehension, yes and no'.[18] This embracing of paradox can be traced to Kathleen Williams's Renaissance 'literature of paradox ... shaped to express ambiguity, to stress the coexistence of apparently irreconcilable truths'.[19] More usually in Scottish criticism (for example, Elphinstone), Sparkian paradox is connected with G. Gregory Smith's 'antithesis of the real and the fantastic ... the "polar twins" of the Scottish Muse'. Smith's 'sudden jostling of contraries' becomes in Spark's work the acceptance of miraculous juxtapositions of the incompatible where the extraordinary and the mundane are in positive conjunction, equivalent and not antithetical.[20]

The Driver's Seat is a novel that proceeds inexorably to the preordained end of Lise's murder, a murder that is being sought by Lise herself, the trajectory of her last days being one of both laying a trail and searching for the suitable murderer as she chooses to leave her alienated and dysfunctional place in modern city and office life, embracing death as a way of gaining control, or the driver's seat. Spark thinks it 'my best novel – better constructed than any other', a view that Gerard Carruthers shares: 'arguably ... the greatest of her novels'.[21] He then affirms but complicates this: 'The close alliance of themes with duplicitous narrative and plot structure makes [it] Spark's most shocking and most accomplished work' (522). But for me the alienating effect of Spark's bleakest and most succinct novel carries with it something problematic which comes directly from the shock of the rape at the end of the novel. While Lise orchestrates her own murder, her chosen end is disrupted by her murderer who reclaims his own freedom of will by raping before killing her. '"I don't want any sex," she shouts. "You can have it afterwards". ... All the same, he plunges into her, with the knife poised high. "Kill me"'.[22] The novel ends with the murderer seeing already 'all those trappings [uniforms] devised to protect' the authorities 'from the indecent exposure of fear and pity, pity and fear' (107). Spark cites the origin of the novel as a newspaper report and expresses pity for the murderer ('the poor fellow got a prison sentence') acknowledging that the novel is 'very cold, yes, at the same time a certain amount of pity I think to be read through the lines', connecting it to the pity and fear of Aristotle's definition of tragedy (*Xcess*). In pursuing her fate, Lise exhibits the usual ferocious control of a Spark narrator, but the control is exercised in a reversion of the norm that the murderee is the 'victim'. The troubling nature of a woman truly 'asking for it', as Lise does, excludes the question of the free will of the man to choose not to rape or murder. Chambers reads Lise's provocative search as representing her 'last sad attempt to confirm her own "normality" to the world – and to cover the traces of her own actual victimisation by society which is ultimately more profound than physical abuse' (522), a judgement which is curiously dismissive of the violence that Spark may mock but about which she certainly intends to be both ruthless and 'derisive'. She indicates this when discussing an underlying principle of her writing:

> The art and literature of sentiment and emotion ... has to go ... In its place I advocate the arts of satire and of ridicule ... [W]e should all be conditioned and educated to regard violence in any form as something to be ruthlessly mocked ... I would like to see ... a less indignant representation of social injustice, and a more deliberate cunning, a more derisive undermining of what is wrong. I would like to see less emotion and more intelligence in these efforts to impress our minds and hearts.[23]

Nina Auerbach describes Lise as 'a woman both possessed and in possession, who is no longer the antagonist of masculine "reality" and "truth", but its symbolic embodiment and eternal form, the driving force behind men's violent history',[24] but this is to succumb to the Helen of Troy syndrome, that is, woman as inspirer and cause of male violence. An alternative reading is that women who have the temerity to attempt control of their life and death will be punished with rape. The alienated modern style of the novel in fact conceals this old-fashioned and conventional view and Spark's apparently radical and challenging novel's unsettling nature lies with this unpleasant dissonance. It is 'best' for Spark, perhaps, because it most exemplifies authorial control and the violation of reader expectation. But it is a novel where the intentional pursuit of death by the protagonist excuses and underplays the ferocity of male violence against women. The old-fashioned misogyny of Lise's rape is balanced by the opening words of *Symposium*: "'This is rape! ... This is violation!" It was not rape, it was a robbery.'[25] The precision of the narrator's response to Lord Suzy's cry is extended when Helen Suzy writes to her husband's daughter, 'He says he's been raped, how would he know about rape? In fact in a funny psychological way he wants to be raped, they say we all do!!!' (96–7). Thus, along with society, Spark moves in this later novel to an interrogation of the idea of women 'asking for it', of burglary being as much of a violation as rape, a view that has been common except among women who have been raped.[26]

Lise belongs to that Scottish tradition of 'the dangerous woman' that Elphinstone explores:

> In twentieth-century writing she may sometimes seem to align herself with a feminist perspective, but she refuses to become quite ideologically sound. She is too sinister for that. She has appeared since the ballads as the daughter of the other world, with all the danger and glamour that that implies ... [S]he becomes more than subversive, she is perilous, and perhaps, in terms of accepted moralities, downright evil. (47)

Lise is 'perilous' to herself and to her murderer. With *Symposium*, Spark moves to a protagonist who longs for 'downright evil'. 'I'm tired of being made to feel guilty for no reason. I would like to feel guilty for a real case of guilt'

(160), Margaret cries as she plots the murder of her mother-in-law Hilda Damien; this is the Margaret who had picked up her future husband at the fruit section of Marks & Spencer's, warning him to 'be careful' of the bruised grapefruit, standing in for the apple of knowledge, signifying Margaret's lack of purity, the presence of danger, and of enchantment (158).

Symposium is the later Spark novel which most clearly foregrounds her relationship to the Scottish traditions of the ballads. Magnus, Margaret's mad uncle, is both warlock and devil, the family's 'guru' (67): 'Who do you have ... but me? Out of my misfortune, out of my affliction I prognosticate and foreshadow' (81). Like a Spark narrator, he manipulates the actions of the novel, reciting doom-laden ballads as he goes, and may have fulfilled Margaret's will in murder (of a school friend and of a teacher, 137–40). His commentary on Margaret's letter from the radical nunnery ensures the presence of incompatible possibilities, truth and lies: 'Conceivably ... what she says is true. But some of it may be the fruit of a fertile Scottish imagination. The Murchies of old were great cursers, oath-takers and foul-mouthers; it was known of them on both sides of the Border. I could cite the manuscript sources' (106). Magnus's conjuring of 'both sides of the Border' reminds us of the debatable land in 'Scotch and English', a childhood game, 'c. 1788', described by Spark in *Curriculum Vitae*, 'in which each party tried to rob the other of their play-things', when the little girls were 'compelled to be English, for the bigger girls thought it too degrading' (22). But it also suggests the idea of debatable lands where truth and lies are interrogated, where there is certainty only of sliding and inchoate meanings. Margaret, Magnus tells us, 'probably sees things double, treble, not as they really are' (106). Margaret's dangerous nature, feared by her parents as 'capable of anything', including 'provoking a murder' (80), the hints of witchcraft, 'the days of witch-hunts were over' (78), her 'capacity for being near the scene of tragedy was truly inexplicable in any reasonable terms' (142): all these are part of Margaret's role as a 'dangerous woman'. Of course, Margaret's 'capacity' for being near tragedy can be explained in both 'reasonable terms' (that Magnus accomplishes the murders to Margaret's unspoken or spoken will) and in unreasonable terms, those of faith, symbol or magic (that she carries with her a force field of violence or of destiny, an 'evil eye', her Scottishness a part of her wickedness as Magnus cheerfully asserts (159)) and that the events surrounding her are truly '*awful*' (167), that is full of awe. But they are also part of Spark's usual narrative technique of indirection. We are made aware of alternative realities; 'the menu could so easily have been hot salmon mousse, not cold' (45), lightly suggesting the possibility of alternative plots just before we are told 'but Hilda Damien will not come in after dinner. She is dying now, as they speak' (45). The breaking of the suspense in this novel is a trick to make us read *Symposium* as a dark, inevitable ballad, the sudden death signalled from early as that of the murder of the mother by the betraying woman, when, in fact, it is a murder of casual violence caused by the passing random act of the robbers that proves to be Hilda's destiny ('"I believe in destiny," said Hilda', (170)).

Marigold, unloved daughter of Tom the film director, is the 'dangerous woman' in *Reality and Dreams*: 'Hideous Marigold. Always negative Marigold' (87). Her disappearance when she is rumoured to be 'lying at the bottom of a deep Scottish loch' (103) leads Tom to see her as 'nemesis in drag. She is the Last Judgement' (106). She is behind attempts on Tom's life which lead always to others being harmed (Dave's shooting, Jeanne's fall to her death from the crane in an echo of Tom's original fall (118, 159)). But she is more peripheral to the novel than Margaret is to *Symposium*, a nemesis who fails as Tom survives in his unreal world of film-making, that 'tract of no-man's land between dreams and reality, reality and dreams' (160), another debatable land where meaning is indeterminate. Tom wonders twice 'if we were all characters in one of God's dreams' (7, 63):

> To an unbeliever this would have meant the casting of an insubstantiality within an already insubstantial context. Tom … meant the very opposite. Our dreams, yes, are insubstantial; the dreams of God, no. They are real, frighteningly real. They bulge with flesh, they drip with blood. (63–4)

Thus Tom, in a reversal of the expected, opposes a worldly insubstantiality to a Godly solidity, dreams against reality. This most recent Spark novel was reviewed as 'a little muted – a certain shadowiness' (Boyd, 8), entertaining in its light recycling of earlier darker novels, Marigold a late example of 'dangerous woman', akin not only to Margaret in *Symposium*, but also to Effie, Harvey's 'unattainable ideal' in *The Only Problem*,[27] who becomes an urban terrorist killed by the police. But the later novel is clearly part of the whole. All Spark's works taken together become a kind of metawork, endlessly commenting on fiction, truth, lies, providing commentary on and resistance to each other. Nathan, Ruth and Edward's relationship in *The Only Problem* is a precursor of Luke, Ernst and Ella's in *Symposium*, both Nathan in his urban terrorism and Luke in his complicity in murderous robbery caught and, presumably, punished, the one warning us how to read the other, as 'a matter of justice. A balancing of accounts' (*The Only Problem*, 42). Edward's part in a film with its 'provisional' title '*The Love-Hate Relationship*' (*The Only Problem*, 18) contains the seed of Tom's film in *Reality and Dreams* with its provisional title *The Hamburger Girl* (30), which is changed 'finally, to *Unfinished Business*' (88). The God whose dreams are substantial to Tom (accused of seeing himself as God (13)) has been placed as fictional in *The Only Problem* when Harvey insists 'I said nothing whatsoever about God, I mean our Creator. What I was talking about was a fictional character in the *Book of Job*, called God' (135).

That Spark's narratorial authority and control is like God's is a critical truism. What should also be acknowledged is that Spark's presentation of herself in interview, articulate and aware, provides a disembodied accompaniment to her work, her commentaries resonating with her fictions. She has a ghostlike presence in her own narratives through the frugal re-use of fragments of autobiography, like Dougal in *The Ballad*, gathering together 'for economy's sake …

the scrap ends of his profligate experience – for he was a frugal man at heart – and turned them into a lot of cockeyed books' (142). Aspects of the novels are themselves recycled economically, episodes, themes, style echoed and prefigured within her works until these most succinct of novels end up constituting a grand œuvre, where her continuities lead us back as well as forward. Like Harvey in *The Only Problem*, her work is 'predictable only up to a point' (11). Her tendency to God-like narrators, her interrogation of God-like control, authorial or otherwise, undermines the separation of author and text;[28] the mischievousness of her authority, the foregrounding of reality and illusion ensure that authorial control shadows God's control. Spark always has the last laugh.

Candia McWilliam's Precision and Excess

Candia McWilliam is considered here as both linked to and separate from Spark.[29] Like Spark, McWilliam (b. 1955) was (partly) educated in Edinburgh and has lived her adult life outwith Scotland. In 1996, McWilliam was explicit about her admiration for Spark and her resistance to claiming an influence:

> I admire her enormously for many things – lightness of touch combined with seriousness of purpose. I believe she's one of the very few real novelists now writing and I admire her formal instinct, her cunning angle of vision and her serious interest in matters of conscience allied within an austere Scottish aesthetic. I think her Catholicism supersaturates her writing and one can't burn it out. I love her, read and reread her and have done most of my life, but to say that she has influenced me would be a rather selfaggrandising claim: as if one is attempting to magically borrow the characteristics of the admired.[30]

Connections and continuities, if not influence, are apparent in the strange worlds of the deracinated rich that Spark's late work and McWilliam's fiction share and in the identification of central characters with Scotland. Both their works are coloured by oblique links to Scotland and underpinned by their educations in the literary traditions of Scotland. The presence of 'Scotland' can be traced in their fictions.

They are also linked by their style, unlikely as that seems given McWilliam's reputation for flamboyant vocabulary. Despite McWilliam's verbosity and Spark's succinctness seeming opposed rather than similar, the precision of McWilliam's descriptions links her to Spark's taut style. Spark's vocabulary is sparse, clear, trite. Her extremity lies in narratorial control, her ambiguity in the suggestiveness of the tightly structured repetitions of her slight narratives, everything pared to the minimum, including language. Her style is like the cat in *Symposium* with its capacity 'to concentrate its eyesight intensely on one relevant item, screening out the irrelevant' (31). McWilliam's style, the explicit, obsessive detail of descriptions – for example, the descriptions in *A*

Little Stranger of the 'slender, unpregnant friends', contrasting with Daisy's feeling of being 'barded with a suit of fat'[31] – are like the 'delightfully shattered world, a dazzling reorganised frost-garden' that Alec in *Debatable Land* saw as a child through the modesty pane of the bathroom window:[32] 'everything... exploded into smithereens ... a green fanfare to a newly splintered world' (15) where things and people can be seen in new relationships to each other. McWilliam's over-explicitness is like a citrus fruit turned inside out, its intricate structures exposed, or like the instructional tortoise that Alec meets in the Bruces' living room: one side, 'as you would expect, whorled shell', but the other, with the shell removed, 'clean bone' with a 'harsh division down the centre, from which fixed line the tortoise could hide nothing of its secret, witty, vulnerable and complicated most internal workings ... [T]he life had been explained out of it' (34–5). Here McWilliam embodies within her novel her own style with its attention to detail, explanation and careful vocabulary. It is a style that in her review writing McWilliam recognises carries a danger of 'overexplanation ... and the obscure sense of being insulted that comes of reading exegetic fiction'.[33] Spark too describes obsessively, if more succinctly, asserting her characters' existences in a ritual of identification through precise detail of age, appearance and occupation. These exegetic tendencies, which can irritate as well as illuminate, link their fictions.

In *A Little Stranger*, McWilliam's second novel, the narrator, Daisy, cocoons herself, like the growing foetus in her womb, in the separateness of her pregnant state. Bilingual in Dutch and English, she is aware of the ambiguities of language, sardonic at the New Year celebrations for the big house's staff: 'Optimistic, frail and ignorant of the future, we sang. You might have thought we were all workers in the established legal firm Auld, Laing & Syne' (47) (a joke altered but echoed in the firm's name of Drive, Torque, MacIsmo, in 'Being a People Person', in *Wait Till I Tell* You).[34] Daisy is the only one to hear 'the lower layers of my own remarks' (59). Married into money, she writes of the hierarchy of women within the big house (51), 'the safe world of romance, hierarchy, display, garmentry' (41) among the wives of her acquaintance. Margaret, the nanny, had believed in the 'calm green sea of money. It rocked her ... and then it wrecked her' (124). She, in her desire for Daisy's husband and position, is the justified sinner whose certainty nearly destroys the narrator and her unborn child, though the connection to Hogg's *Confessions of a Justified Sinner* is not made explicit, as it is in McWilliam's first novel when Anne Cowdenbeath – the only Scottish character in *A Case of Knives* – asserts, 'I am a Scots Calvinist, so used to the idea of there being unjustified sinners'.[35]

The narrator of *A Little Stranger* is not named until late in the novel. Until then she is her husband's wife, her son's mother, seen by Margaret not as an individual woman but in her 'position as mother of her source of income, wife of her source of payment' (16). She is the unreliable narrator who, as she says at the end, has lived without knowing 'at the margin of [her] own life' (135). She leads us through her 'womaned' (57) world of pregnancy, and misdirects us. 'I

did not cease to exist when they were away ... We took a great deal in. We
grew together' (88) we are told in the one paragraph that makes up chapter
17. But in chapter 27, she returns to that lost weekend when Margaret and
John Solomon, Daisy's son, had been in London with her husband:

> What we did together, I and my conscript accessory to the fat, was attend a
> children's party lasting twenty-four hours, a party for ourselves alone ... Soon
> after Margaret came into our house, I began my secret eating ... Our house,
> that long full term of pregnancy, contained two countervalent madnesses, both
> to do with food. (126–7)

Margaret the nanny, bulimic and fixated on taking Daisy's place in the house-
hold, hides her food in her suitcase, getting thinner as Daisy gets fatter, carrying
out her 'inverted worship of the same god' (128). McWilliam weaves a Grimm
brothers' fairy story in which no-one is innocent, recording the madness of
pregnancy and the distorting effects of riches, with a narrator who stands 'outside, alone, at the margin of house and park' (25), incompletely absorbed into
her social setting, before casting herself off into the tide of her pregnancy.
Together, she and Margaret 'had turned the gingerbread house of family life
into the smelt blood and ground bones of the most cruel tales' (135). This is
the conclusion of McWilliam's Gothic tale of class, obsession and pregnancy.
It foregrounds the novel's relationship to the harsher kinds of fairy-tales and
links with the ballad world of betrayals and murders within families.

McWilliam's first novel, *A Case of Knives*, is likewise a tale of class, obsession
and pregnancy, but also of betrayal and violence, told by four narrators (Lucas,
Cora, Anne and Hal), unreliable and partial, the limited view of each building
into an ambiguous whole. Mandy Merck sees it as 'a novel saturated in genre
(the romance and its Gothic ancestor, as well as the crime thriller)' which
'executed an impressive crossover in the literary honours of 1988', critics sin-
gling out McWilliam's writing 'for its art, technique, accomplishment,
brilliance, extravagance', with 'occasional dissenters' complaining that it was
'*too* brilliant'.[36] Merck is more troubled by its 'matching of a hyperstylized
narrative with an equally stylized narration', its 'surprisingly decorous melodrama' (46) disguising an ambivalent attitude to AIDS and homosexuality,
'compact with our most popular narratives of sex, class and disease' (47),
reserving 'a safe space for the straight liberal, uncontaminated by bigotry *or*
disease' (53). But McWilliam's quartet of narrators distances her from any
certain accusations; AIDS as a metaphor for unexpected danger, language presented as 'a case of knives' (216) are part of Anne's narrative. This is the Anne
who controls and folds her life like her vast London wardrobe room's contents,
who has faith in 'the limiting of chaos by external control, the absolute control
of passion by ritual' (14), and who had killed the husband who came to her
'trusting to my courage and my cold blood' (246) after a botched suicide
attempt. Real violence, not the 'melodramatic, erotic danger, to be feinted but
not fulfilled' (240) sought by Lucas in his masochistic trysts with violence,

underlies the novel. It becomes a violence which surprises and violates when Lucas's beloved Hal is exposed retrospectively as Lucas's attacker. There is also the violation of feeling and impending death by AIDS for Tertius. Lucas had seen Tertius (the only 'out' gay and only main character to have no narrative of his own)[37] as his guide in their 'small world, with its four corners, trade and sex and money and class, enclosing a formal maze' (72) but he also links the four narrators with gossip and hidden knowledge. McWilliam's quartet of narrators, in their ambiguous dance with 'trade and sex and money and class', are an unsettling foursome. Scotland, in this world, is Anne's place of refuge; her husband's estate, place of his and their son's deaths, provides the safe haven to which she can sweep away Cora and the damaged Lucas, 'home to Stone' (246). For Anne, Scotland is 'the only serious place to be' (248). Her feelings are rooted in this house 'of secret-bearing stone' (246) which lay between Glasgow and Edinburgh in the Lowlands, approached by 'an irregular drive' (249). It represents a microcosmic if precarious point of balance between Scotland and England and Anne's two worlds: of safety (in this place of murder and death) and of disguise and deceit in London.

Scotland has a complicated presence in *Debatable Land*. McWilliam has talked of the novel making 'explicit what lay unexplicit between' her and her father, and has written of her mother's 'particular flavour' and her parents' middle-class frugality and poverty.[38] In this novel McWilliam writes what amount to elegies for her dead parents in the intense detail of Alec's childhood wanderings around the streets of Edinburgh, the stones and setts evoked in his view from the Camera Obscura (25–6), and in Elspeth's memories of her childhood trip to Culloden with her eccentric and poor middle-class parents. These stories of their Scottish upbringings are embedded in the narrative memories of Alec and Elspeth. They have 'different cities' (146), as Alec says; Alec's moves between the working-class (edging into lower middle-class) scoured cleanliness of his parents' lives and the overcrowded bourgeois world of the Bruces' tenement flat in central Edinburgh; Elspeth's is an Edinburgh of daytrips from the Borders for shopping, dancing and the theatre. But Alec recognises her as a fellow Scot nonetheless by her pronunciation of 'Post Office' (135). 'Admit', he says to her about her otherwise English accent, 'you like the feeling of being different in either country' (135). Alec and Elspeth are the main site of narrative concentration in *Debatable Land* though its technique is also to move between the internalised thoughts of all the characters so there is an intricate pattern of observation and self-reflection throughout the novel. They are all outsiders to each other, constrained from intimacy by the small intimate space of the confines aboard the Ardent Spirit. McWilliam deploys their internalised observations on each other until their final survival through the catharsis of the last part of the voyage through a violent storm. Then Alec is told '"It's ... like it's Scotland you found at the back end of the Pacific"... It took the clear sight of an outsider to show him his own future' (215). This returns us to the opening page of the novel ('he had come so far from home in order to see it clearly' with Alec described as at the 'edge of the Pacific, docile and oily at this margin against the sea wall' (1)) which presages Alec's own voyage from marginality to his newly found ability to return to Edinburgh and the centre of his life.

Debatable Land is McWilliam's conscious attempt 'to convey the strong sense of home ... refracted through a voyage across the south-pacific which is more than a nod to Stevenson' ('Usual Suspects'), emphasising this with the novel's epigraph from Stevenson's *Songs of Travel*. She had 'tried writing ... plain narrative ... and it didn't work. Folding in the discussion of one place while in another place seemed to work much better, like mirrors facing each other'.[39] It is a voyage through islands colonised by Europe, reflecting a Scotland which itself has a complicated relationship to colonising and being colonised. This is emblematised in the 6-year-old Elspeth's subliminal awareness of the 'complicated terror' (162) residual in the stones on Culloden, that last battlefield on British soil with English and Lowland Scots complicit in the defeat of the Jacobite forces and the following repression of Highland clan culture, itself equivalent to many later cultural destructions imposed by colonial British (including Scottish) administrations. McWilliam has spoken of the debatable land as the 'underlying theme' in the novel, describing it as 'no matter how close we are to each other there is a gap between us which for want of a better word I might call the debatable land but love is having the faith to cross that gap' ('Usual Suspects'). In the novel itself, she also inserts the idea of a 'Debatable Land' into a discussion between Alec and Elspeth about Scotland and England, Elspeth speaking first:

> 'There is less place for Anglo-Scots, whatever the word is, than there was. Things are bad. There could be a split. People want it. They sing about it. There was the fish, there is the oil. The stupidity of the South has hurt, the tactlessness that has looked like pillage, the willingness to treat the place like a plaid, to throw on for its ancient rustic glamour and to throw over puddles to save them getting their feet dirty. I fear for the border, I really do.' He laughed at her. 'Here we are,' he said, 'on debatable lands.' (135–6)

So Elspeth, the child of the borders, considers the dangers and falsities of cross-border, Southern upper-class interest in Scotland, and Alec, child of fishing folk on the edge of Edinburgh, names this the debatable lands, that old area of dispute in the borderland that is neither Scotland nor England. The debatable land of the novel becomes these areas of dispute, containing ambiguity and exploitation, the space between classes, and, in the South Seas, the exploited and the exploiters, whether the old colonisers or the new tourists. But it is also McWilliam's gap between people, the gap over which at the end of the voyage Alec finds the faith to return to Edinburgh and to his partner Lorna and their son Sorley.

McWilliam is also a reviewer of others' work. Her reviews are generous, giving careful and intelligent responses. Of Vikram Chaudry's *Love and Long-*

ing in Bombay (1997) she writes that it is 'like a beautiful reduced map that joins its fluidity to that of the reader's imagination and in so doing swells in suggestion and memorableness to become increasingly impressive'.[40] McWilliam's own writing can be both syntactically awkward and accurate; for example, in one of the sharp looks at gender roles in *Wait Till I Tell You*, the wife in 'Seven Magpies' thinks:

> She thought these small acts of abnegation would attune her children at an early age to the deceits of family life and, even more importantly, the real place of women: these inoculations, she, being ironic, took as salutary, and they, being innocent, took for example. (136)

Her writing also revels in its vocabulary of 'the *right* words for the thing I wanted to describe ... very specific words' (Mitchison, 16). Taken together the three novels and her short stories, *Wait Till I Tell You* (the title perhaps acknowledging Lochhead's opening to 'Mrs Abernethy: Festive Fayre': 'Well ... *wait* till I tell you'[41]), as a body of work, is 'increasingly impressive'. Her fiction's ambiguities of narrative and precision and excess of style have exactly the kind of resonant memorableness that she extols in Chaudra.

'For an exile, there are no continuities, merely succession', thinks Alec in *Debatable Land* (59). Those in self-chosen exile, such as Spark and McWilliam, are inevitably outsiders, onlookers by default or choice. Like Alec, the artist, who chooses sight above hearing at the revelation of Edinburgh, 'voiceless' and 'displayed' from the Camera Obscura (26), they are watchful; they observe and describe, negotiating class and gender, North and South (as the two sections of *Wait Till I Tell You* are named). Despite her disclaimer, McWilliam represents a continuity, if not a succession, as an inheritor of Spark's self-created tradition, in that shared intense self-consciousness of style, and the way in which her writing also foregrounds language and intricate ambiguities of meaning.

Notes

1. Alan Bold (ed.), *Muriel Spark: An Odd Capacity for Vision* (London: Vision Press, 1984), p. 7; and Janice Galloway, 'The Vital Spark', *Sunday Herald M*, 11 July 1999, pp. 6–10 (8).
2. *The Prime of Miss Jean Brodie* (1961; Harmondsworth: Penguin, 1965), p. 88. See also Candia McWilliam, 'Introduction' in Muriel Spark, *The Prime of Miss Jean Brodie* (Harmondsworth: Penguin, 2000), pp. v–xiii.
3. For a longer discussion, see A. Christianson, 'Certainty and Unease in Spark's *The Ballad of Peckham Rye*', in Carol Anderson and A. Christianson (eds), *Scottish Women's Fiction, 1920s to 1960s* (East Linton: Tuckwell Press, 2000), pp. 135–46.
4. *Curriculum Vitae* (London: Constable, 1992), p. 98.
5. Galloway, 'The Vital Spark', p. 8; for further discussion of Spark's 'Scottishness', see Alan Bold, *Muriel Spark* (London: Methuen & Co., 1986).
6. Alan Taylor, 'Home Fires Still Burning', *Scotsman Weekend*, 1 January 2000, p. 3.

7. Frank Kermode, 'Myth, Reality, and Fiction', *The Listener*, 30 August 1962, pp. 311–13 (312).

8. 'My Conversion', *Twentieth Century*, 170 (Autumn 1961), pp. 58–63 (63).

9. *A Far Cry from Kensington* (1988; Harmondsworth: Penguin, 1989), p. 98.

10. *The Ballad of Peckham Rye* (1960; Harmondsworth: Penguin, 1963), p. 76.

11. *Muriel Spark: A Biographical and Critical Study* (Fontwell: Centaur Press, 1963).

12. *Loitering with Intent* (1981; Harmondsworth: Penguin, 1995), p. 9.

13. *Moral Absolutism in the Novels of Robert Louis Stevenson, Robin Jenkins and Muriel Spark: Challenges to Realism* (unpublished Ph.D. thesis; Edinburgh: University of Edinburgh, 1985), p. 335.

14. Jonathan Coe, 'Conversions' (review of *Symposium*), *London Review of Books*, 13 September 1990, pp. 15–16 (15).

15. William Boyd, *Independent Weekend*, 21 September 1996, p. 8.

16. For example, *Memento Mori* (1959), *Symposium* (1990) and *Reality and Dreams* (1996).

17. Summarised from Norquay, 'Calvinism and Scottish Writing', 'Scotland and the Foundations of Modernity' series, 'Calvinism and Modernity' symposium, University of Edinburgh, 14 February 1997.

18. *Reality and Dreams* (1996; Harmondsworth: Penguin, 1997), p. 111.

19. Introduction, *Twentieth Century Interpretations of the Praise of Folly* (1969), p. 8, cited by Jennifer Lynn Randisi, *On Her Way Rejoicing The Fiction of Muriel Spark* (Washington, DC: Catholic University of America Press, 1991), p. 111.

20. Margaret Elphinstone, 'Contemporary Feminist Fantasy in the Scottish Literary Tradition', in Caroline Gonda (ed.), *Tea and Leg-Irons: New Feminist Readings from Scotland* (London: Open Letters, 1992), pp. 44–59 (48); G. Gregory Smith, *Scottish Literature Character and Influence* (London: Macmillan, 1919), p. 20.

21. *Xcess*, BBC Scotland, 29 January 1996; Gerard Carruthers, 'The Remarkable Fictions of Muriel Spark', in Douglas Gifford and Dorothy McMillan (eds), *A History of Scottish Women's Writing* (Edinburgh: EUP, 1997), pp. 514–25 (521).

22. *The Driver's Seat* (1970; Harmondsworth: Penguin, 1974), p. 106.

23. 'The Desegregation of Art', American Academy and Institute of Arts and Letters, 1971; reprinted: Joseph Hynes (ed.), *Critical Essays on Muriel Spark* (New York: G. K. Hill & Co., 1992), pp. 31–7 (35).

24. Nina Auerbach, *Communities of Women An Idea in Fiction* (Cambridge, MA: Harvard University Press, 1978), p. 181.

25. *Symposium* (1990; Harmondsworth: Penguin, 1991), p. 7.

26. My reading of *The Driver's Seat* is undoubtedly linked to my work with Edinburgh Rape Crisis Centre, 1978–96.

27. *The Only Problem* (London: The Bodley Head, 1984), p. 131.

28. Roland Barthes, 'The Death of the Author', in Barthes, *Image Music Text*, trans. Stephen Heath (London: Fontana, 1977), pp. 142–8.

29. This section on McWilliam is partly based on my 'Elspeth Barker, Candia McWilliam and Muriel Spark: Writers in Exile', in Susanne Hagemann (ed.), *Terranglian Territories: Proceedings of Seventh International Conference on the Literature of Region and Nation* (Frankfurt am Main: Peter Lang, 2000; pp. 339–47).

30. Anne Donald, 'Spark of Humanity', *Scotland on Sunday, Spectrum*, 28 January 1996, p. 10.

31. Candia McWilliam, *A Little Stranger* (1990; London: Picador, 1990), pp. 63.

32. Candia McWilliam, *Debatable Land* (London: Bloomsbury, 1994), p. 14.

33. Candia McWilliam, review of Anne Haverty, *One Day as a Tiger*, *The Sunday Review*, *The Independent on Sunday*, 23 February 1997, p. 29.

34. Candia McWilliam, *Wait Till I Tell You* (London: Bloomsbury, 1997), p. 195.

35. Candia McWilliam, *A Case of Knives* (1988; London: Abacus, 1989), p. 242.

36. Mandy Merck, 'A Case of AIDS', in Merck, *perversions: deviant readings* (London: Virago, 1993), pp. 45–58 (46).

37. Ibid., pp. 51–2.

38. Interview, 'The Usual Suspects', BBC Radio Scotland, 15 June 1994; 'The Many Colours of Blood', *The Scotsman Weekend*, 4 July 1998, pp. 12–15 (13).

39. Amanda Mitchison, 'The Folding Starlet', *The Independent Magazine*, 4 June 1994, pp. 14–18 (16).

40. 'Et in India ego', *The Sunday Review*, *The Independent on Sunday*, 30 March 1997, p. 34.

41. Liz Lochhead, *True Confessions and New Clichés* (Edinburgh: Polygon, 1985), p. 126.

CHAPTER EIGHT

Agnes Owens's Fiction: Untold Stories

Lynne Stark

Agnes Owens (b. 1926) came to writing late in life after joining a local writing class in the Vale of Leven in the mid-1970s. Liz Lochhead, after reading 'Arabella' (a short story by Owens), showed it to Alasdair Gray and James Kelman who were equally impressed. Gray describes instructing Owens in the harsh realities of a writing life:

> Our first reaction was to call her a natural writer, which on second thoughts was silly. Nobody writes naturally ... They had to teach her that if she steadily posted her work to a certain number of small magazines, always with a stamped addressed envelope for return, she might get two or three stories published in four or five years.[1]

Owens's first novel, *Gentlemen of the West*,[2] was published in 1984; *Lean Tales*, the collection of short stories written by Gray, Kelman and Owens, came next. This joint publication was accidental but Owens's name remains linked to theirs, her work framed by their social preoccupations. Kelman and Gray belong to the community of Scottish writers who emerged in the 1980s with a distinct artistic agenda. Conscious that the new environment of industrial decline, structural unemployment and social fragmentation demanded innovative narrative patterns, their writing went well beyond the confines of conventional social realism, redefining the model of 'working class' writing, the alienated social subject replacing the community as centre of attention. There was a determination to bring to fiction the unimagined: voices, people and places denied cultural existence. In tune with this, Owens's characters are drawn from the margins of working-class life: alcoholics, petty criminals and down-and-outs. Mac, the main character of *Gentlemen of the West*, is representative of the new type of working-class protagonist. Unlike his fictional forefathers who tried to escape their surroundings through education or transform it through social revolution, Mac is politically apathetic. Short-term self-interest rather than socialism motivates him. The title mocks the idea of social improvement. The 'gentlemen' in question are a group of alcoholic itinerants: 'generous, treacherous, vicious and kindly with no admiration for the rich and successful' (124). Their aimless, peripatetic lifestyle symbolises the existential

quality of contemporary working-class existence. Owens registers her characters' inability to move upwards or outwards at a stylistic level through the
extensive use of repetition within and between her novels. *Gentlemen of the
West*, for example, begins and ends with the funeral of Paddy, the most famous
gentleman of them all, prompting Mac to leave his depressed hometown and
travel north in search of employment. His journey into a surreal Scottish hin-
terland forms the subject of Owens's next novel, *Like Birds in the Wilderness*,[3]
looping back on the first novel in defiance of the serial logic of the sequel. No
wiser or richer for his travels, Mac ends up exactly where he started: unemployed and living in the west with his mother, ironically pinning his hopes for
domestic escape on a mobile home, that perfect symbol of illusory movement.

Like Birds in the Wilderness depicts an ordinary individual caught up in a
web of intrigue and deception that is beyond his ability to understand. After
losing his job on a building site, Mac volunteers to be a get-away driver for
some sort of illegal activity, possibly a robbery, only to become the unwitting
dupe of the two conmen who recruited him. He wakes up in a police cell,
minus his pay packet, and facing trumped-up charges. After a short period of
incarceration in a private hospital, Mac tracks down the conmen to the Highlands where they are setting up another shadowy scheme. When confronted
by Mac, they claim to be government-sanctioned political agitators whose job
it is to entrap terrorist elements on the mainland. Mac's inexplicable incarceration in a private hospital and equally mysterious release certainly suggest
influential powers at work but Mac suspects that he is being fed yet another
lie. Unsure who or what to believe, reeling from alcohol and hunger-induced
hallucinations, Mac is as disorientated as the birds of the title. Surreal incidents
and a consistently comic tone undercut the potential terror of Mac's situation
and the novel's suggestion of covert state surveillance.

Owens's ability to render familiar elements of Scottish landscape uncanny
is redolent of Alasdair Gray. Here, sheep move across a hillside like 'lice on a
shaved head' and reality is deceptive. Mac sees a man with a grossly disfigured
face and assumes that he is wearing a Halloween mask. On second thoughts he
revises his opinion and describes the man as a 'burnt-out case, maybe caused
by the war or a car crash' (*Like Birds*, 24). Later the same man accosts Mac and
to Mac's horror peels off his skin. Underneath is the grinning face of Dad, one
of the two conmen. A fellow lodger's suspicion that 'he's workin' for the polis
and the mask is tae disguise himsel, where he's known' (*Like Birds*, 27) catches
the novel's atmosphere of distrust, duplicity and paranoia. The weakest members of society are not simply trapped by their environment; all too often they
are incarcerated physically. A striking number of Owens's characters experience forcible imprisonment within institutions: in the course of his journey
Mac is held in a police cell for a crime he did not commit and then sedated in
an unspecified hospital. The narrators of Owens's last two novels, *People Like
That* and *For the Love of Willie*,[4] are mental patients. For Owens the reality of
working-class experience is dystopian if not Kafkaesque in character: 'people

do live in a state of fear, but still cope with ordinary life. I try to write about what's behind it all, portray people living in this state of fear'.[5] The theme of entrapment dominates her work just as it does that of Kelman and Gray.[6] *Like Birds in the Wilderness* is Owens's most overtly political piece of writing. Only here is there any suggestion, however indirect, of a large-scale, organised political system at work.

In an interview in 1996, Owens expressed frustration at being forced to conform to a narrow political agenda: 'I don't consciously try to write about bad conditions, although that comes into it – but I'm sick of that right now.' Her real interest lies in what she refers to as 'the treacheries of attitude, the small treacheries of human nature'.[7] Consequently, her recent fiction is markedly different from her early work. Whereas *Gentlemen of the West* carefully brought to life a small, economically depressed town on the west coast of Scotland, *A Working Mother* provides minimal description.[8] Only the narrator's comment that 'ten years after the war he [her husband] still looked as if he had just come home from the battlefield' (1) places it in the context of the 1950s. The most recent novel, *For the Love of Willie*, on the other hand, returns to wartime Glasgow to tell the familiar tale of a young pregnant girl's abandonment by her married lover. Significantly, both narrators are elderly women. Owens's early writing was exclusively male-orientated, in keeping with the kind of working-class writing then prevalent. The author's age and gender were often overlooked in critical discussions because of her association with Kelman and Gray. Perhaps by using narrators whose profile matches her own Owens is signalling that she is finally comfortable with her own voice.

However, even at an early stage, stylistic differences existed between Owens and her collaborators. Kelman, for instance, objects to the traditional third-person narratorial voice on the grounds that it masks the unequal relationship between (bourgeois) narrator and (working-class) subject. His own writing works to dismantle the 'wee game between the reader and writer' by the extensive use of interior monologue.[9] Characters are perceived from within, rather than observed from without, the working-class subject, not the writer or implied reader, becoming the arbiter of values. By contrast, Owens adopts the third-person narrative voice in order to accentuate the perceptual distance between reader and subject. The reader alone recognises the tragic dimensions of a given situation, characters do not; it is a measure of how little control they have. Kelman explodes working-class stereotypes by granting his creations layers of intellectual and emotional complexity: Owens's subject *is* the disparity between social and individual perception. The gulf between how we see ourselves and how others see us is standard comic fare but Owens adds extra satiric bite. Lack of recognition is what connects reader to character: we do not recognise ourselves in these shambling, derelict figures and neither do they. In 'People Like That', a woman waits at a railway station for Brian, her son. The narration is in bland Standard English and it moves from third-person observation to third-person reflective. Coupled with the absence of any physical description, this prevents us identifying her as homeless and mentally ill. Only the hostile reactions of passers-by hint that Mary is in some way physically unappealing. She has no awareness of how she is perceived: 'Perplexed, Mary watched her go, wondering what she'd said to annoy this woman with a face like a pig and legs as thick as tree trunks. Likely she was off her head. You were bound to meet people like that in a railway station' (*People*, 79). Compelled to exist in a hopeless environment, characters respond by creating their own strange, self-contained universe. Owens allows the reader to enter this private landscape and then exposes it, and them, to a brutal public gaze. More often than not, the mutual incomprehension fostered by imposed social categories has tragic consequences. In 'Bus Queue', a young boy is prevented from escaping his attackers by a group of older people who think he is a 'young thug' jumping the queue. As the bus pulls away he is stabbed. 'There's a boy hingin ower the fence. Looks as if he's hurt bad', observes one. 'Och they canny fight for nuts nooadays', responds another with unintentional irony, 'they should be in Belfast wi' ma son'. With that 'the boy was dismissed from their thoughts. They were glad to be out of the cold and on their way' (*Lean Tales*, 125). Owens's protagonists can be amnesiac (Peggy and The Duchess in *For the Love of Willie*), delusional (Betty in *A Working Mother*), or clinically insane (Arabella in 'Arabella'). Owens exploits the gaps in her characters' understanding to produce narratives hinting at untold stories, unanswerable questions and unrealised possibilities.

Owens's interest in 'the treacheries of attitude' ('Finding Truth'), the dynamics of betrayal, links her thematically to the earlier (but near-contemporary) writer Muriel Spark. These two writers are seldom associated with each other. However, a comparison highlights aspects of Owens's work missed by any exclusively class-orientated approach. The connection is most apparent in Owens's last two novels where she combines a deliberately pared-down style with dark, frequently violent, subject-matter. With its terse dialogue, bitter humour and cast of grotesque characters, *A Working Mother* recalls Spark's grimly comic novellas of the mid-1970s; there is Mrs Rossi, the tarot-reading boss of a recruitment agency, and Betty's boss, Mr Robson, is an elderly sexual voyeur who pays Betty to sit on a bed naked while he masturbates behind a screen. It comes as no surprise to learn that he is writing a study on 'Human Behaviour in Animals'. There is Betty herself, a recognisable Spark 'type', the ill-fated plotter. Unhappily married to an alcoholic war veteran, Betty spices up her life by manipulating others. She embarks on an affair with her husband's slow-witted best friend, Brendan. In return for her invented stories of sexual intrigue Mr Robson agrees to employ Brendan as his gardener, a decision Betty will come to regret.

The grotesque is an index of the world's imperfection. Here the 'natural' order of the family is reversed. Betty provides for the family while her husband, traumatised by his wartime experiences, crawls 'round the floor like an animal or a gigantic baby, moaning and grinding his teeth' (130). The pattern is repeated in society at large: men are unemployed and ineffectual whilst the female characters like Betty or Mrs Rossi are shown as arch-manipulators. Betty is an unusual figure in Owens's fiction: an active, decisive individual. Her first words are, 'I'll have to get a job' (1). But her belief in her capacity for self-determination is shattered by the unexpected turn of events. In a play on gender stereotypes, her husband takes the wife's prerogative and walks out with the children. Meanwhile, Brendan murders Mr Robson. Brendan is arrested but Betty is widely suspected to be the real culprit. Her protests of innocence are in vain as Betty finds herself forced into a role she did not choose. Out-manœuvred by the weak, she turns to drink and slips slowly into madness.

A *Working Mother* and *For the Love of Willie* explore what might be thought of as quintessential Sparkian themes – the status of fictional 'truth' and the relationship between reality and fiction. There is an unexpected twist in the final quarter of A *Working Mother*:

> I'm looking over the veranda of the cottage hospital to where a bus shelter stands covered in graffiti ... Lady Lipton is asleep. She's been asleep for most of my tale ... 'Weren't you listening?' 'I heard most of it, though I may have dozed off at the boring parts. Please do go on.' 'It's not true anyway', I said off-handedly. 'It sounds to me like a whodunit where you have to plough through a lot of red herrings before it gets to the point.' (164–5)

What we think is happening has already happened; or perhaps never happened at all. Confined to a mental hospital, Betty still tries to control events by shaping and remaking them into a narrative of dubious authenticity: 'When you're in here everything gets so jumbled up it is hard to know the truth', she complains (182). *For the Love of Willie* establishes the same scenario in the foreword. Peggy, 'stoutly built, middle-aged, and with a hard set to her jaw', informs her fellow patient that she is writing a book 'about my life before they put me inside' (1). Here the dual narrative is integrated and the novel alternates between the hospital and wartime Glasgow. The emphasis on the process of storytelling highlights what is not told. Peggy and Betty's accounts are riddled with gaps, both accidental (the result of memory loss) and deliberate. Betty narrates her own story but refuses to analyse her actions. Consequently, her capricious and mean-minded behaviour is never explained satisfactorily. Peggy omits any mention of the most important event in her life. We learn the real reason for her incarceration from a casual comment:

> The couple arrived on time but had to wait ten minutes before Peggy came into the hall carrying the child ... The next moment they were leaving ... Only now that she was safely on the tram did she allow herself the luxury of wondering how long it would take the couple to discover the baby was dead. (116)

No details are given either of the circumstances of the murder or the scandal that must have followed. In this absence Owens evokes the sheer, purposeless waste of not one but two prematurely terminated lives. Yet, despite being denied the right to live her life, Peggy reclaims the right to tell it. The ending is surprisingly optimistic. In contrast to *A Working Mother* which ends with Betty's incarceration, *For the Love of Willie* concludes with Peggy's release.

A *Working Mother* and *For the Love of Willie* ironically counterpoint the large-scale destruction of war with the everyday damage of domestic life. Yet there is no indignant tone, no authorial condemnation: 'People say, my writing is compassionate, but I don't intend that', says Owens ('Finding Truth'). Like Spark's, her novels fall into the category of tragi-comedy: a genre that demands a detached observation of suffering. Although they are invariably the victims of tragic circumstances, Owens's characters are not capable of tragedy themselves. They are largely passive; bewildered but not angry at the invisible structures containing them. Alcoholism and addiction are pleasurable substitutes for action: 'it's the life we lead', observes Betty in *A Working Mother*, 'it's so pointless. All we do is drink' (129). Mac's cry for 'anything, just anything to give me a hint of something beyond' after Paddy's death is a rare moment of angst (*Gentlemen*, 116). Owens's characters, unlike Kelman's narrators, refuse the burden of consciousness. Peggy is given a copy of Camus' *The Plague* but forgets to read it. This small but telling incident sets the pattern for all Owens's writing: amnesia replaces alienation. Potential dilemmas of conscience are transformed into comedies of confusion. Mac and his kind stumble through a world that is terrifying not because it is violent but because it is arbitrary. 'There's terrorists everywhere nooadays', says one of Mac's friends after hearing a loud explosion, 'It's the new craze' (*Like Birds*, 29). A blind force not unlike terrorism underpins Owens's fictional universe. The chance turn of events may result in terrible suffering and there is, Owens seems to suggest, no viable alternative. Surface absurdity hides a bleak vision. Spark's characters are tragi-comic because they pursue their plots in defiance of the presence of God: Owens's characters are tragi-comic because they do so in his absence. Everyone is a citizen of this 'state of fear' ('Finding Truth').

Notes

1. 'Postscript', Agnes Owens, James Kelman and Alasdair Gray, *Lean Tales* (Edinburgh: Polygon, 1985), p. 284.
2. Agnes Owens, *Gentlemen of the West* (Edinburgh: Polygon, 1984).
3. Agnes Owens, *Like Birds in the Wilderness* (London: Fourth Estate, 1987).
4. Agnes Owens, *People Like That* (London: Bloomsbury, 1996); *For the Love of Willie* (London: Bloomsbury, 1998).
5. Joy Hendry, 'Finding Truth in Hard Times', *The Scotsman*, 11 May 1996, p. 16.
6. Robert Crawford, 'Introduction', in R. Crawford and T. Nairn (eds), *The Arts of Alasdair Gray* (Edinburgh: Polygon, 1991), pp. 1–9 (4–5).
7. Hendry, 'Finding Truth'.
8. Agnes Owens, *A Working Mother* (London: Bloomsbury, 1994).
9. Duncan McLean, 'James Kelman Interviewed', *Edinburgh Review*, 71 (1985), p. 77.

CHAPTER NINE

Emma Tennant, Elspeth Barker, Alice Thompson: Gothic Revisited

Carol Anderson

In an influential essay of 1972, 'When We Dead Awaken', whose title is drawn from Ibsen, American poet and critic Adrienne Rich argues that women, particularly, must attempt a 'radical critique' of literature:

> Re-vision – the act of looking back, of seeing with fresh eyes, of entering an old text from a new critical direction – is for us more than a chapter in cultural history: it is an act of survival. Until we can understand the assumptions in which we are drenched we cannot know ourselves.[1]

Since then, there has been much revisioning, critical and creative. As Steven Connor observes, 'the practice of rewriting earlier works of fiction' has become a marked feature of post-war fiction generally,[2] and notably among female writers who 'rewrite' specific male texts, offering an interpretation – often feminist – both of the texts and the culture which produced them. Alison Fell has reworked Swift in *Mistress of Lilliput* (1999), for instance. Other novelists revisit dominant cultural traditions and myths more generally.[3]

This chapter looks at three novels signalling a significant relationship with an earlier male text: Emma Tennant's *Two Women of London* (1989) engages with Stevenson's *The Strange Case of Dr Jekyll and Mr Hyde*, Elspeth Barker's *O Caledonia* (1991) with Scott's *The Lay of the Last Minstrel*, and Alice Thompson's *Justine* (1996) with Sade's *Justine* and *Juliette*.[4] Their interaction with the earlier texts varies in method and degree. Tennant makes detailed response to Stevenson, while Barker and Thompson depart considerably from their male predecessors in their 'revisioning' of myth and tradition. All three novels also refer to numerous other texts, including female ones.

These three intensely literary novels can be seen as engaging with a specific *kind* of fiction, Gothic, partly in response to the works on which they draw: Stevenson called his novella 'a Gothic gnome', Scott described his long poem's characters as 'Gothic borderers', and Sade is one of the 'father-figures' of Gothicism.[5] Gothic fiction is most narrowly interpreted as a cultural phenomenon of the late eighteenth and early nineteenth centuries, initially portraying fear and the supernatural in medieval settings including the sinister castle or mansion, though work by mid- to late nineteenth-century writers including the Brontës and Poe is also often viewed as Gothic. More broadly, Gothic represents the demands of the unconscious, the imagination and desire, transgressing literary and social conventions and provoking unease, and it is difficult to separate from related modes such as 'horror' fiction and fantasy.

The three writers considered here can be seen, too, in the context of a wider contemporary attraction to 'the Gothic'. Gothic has gained renewed currency; according to the late Angela Carter, 'we live in Gothic times'.[6] Historical parallels are discernible between the period of 'Old Gothic' and the late twentieth century;[7] that Gothic, itself arguably a parodic form, is so easy to parody also makes it attractive in an age of parody and pastiche. Its presence is detectable in many post-war fictions through 'structural or verbal allusion, or wholesale rewriting' (Sage and Smith, 1), and it is fashionable among critics.[8] Contemporary novelists, attracted to typically Gothic subject-matter – violence, tabooed desires, paranoia, the nature of evil – explore, like their antecedents, contemporary anxieties. Modern Gothic fiction, including work by various Scottish writers, offers cultural self-analysis, and examination of the relationship between past and present.[9] Some of these writers are female. A. L. Kennedy's *So I Am Glad*, with its portrayal of psychological damage and sado-masochistic sex, can be seen in a Gothic light, as can the deadpan horror of Agnes Owens's *A Working Mother*. Emma Tennant and Janice Galloway are included in McGrath and Morrow's *The Picador Book of the New Gothic* and are also discussed by David Punter.[10]

Characteristically ambivalent, Gothic literature can be viewed differently as either 'disturbing but conservative' or 'radical and subversive',[11] in relation to gender amongst other things. Women in male-authored Gothic fiction are often represented voyeuristically as sexual victims or predators; yet Gothic fiction can also be seen as 'questioning the absolute nature of sexual roles' (Punter, 191). It was, from the start, often written both by and for women, and 'female Gothic' has its own characteristics.[12] The novels discussed here, by Tennant, Thompson and Barker, may be seen in a Gothic fictional tradition, deliberately exploiting its potential subversiveness, yet making visible 'the socially and politically conservative discourses coded into traditional genre conventions',[13] self-consciously reworking Gothic to explore the construction of femininity, the importance of the visual, and the dominance of the 'male gaze'.[14] They revisit the psychological aspects of Gothic, its concern with 'interior entropy – spiritual and emotional breakdown' (McGrath and Morrow, xii), and the darker sides of sexuality, 'incest, sexual violence, rape' (Punter, 191), exposing damaging attitudes to women. The 'victimisation and the anger' identified by Adrienne Rich (98) are both expressed and examined.

Novelists who both use *and* criticise past art, who both work within *and* abuse convention, risk being implicated in the models they employ.[15] Displaying self-awareness, 'self-conscious masquerade' (Waugh, 189), is one countering strategy:

To play with mimesis is thus, for a woman, to try to recover the place of her exploitation by discourse, without allowing herself to be simply reduced to it. It means to resubmit herself ... to ideas about herself, that are elaborated in/by a masculine logic, but so as to make 'visible', by an effect of playful repetition, what was supposed to remain invisible.[16]

'The double voice of irony' is characteristic of both postmodern and feminine art, women writers revisiting Gothic often presenting a 'combination of gendered critique and ironic humour'.[17] Each of the novels discussed here playfully features that arch-mimic, the parrot. A traditional heraldic symbol of rhetoric which has appealed also, notably, to Julian Barnes (*Flaubert's Parrot*, 1984), it emblematises, perhaps, these works' literary and parodic qualities, hinting at their 'doubled' and ambiguous nature.

Many of Emma Tennant's novels are openly intertextual revisionist fantasies. *The Bad Sister* (1978), for instance, responds to James Hogg's *The Private Memoirs and Confessions of a Justified Sinner* (1824). Tennant, resident in London but raised in Scotland,[18] turns again to Scottish tradition in *Two Women of London*. Its plot and characters derive directly from Stevenson's *The Strange Case of Dr Jekyll and Mr Hyde*, a novella with the status of cultural myth, which has attracted considerable 'revisionist' attention.[19]

Set, like Stevenson's novella, in London, Tennant's re-reading overtly places itself in a Gothic tradition. The novel opens with a death, and the night sky 'seems permanently overheated' (181), creating unease: this is the city as Gothic location (as in Stevenson). Interiors are significant, too; Eliza Jekyll's house has a hall 'mirrored with old glass so that it was impossible to tell where it ended and the rest of the flat began' (227), suggesting, like the 'Pompeiian mural' (228) – the 'painted room of trick colonnades and marble ante-chambers' (234) – the labyrinthine structures of Gothic. But this Gothic may be seen also as Scottish, not only because of Stevenson's background but because Tennant shares the view with her novel's dedicatee, Karl Miller, that the Gothic mode is especially strong in Scotland, arriving initially via the influence of German literature.[20] Such a context for reading is suggested here through pointed allusion to 'the old tales of the Germans and the Scots' (224) and the way in which Scottish- and German-speaking characters are foregrounded. The novel invites reading in terms of female Gothic as well. A character called Grace Poole connects *Two Women* not only to *Jekyll and Hyde*, with its manservant, Poole, but to Charlotte Brontë's *Jane Eyre*. References to 'Victorian madwomen' (257) and 'female' maladies like hysteria (205) also point to feminist interpretations of Gothic.[21]

This deliberate revisiting of Gothic focuses the reader's attention on gender, picking up anxieties implicit in *Jekyll and Hyde*, and creating what Elaine Showalter calls a 'brilliant feminist version of Stevenson's novel'.[22] Stevenson's middle-class professional men are translated into a group of women in 'one of Notting Hill's most desirable quarters' (181), discussing an anonymous rapist prowling their gardens. This highlights the sexual threat to women that pervades Gothic, obliquely hinted at by Stevenson, whose novella prefigured Jack the Ripper. Tennant's women turn to 'the topic of women in general; and the change (if any) in society's attitude to physical violence and social discrimination against them' (200), expressing their 'rage and dissatisfaction with society' (207); thus feminist issues are foregrounded.

Tennant's reworking of Stevenson's 'split' figure as metropolitan Ms Eliza Jekyll, 'doubled in her self and craving a true mirror image' (270), and Mrs Hyde, an ageing, poverty-stricken single mother, also invites feminist interpretation. Stevenson's pattern is inverted, the key figure transforming aspirationally *from* Hyde, *into* the glamorous Jekyll. The novel directs attention to society's emphasis on female youth and beauty and explores women's problematic relationship with the visual, especially the objectification of women by film, photography and the media, echoing Laura Mulvey's analysis: 'in a world ordered by sexual imbalance, pleasure in looking has been split between active/male and passive/female. The determining male gaze projects its fantasy onto the female figure, which is styled accordingly' (Mulvey, 436). The gulf between exploitative images and the reality of women's experiences of poverty and marginalisation is suggested in an emblematic scene where Mrs Hyde walks behind 'Canalot' film studios 'in a street as rough and garish and abandoned to the poor as that great warehouse behind her is a haven for creativity and wealth' (219–20).

Women's own creativity is beset by problems; significantly, Eliza Jekyll is not a medical doctor, as in Stevenson, but the Art-School-trained manageress of the (Gothically named) Shade Gallery (186), whose career crumbles after marriage, children and abandonment; her friend Robina Sandel, potentially a talented film-maker, lacks opportunities (196, 198), while Mara Kaletsky's photomontages of rape-victims are full of '*hate*' (192), suggesting (self-referentially?) the difficulties of portraying women's experience (197). Mara, like several other characters, may herself be exploitative or hypocritical, but the novel also stresses the difficulties for women attempting to reconcile the different stresses on them in patriarchal society.

Tennant's 'two women', 'Yuppy ... and avenging slattern' (276) suggest 'all the divisions we are in the midst of suffering in this country' (201), but binary oppositions (as in Stevenson) are challenged (274). While gender is foregrounded, so, too, is the power of capitalism. Even Eliza Jekyll lacks the power of Sir James Lister, owner not only of the Shade Gallery but 'the massive new supermarket up by Kensal Road' and much other property (192). When he unexpectedly closes the Gallery 'and announced plans to develop the site' (248), Eliza loses her job. Tennant shows the insecurities of an unequal society; as the (fictional) editor – perhaps an echo of Hogg – comments: 'The media leave us in no doubt that rapaciousness and a "loadsamoney" economy have come to represent the highest values in the land' (184).

Tennant's short novel is set self-consciously in the 1980s but alludes to the 1880s when Stevenson's novella appeared, with the image of saplings in the gardens 'in crinolines of wire netting' (181), references to Victorian fogs (231), and Victorian-sounding names like Eliza. 'Mara', too, is the name of a character from George MacDonald's fin-de-siècle fantasy *Lilith* which splits 'Woman' into 'good' and 'bad'. *Jekyll and Hyde* is now seen as a text emblematic of its time, and Tennant's novel draws attention to the spirit of its age; 'The Zeitgeist is not to my liking' comments one character (198), and in an 'afterword', the Scottish doctor Jean Hastie refers to Mrs Hyde as 'this tragic victim of our new Victorian values' (280). The 1980s were a period of intense Thatcherite Conservatism; Tennant's satiric purposes are clear.

Yet *Two Women* also offers a critique of late twentieth-century use of 'Heritage stuff' (191). Prosperous Londoners may take from the past its appealing features, like 'lamp-posts, facsimiles of the Victorian originals and insisted on by rich residents of the borough' (224), but they are appalled when the past's unpleasant aspects reappear – when a rapist stalks their gardens or poverty intrudes. If Gothic ransacks 'an imaginary museum of pastness', arguably postmodern culture, too, cannibalises images 'from the detritus of global history in which the past, in Jameson's words, has itself become a vast collection of images'.[23] The novel suggests such ideas; Mara's photographic art, disliked notably by Robina Sandel who has lost most of her family to the Nazis in World War II (192), may be 'no more than a presage of a world where the sole survivors are machines' (270). Although postmodern in its use of tradition, *Two Women* is both implicitly critical of the late twentieth century's often casual and exploitative use of history and imagery, and self-aware about its own strategies.

Like Stevenson's novella, Tennant's raises moral questions. If the murder of Sir Danvers Carew seems motiveless, Mrs Hyde's murder of the 'innocent' Jeremy Toller is highly problematic. Is this 'Murder? Manslaughter? Execution?' (185). As with Stevenson, there are no clear answers. Steven Connor sees *Two Women of London* as failing to escape Stevenson, whose 'fear of reversion *into* the female resurfaces as a fear of reversion *in the female* into pure and unrepresentable "evil"' (Connor, 182). However, the novel, overtly debating the nature of evil (with the garden crime-scene a self-conscious reminder of Original Sin), foregrounds social injustice, presenting the killing in a context that makes it explicable (277). Tennant's mimicry of Stevenson's range of narratives, providing no single reliable voice, also results in a quality of indeterminacy common to Gothic and postmodern fictions, undermining didacticism. None of the characters are fully endorsed, including Jean Hastie, whose name may echo that of the intensely Presbyterian Scot Hastie in Stevenson's *The Master of Ballantrae*. Uncertainty is heightened by the uneasy mixing of subject-matter and sometimes playful tone; the supposed rapist is killed by a parrot, we are told: 'deep into his throat, with its beak' (238). The parrot is the head on Eliza Jekyll's umbrella. The real mimic is Tennant herself, whose double-voiced response to Stevenson's 'master-text' is deadly serious in its gendered themes, yet shot through with satirical humour.

Like *Two Women of London*, Alice Thompson's (first) novel *Justine* has a metropolitan setting. Of one key location, the 'London Library', we are told, 'People
are always putting it into their novels' (48), a typically self-reflexive touch.
But London, 'the centre of cultural and political greatness' (72), intertwining
in the nameless male narrator's mind with the Justine of the title (72), is
revisioned disturbingly as a psychological locale that through 'deliberate echoes
of Hogg and Stevenson' connects with Scottish tradition.[24]

As in Tennant's novel, period is significant. Initially *Justine* appears set in
the late nineteenth century because of its lush prose and its narrator, an opium-
smoking aesthete whose room is decorated with tapestries and 'lilies of the
holiest white' (2). References to Oscar Wilde's *The Picture of Dorian Gray* (13),
Lewis Carroll (43) and the painter Moreau (52) further suggest a fin-de-siècle
context; but this is 'the maelstrom of the twentieth century's final decade' (8).
Darkly apocalyptic images of 'black skyscrapers … like monoliths to an urban
god' (73), urban tension (85), violence and homelessness (100–2) imply, like
Two Women, the 'decadence' and spiritual lack of recent times.

Thompson's *Justine* also signals a relationship with another end of century
through its relationship with Sade's *Justine* (1791–7) and *Juliette* (1797) –
both explicitly named (54, 117). Sade's libertines are echoed in Thompson's
male narrator, with his sexual obsessiveness, his erotic and 'sadistic' fantasies. Byronically club-footed yet 'angel-faced', he embodies the novel's many
Gothic dualities and doublings. Self-conscious references to the recurring
dream of a 'huge Gothic house' (9, 49, 103), 'an uncanny feeling' (103),
the occult and surreal, and Gothic 'props' like the cat Lethe (33, eventually
burnt alive) and a stuffed raven (44) all signal the nature of this literary
universe. It accords with Carter's description of Gothic tales, whose 'characters and events are exaggerated beyond reality, to become symbols, ideas,
passions …', their 'ornate, unnatural' style undermining realism (*Fireworks*,
122); but the novel's self-conscious use of an already 'exaggerated' form draws
attention to its own fictiveness and critical awareness. The pages of its first
edition even required to be slit open in an act suggestive of Sadeian or Gothic
violence.

The Marquis de Sade, a troubling figure for women, was reinterpreted by
Angela Carter in a controversial essay as importantly 'shaping aspects of the
modern sensibility'.[25] Following Carter's lead, *Justine* is a witty engagement
with the conventions of Sadeian Gothic. Like Carter, whose influence also pervades Thompson's second novel *Pandora's Box*, she is interested in the debunking
of myths, especially those relating to gender. *Justine* engages with prevailing
constructions of femininity, alluding to enduring myths: Aphrodite, Diana,
the Lorelei (26–7), Botticelli's *Venus* (36). Rather than revisiting Sade in detail
– he authored 'the lengthy, picaresque double novel: *The Adventures of Justine
and of Juliette, Her Sister*, and the three different versions of *Justine*' (*Sadeian
Woman*, 36) – Thompson's novel, like Carter's essay is 'a late-twentieth-
century interpretation of some of the problems he raises about the culturally

determined nature of women and of the relations between men and women that result from it' (*Sadeian Woman*, 1).

Justine again pivots around 'two women'; here, physically identical opposites. The narrator, who first encounters the elusive Justine at his mother's funeral, becomes obsessed with her, but sexually embroiled with her twin sister, Juliette, first glimpsed in an art gallery. These two figures, linked to Death and Art, echo Sade's characters as interpreted by Carter: 'Justine is the holy virgin; Juliette is the profane whore' (*Sadeian Woman*, 101); opposites 'like shadow and light' (*Justine*, 42); a male vision of 'Woman' split between limiting stereotypes. The narrator opens, tellingly, with memories – or fantasies – of his mother, imaged, like a figure in a symbolist painting, as a beautiful predator, plucking a man's heart out 'through his open lips' (6), recalling Carter on the Sadeian libertine's terror of the mother (*Sadeian Woman*, 135). Throughout he presents women as Madonna-like (15), as 'Sleeping Beauty' (57); or as deadly (26–7) and corrupt: 'the need of a woman was rotten at the core' (35).

Power and domination, as in Tennant's novel, are explored in visual terms. The narrator, an art-collector, is obsessed with Justine's portrait: 'Her gaze did not look directly at me, but coyly, to one side. This meant I could look at her to my heart's content. By looking away she put herself even more on display to me' (10). He sees women, like artworks, as 'objects' to possess, saying of Justine: 'As soon as I saw her, I wanted her for my own' (15). Similarly of the painting: 'Visually, she was mine. As long as she didn't look up and see me, I had the upper hand. I was in control' (75). The continuing problematic dominance of the 'male gaze' is evoked through references to the visual arts, including film, such as Hitchcock's (Gothic?) *Vertigo* (24, 53).

Many male Gothic writers have performed acts of 'female impersonation' (Punter, 191); Thompson inverts – and subverts – the tradition. Trapping the reader inside the mind of a sadistic man is a dangerous strategy, but this narrator is 'transparent', like the pages of the books he reads with paper so thin 'that the words of the other side strike backwards, through' (*Justine*, 2). His need to control women is explicitly related to his fear of mortality; and his conflation of women with death (93) is exposed by Justine's – or is it Juliette's? – novel *Death Is a Woman* which, it transpires, is in every sense a fiction.

Gothic 'cannot afford irony' (Smith, 12); but although the narrator of *Justine* lacks irony (88–9), the novel itself is highly ironic, often at his expense. As in Tennant's Stevenson-inspired novel, the two women are revealed as one. She mocks the narrator and his alter-ego, the artist, Jack (90) – 'Did … you really think you could divide me up that easily?' – exposing the characterisations of 'Omnipotent Justine and needy Juliette, virgin and whore' as constructions: 'While the real me was climbing between the two phantoms of Justine and Juliette, living somewhere in the space between the two and neither you nor Jack noticing' (123). The real woman is much more complex – and free. Significantly Juliette is first seen in a dress disliked by the narrator because 'covered in a grotesque pattern of flying birds' (19), and she releases a trapped bird: '"I hate seeing things imprisoned," she said' (32).

Juliette counters the narrator's view of women as dangerous with an ambiguous retort: 'Men *make* women dangerous' (27). Men create images of feminine danger? Or men force women to become dangerous? Both seem true here. The Gothic mansion finally appears (109) as the location of the narrator's own imprisonment and Sadeian-style torture by the female protagonist, a vengeful and morally ambiguous figure who is finally figured as creator. The narrator, initially believing that the novel 'is the writing out of my desire' (18), slowly notices the woman's role. 'My plot was being rewritten by *her*' (39); she was 'complacently rewriting my history. Telling me the story that I had been in was not mine, but hers all along' (46). Towards the end references to Charlotte Perkins Gilman's *The Yellow Wallpaper* create a sense of a male-dominated text becoming feminine (129). Taking Sade as a provocative starting point, this intellectually and morally challenging novel is resistant to any simple reading.

Justine is about the processes of creating and interpreting. In one of his many dreams, the narrator sees books falling and opening 'like birds taking flight, revealing that they too were full of blank pages' (63); the novel's first edition, too, included blank pages – for the reader's imagination. Announcing itself as artifice, this is a work which, like the painting described self-reflexively as being 'about such primitive themes as desire and death and myth', is 'constructed with ... elaborate control' (23), both using and mocking tradition. The deluded male narrator, seeking Juliet in her apartment above the pet-shop, finds the apartment empty: 'As the door swung shut behind me, the parrot let out a piercing peal of laughter' (78). Thompson's novel invites the reader both to smile and ponder on 'the story of life. And the story of death' so beautifully and chillingly presented by her unwitting 'ghost writer' (123).

Elspeth Barker's *O Caledonia*, the only one of the three novels to be set primarily in Scotland, takes its title from the opening of Canto VI, Verse 2, of Scott's narrative poem *The Lay of the Last Minstrel*: 'O Caledonia! stern and wild, / Meet nurse for a poetic child!'. 'This octosyllabic couplet', comments Karl Miller, 'has given satisfaction in Scotland, and has become almost proverbial. When we think of some Scottish orphans, both real and self-made, it has a grim cogency' (Miller, 213).[26] Barker's first novel portrays Janet's childhood and adolescence, mainly at her family's baronial home in the north-east of Scotland in the years after World War II, and celebrates the beauty of place. However, Janet, this 'poetic child' (a metaphorical orphan) is badly treated by Caledonia – no 'meet nurse' – and the title invites ironic reading.

When written, Scott's poems were noted for their 'poetical fusion of landscape with the sentiment of nationality',[27] and Barker's landscapes, too, are lyrical: 'Winter descended on the glen; in mid-October came the first thin fall of snow, gone an hour later in the wet wind. The deer ventured down from the hills at dusk, tawny owls shrieked as they hunted through the darkness and shooting stars fled across the night sky' (52). With its vivid imagery, alliteration and onomatopoeia Barker's poetic prose appeals to the senses. The balladry which inspired Scott is important not only to Janet, but to the novel itself, with its landscape and characters, its 'lonely figures driven by passion and savagery' (47).

But while national identity, following Scott, is self-consciously evoked early on in the Saint Andrew's Day celebrations (11–14), Barker mocks the clichés of Scottish culture: the name of Janet's home, 'Auchnasaugh' – meaning 'the field of sighing' (32) – sounds parodic, like the village's 'Thistle Inn' (33). The novel undermines Scott's implied complacency; Barker's Caledonia is a place of grim, dutiful repression, evoking 'Sunday afternoon tea in the cold parlours of outlying crofts, where the Bible was open beside a ticking clock and rock buns were assembled on snowy doilies, malignly aglitter with the menace of carbonized currants' (3). A landscape of great beauty surrounds a bleakly unforgiving Calvinist culture personified by Janet's Nanny, sucking 'a vengeful Pandrop'(7), her hat spiked with hatpins (8). This culture of extremes is emblematised by the paradoxical image of the 'wild tattooed men' from the Ship Inn 'as homely and douce with their scones and jam as the fat-bellied tea cosies clothing the brown teapots. O Caledonia' (14).

The novel reworks the Gothic elements of *The Lay* in the exaggerations of the 'gaunt place' Auchnasaugh with its moaning winds (32), 'dim and vaulting hall' and 'Gothic arch' (1). Janet's own attraction to Gothic, suggesting her youthful taste for the extreme, illustrates the novel's playful self-consciousness. Drawn to the 'holy splendour of all the purples' (9) in reaction against a colourless Presbyterian environment (33), she plans as an adolescent to decorate her bedroom with 'lengths of purple taffeta which she would nail to her walls as a start to redesigning the room in the manner of Edgar Allan Poe' (136). Janet's adopted jackdaw, Claws, installed in a doll's house endowed with a suburban name, fails to repeat 'Never more' like Poe's Raven, learning instead (from her brother Francis) to say 'Never mind' (136, 145). There is humour, too, in the sinister-sounding Goblin Teasmaid (110), slyly recalling the Goblin Page of Scott's poem.

But there are serious threads. Young Janet imagines God as 'clad in a butcher's striped apron' (8), and the novel's grotesque images are disturbing. This society's responses to Janet's premature death – 'The lass had only herself to blame' (3) – are cruelly prejudiced. *O Caledonia* self-consciously foregrounds ideas about femininity, highlighting the sexual menace in Gothic by heightening its characteristic gendered roles. Figured from the start as a victim, Janet is taunted by the boys (59) and fends off the sexually rampant Raymond Dibdin (68). When she finally play-acts the black-garbed *femme fatale*, feeling 'strong and bright and beautiful' (150), this provokes her violent, Gothic-tinged demise at the age of sixteen, as she enters womanhood. Janet is stabbed by the pornography-hoarding gardener with his rabbit-skinning knife (a warped Adam or serpent in her Eden), becoming another of his 'slaughtered innocents' (37), found 'oddly attired in her mother's black lace evening dress, twisted and slumped in bloody, murderous death' (1). Jim's hissed words – 'You filthy wee whore' (152) – suggest the misogyny and repression of a life-denying culture. Jim had 'come in to turn off the music and the lights and so he turned them off' (152).

Female madness, identified by feminist critics in women's Gothic as a response to the destructiveness of patriarchal society is an important under-current.[28] Janet's role models include Lila, the family's resident 'madwoman in the attic'; Janet, herself dreaming of being 'the madcap of the Fourth' at school (64), is merely considered 'mad' (72, 75) for her intellectuality. Society's con-ventional ideals of womanhood are questioned in a comic yet disquieting scene when Vera, seeking her daughter's transformation into a more traditionally acceptable girl (120), takes Janet to a hairdresser's salon. It 'reminded Janet of the lunatic asylum' (to which Cousin Lila is assigned), its 'neon-lit inner torture chamber of throbbing machines' seeming like a place of sacrifice, 'the dim, blood-boultered altar of womanhood' (130) – ominous, given Janet's fate.

Through overt reworking of Gothic, the novel both critiques a culture, and, implicitly, a literary mode. However, how are we to view Janet's death? We may react as she does to Raymond's assault, with a 'great tide of anger' (69): 'how dared he ... All her dreams and yearnings for high romance ... pitted against his miserable filthy mind' (69). Janet, longing in childhood to be Snow White (17) or a princess (11), is both endearing and absurd; yet the third-person narrative, with its shifting perspectives, creates distance and undercuts sympathy (100). Janet is wrong to believe 'she could control her destiny', for 'the gods whom Janet had chosen played tricks on mortals for their pleasure' (135), and her death, prefigured at the outset in Sparkian fash-ion, implies a deterministic – even Calvinist – vision.[29] Should we feel outraged or resigned, feel 'pity like a naked newborn babe' (108), or, in Janet's own words, say 'tant pis to that' (151)? The combination of tragedy and playfulness is unsettling. Ballad-like, the novel is 'mournful, cruel, tender' (48), implying a 'moral code of pagan nobility without pity' (48); it is classically 'mournful and tender, cruel and foreboding, beyond all else noble' (146). O Caledonia's curious blend of tones deliberately echoing tradition, achieves an effect of postmodern indeterminacy.

The novel also invites mixed responses to Caledonia. When away from Auchnasaugh, Janet feels 'maimed, deprived of her identity, living in two dimensions only' (79), and the portrait of her home is vivid; echoing Scott's desire to preserve something of his native culture for posterity,[30] Barker, born in Scotland but now an English resident, wrote O Caledonia 'in part as an elegy for places, people and a form of education now largely gone from the world'.[31] Dorothy McMillan is dissatisfied: 'if Caledonia is merely, for the passionate female imagination, a place fit to die in, should not outrage overpower lament?'[32] Yet if Barker's novel withholds absolute judgement, its Gothic castle and history-haunted region (34–5) suggest how 'the Past haunts, critically, ironically, and embarrassingly, the Present',[33] with grim reminders of ancient violence and the Scottish Play (Macbeth) brooding in the background (19, 61). *O Caledonia* is shadowed especially by World War II, and peopled by its physically and mentally maimed victims and exiles. There are also bullish survivors, like heartless Vera, whose headscarf is 'printed with the flags of the allied nations', bearing 'the slogan "Into Battle" many times repeated' (53). An anti-war thread is discernible in the portrayal of a destructive period. At Hogmanay, Janet, praying for a visitor 'bearing memories of love and loyalty and the irredeemable unquenchable past' (143), instead gets her bosom pinched by an elderly member of the war-wounded.

There is anger within the comedy. The novel's frequently flippant tone regarding serious events may resemble Janet's reaction into jokiness and apparent indifference. Knowledge of the Holocaust and the atomic bomb's destructiveness (107) feed Janet's perceptions of animal suffering: 'Anger rose in her and merged with her grief, confusing her utterly. She had had enough, she could not cope' (109). Despair, although not directly stated, is implicit. The image of Janet's pet jackdaw, killing himself 'like a tiny kamikaze pilot' (2) is a reminder of the war, while the absurd familial emblem of the dying cockatoo, hovering 'like the paraclete' (80), suggests an exhausted tradition and the vacuity of a family, a nation, and the age. Is this what the world has come to in spiritual terms?

Like the other novels examined here, Barker's fiction, refusing closure, is highly self-conscious. Janet's comically parrot-keeping family raises serious questions about attitudes to the past. Grandpa's belief that 'ancient parrots should be fêted ... as true archivists' (15) is countered by the narrative itself,[34] which implies the dangers – especially for women – in allowing history to consist of uncritical repetition (violence, madness or death). The dangers of forgetting are implied, too; we know of mad, Russian born Lila that 'all her past was gone' (42); that Janet herself 'was to be forgotten' (2) seems callous. Yet it is 'Janet's view that forgetting was the only possible way of forgiving' (87); perhaps this is the only way to deal with the terrible past, better than exploiting it like Francis with his photographs (81). In the closing lines Janet's spirit is borne away by the 'wild winds of dawn' (152); this recalls an earlier description of the dawn wind, 'which brought the next day, and whirled the past off into the breaking clouds: a wind thrilling and melancholy, tender and cruel, a wind of beginning and ending' (109). Characteristically ambivalent, the novel leaves open the possibilities of a fresh start.

O Caledonia, rejecting Scott's Romantic myth of Scotland, arguably bolsters that of the Calvinist nation. But it would be unfair to see this, or indeed any of these novels, as simply bound by the tired past. At once fascinated by history and critical of it, Tennant, Barker and Thompson use tradition yet remake it, playing seriously with Gothic, 'the literary tradition that contemporary writers have found most resonant in their attempts to break up "conventional pedestrian mentality and morality"' (Smith, 14). All three may be seen in the context of postmodernism, although criticising its reduction of the past to images.

Their concern with power structures and with female identity is informed, to differing degrees, by feminist ideas and theory, both using and interrogating ideas of 'sisterhood', literal and metaphoric.

There are links with recent fiction. Angela Carter's 'The Company of Wolves' and 'The Erl-King' were first published in Tennant's magazine *Bananas* in the 1970s. Tennant's own fiction has been compared with Carter's,[35] and the latter's vision may underlie the sinister fairy-tale allusions of *O Caledonia*. Muriel Spark's influence on contemporary Scottish fiction has yet to be fully assessed, but the writers considered here, with their precise prose and refusal of realism, may also be indebted to her. And while the social milieux of these three novels may seem distant from those of many writers working in Scotland, Tennant, Barker and Thompson share the 'dark sense of humour' observable in a range of Scottish novelists.[36]

Yet these three – each at different stages in their careers – present a distinctive achievement. Adrienne Rich's call for revisioning, answered so brilliantly in poetry by Liz Lochhead and Carol Ann Duffy (most recently Duffy's *The World's Wife*, 1999), is met in fiction by the richly disturbing novels of Emma Tennant, Elspeth Barker and Alice Thompson, inviting us to face our shadow selves, while shedding light on the long dark twentieth century.

Notes

1. Adrienne Rich, 'When We Dead Awaken: Writing as Re-Vision', first published in *College English*, XXXIV:1 (October 1972), pp. 18–25; reprinted in Barbara Charlesworth Gelpi and Albert Gelpi (eds), *Adrienne Rich's Poetry* (New York: Norton, 1975), pp. 90–8 (90).
2. Steven Connor, *The English Novel in History 1950–1995* (London: Routledge, 1996), ch. 5, 'Origins and Reversions', p. 166.
3. See Patricia Waugh, *Feminine Fictions: Revisiting the Postmodern* (London: Routledge, 1989), p. 213.
4. Emma Tennant, *Two Women of London* (1989; reprint in Tennant, *Travesties*, London: Faber & Faber, 1995). Elspeth Barker, *O Caledonia* (1991; Harmondsworth: Penguin, 1992) (Copyright © Elspeth Barker. Reproduced by permission of Penguin Books Ltd.); Alice Thompson, *Justine* (1996; London: Virago, 1997) – originally published in 1996 by Canongate Books, 14 High Street, Edinburgh.
5. Stevenson, Letter to Will Low, 2 January 1886, Bradford A. Booth and Ernest Mehew (eds), *Letters* (New Haven and London: Yale, 1995), vol. 5, p. 163; Scott to G. Ellis, 21 August 1804, *Letters* I, 226–7, cited in Thomas Crawford (ed.), 'Introduction', Sir Walter Scott, *Selected Poems* (Oxford: Clarendon Press, 1972), p. x. On Sade as father of Gothic, see Beate Neumeier, 'Postmodern Gothic: Desire and Reality in Angela Carter's Writing', in Victor Sage and Allan Lloyd Smith (eds), *Modern Gothic: A Reader* (Manchester: Manchester University Press, 1996), pp. 141–51 (145).
6. Angela Carter, Afterword to *Fireworks: Nine Profane Pieces* (London: Quartet Books, 1974), p. 122.

7. 'The literary declension of terror is an inevitable response to the atrocity exhibition of the twentieth century, just as it was for the writers of the late eighteenth and early nineteenth centuries as they confronted the social, economic, and political instabilities of a new order, and the mayhem of a revolutionary period'; 'Introduction', Sage and Smith, *Modern Gothic*, p. 5. See also 'Introduction', Patrick McGrath and Bradford Morrow (eds), *The Picador Book of the New Gothic: A Collection of Contemporary Gothic Fiction* (1991; London: Picador/Pan, 1992), p. xiv.

8. Terry Eagleton, 'Allergic to Depths' (review of *Gothic: Four Hundred Years of Excess, Horror and Evil* by Richard Davenport-Hines), *London Review of Books*, 18 March 1999, pp. 7–8 (7).

9. Victor Sage, 'The Politics of Petrifaction: Culture, Religion, History in the Fiction of Iain Banks and John Banville', in Sage and Smith, *Modern Gothic*, pp. 20–37 (20).

10. David Punter, *The Literature of Terror: A History of Gothic Fictions*, vol. 2: *The Modern Gothic* (2nd edn; London: Longman, 1996), pp. 156–9.

11. 'Introduction', Clive Bloom (ed.), *Gothic Horror: A Reader's Guide from Poe to King and Beyond* (London: Macmillan, 1998), p. 13.

12. On female Gothic, see for instance Susan Wolstenholme, *Gothic (re)Visions: Writing Women as Readers* (Albany: State University of New York Press, 1993); and Alison Milbank, *Daughters of the House: Modes of the Gothic in Victorian Fiction* (London: Macmillan, 1992). On contemporary female Gothic, see for example Waugh, *Feminine Fictions*, pp. 168–217.

13. Anne Cranny–Francis, *Feminist Fiction: Feminist Uses of Generic Fiction* (Cambridge: Polity Press, 1990), p. 19. For detailed discussion, see Susanne Becker, 'Postmodern Feminine Horror Fictions', in Sage and Smith, *Modern Gothic*, pp. 71–80 (72).

14. On the 'male' gaze, see Laura Mulvey's influential essay 'Visual Pleasure and Narrative Cinema', *Screen* 16:3 (Autumn 1975); reprinted in Robyn R. Warhol and Diane Price Herndl (eds), *Feminisms: An Anthology of Literary Theory and Criticism* (New Brunswick: Rutgers University Press, 1991), pp. 432–42. On Gothic and the visual, see Wolstenholme, *Gothic (re)Visions*, ch. 1.

15. See Cranny-Francis, *Feminist Fiction*, p. 15. African-American, gay and post-colonial writers are among those who 'rewrite' narratives. See also Linda Hutcheon, *A Poetics of Postmodernism: History, Theory, Fiction* (London: Routledge, 1988), p. 16, p. 23 and also ch. 4.

16. Luce Irigaray, 'The Power of Discourse', in Margaret Whitford (ed.), *The Irigaray Reader* (Oxford: Blackwell, 1991), pp. 118–32, p. 124.

17. Becker, 'Postmodern Feminine Horror Fictions', pp. 71–80 (73).

18. *The Bad Sister*: copyright © Emma Tennant, 1989; first published by Faber and Faber Ltd. See Tennant's family history, *Strangers: A Family Romance* (London: Jonathan Cape, 1998), where she describes the family home as a 'mock-Gothic castle', p. 86.

19. Other fictional reworkings include Valerie Martin, *Mary Reilly* (New York: Doubleday, 1990). For critical responses, see William Veeder and Gordon Hirsch (eds), *Dr Jekyll and Mr Hyde: after One Hundred Years* (Chicago and London: Chicago University Press, 1988).

20. See Karl Miller, *Cockburn's Millennium* (Cambridge, MA: Harvard University Press, 1975), pp. 221–3; also pp. 212–13 on Stevenson as Gothic.

21. See Sandra M. Gilbert and Susan Gubar, *The Madwoman in the Attic: The Woman Writer and the Nineteenth-Century Literary Imagination* (New Haven: Yale University Press, 1979); also Elaine Showalter, *The Female Malady* (New York: Pantheon Books, 1985). Tennant mentions Showalter's work in interview; see Olga Kenyon, *Women Writers Talk* (Oxford: Lennard Publishing, 1989), pp. 173–87 (186).

22. *Sexual Anarchy: Gender and Culture at the Fin de Siècle* (1990; London: Virago,1992), p. 124.

23. Allan Lloyd Smith, 'Postmodernism/Gothicism', in Sage and Smith, *Modern Gothic*, p. 11.

24. Douglas Gifford, 'Autumn Fiction: Clever Books and Sad People', *Books in Scotland*, no. 59 (Autumn 1996), p. 3.

25. Angela Carter, *The Sadeian Woman: An Exercise in Cultural History* (London: Virago, 1979), p. 32; *Pandora's Box* (London: Little, Brown & Co., 1998).

26. Emma Tennant quotes this couplet in interview; see Sue Roe and Emma Tennant, 'Women Talking about Writing', in Moira Monteith (ed.), *Women's Writing: A Challenge to Theory* (Brighton: Harvester Wheatsheaf, 1986), p. 128.

27. Thomas Crawford, *Walter Scott* (1965; rev. edn, Edinburgh: Scottish Academic Press, 1982), p. 41.

28. See Gilbert and Gubar, *The Madwoman in the Attic*; Shoshana Felman, 'Women and Madness: The Critical Phallacy', *Diacritics*, 5 (1975), pp. 2–10.

29. Compare 'God had planned for practically everybody … a nasty surprise when they died' – Muriel Spark, *The Prime of Miss Jean Brodie* (1961; Harmondsworth: Penguin, 1965), pp. 108–9.

30. See T. F. Henderson (ed.), Walter Scott, *The Minstrelsy of the Scottish Border* (1902; 1932); cited by Crawford in *Walter Scott* (1982), p. 48.

31. Elspeth Barker, 'What if?', in *Book News* (published by Scottish Book Fortnight), 19 October–2 November 1991, p. 5.

32. Dorothy McMillan, 'Constructed out of Bewilderment: Stories of Scotland', in Ian A. Bell (ed.), *Peripheral Visions: Images of Nationhood in Contemporary British Fiction* (Cardiff: University of Wales Press, 1995), pp. 80–99 (95).

33. Victor Sage (of Iain Banks's work), 'The Politics of Petrifaction', p. 23.

34. There are intriguing echoes (whether conscious or not) of Sir David Lindsay's long poem *The Testament and Complaint of the Papyngo* (1538).

35. See Linda R. Williams (ed.), *The Bloomsbury Guide to English Literature: The Twentieth Century* (London: Bloomsbury, 1992), p. 297.

36. Angus Calder quotes Alison Kennedy from the ScotRail free magazine, February 1996, on herself, Kelman and Welsh: 'We have a dark sense of humour, are politically left-of-centre and not afraid of nastiness in our writing.' Calder sees these characteristics linking all three with Janice Galloway, Duncan McLean, Alan Warner, Alasdair Gray and Iain Banks, in 'By the Water of Leith I Sat Down and Wept: Reflections on Scottish Identity', Harry Ritchie (ed.), *New Scottish Writing* (London: Bloomsbury, 1996), pp. 218–38 (236–7).

CHAPTER TEN

Janice Galloway's Novels: Fraudulent Mooching

Glenda Norquay

In Janice Galloway's second novel, *Foreign Parts*, the friends Cassie and Rona, newly arrived in France, encounter the term 'BRICOLAGE'.[1] Reproduced in capitals, surrounded by white space, the text mimics this word's status: letters on a hoarding, out of context, signifier of otherness, the foreign. In French, 'bricolage' has a number of meanings: odd jobs, trifles; in a commercial sense, handicraft, do-it-yourself. In its everyday usage then 'bricolage' carries connotations of both 'fragments' and 'construction'.

Galloway is a writer who explores states of brokenness and fragmentation: *The Trick Is to Keep Breathing* (1989), a dark, ironic and witty novel, traces recovery after a nervous breakdown.[2] *Foreign Parts* (1994), in some senses a more relaxed book, takes as its subject a series of moments from Cassie and Rona's driving holiday in France, exploring not only the breaking- and making-ups that are part of their daily routine, but also, through snapshot flashbacks to other holidays, interpreting Cassie's disastrous relationships with men. If fragmentation is a theme in Galloway's fiction, fracture is also its predominant technique. She works with broken narratives and syntax, breaks in chronology and unfinished sentences. The text is broken on the page into different typefaces, spacing, layout – even half sentences in the margins, disappearing off the page. The past in both novels breaks into the present through memories and photographs; the present itself is frequently broken into lists of mundane details and insignificant moments. Both novels are discursively fragmented: different discourses compete for attention, often blocked out visually to indicate their separateness. In *The Trick Is to Keep Breathing* the institutional discourses of hospitals, doctors, health visitors, compete with phrases from women's magazines, dietary advice, romantic fiction, horoscopes and the clichés surrounding death. In *Foreign Parts* foreign voices break into the narrative, the guidebook excerpts structure the women's journey, they read letters from Rona's grandfather (killed in France in the First World War) to his wife, and rehearse words and phrases used many times before. So while both texts are obviously dealing with states of brokenness in their themes, they could also be described as 'deconstructive texts' with a specific agenda in exposing and undermining the language, textual practices and discourses we live by.

The Trick Is to Keep Breathing is an exploration of the subject caught in institutionalised discursive practices. Joy Stone, whose oxymoron of a name indicates
her ambiguous identity, has, in a sense, no existence. As the mistress of her
dead lover, society allows her no place to mourn. Time, her work, eating, are
all emptied of meaning; the book traces her attempts to fill that emptiness, to
establish control in a context where she has none. The void which defines her
is signalled in various ways; time has lost significance: 'What will I do while
I'm lasting, Marianne? What will I do?'(15) is her cry throughout the novel.
Her attitude to food has become a way of emptying herself: baking and buying
food is an obsession, but eating has to be avoided at all costs; if she does eat she
must make herself sick. This in itself is an attempt to empty – both physically
and psychologically – the rituals and practices we live by, a negation made
manifest by the image of Joy in the bath: 'I trace the hairline, the swollen jaw,
the neck and breastbone, the sour nipples, concave saucer of stomach. Nothing
there at all' (166). Likewise as a woman she is empty – when a doctor suggests
her lack of menstruation may be due to pregnancy she is given a scan but it
shows '[e]mpty space. I had nothing inside me'. (This scene is between pages
145 and 147, on a page without a page number, one of several which are
'blank'.) So Joy has become an empty space, an absence, outwith conventional
social and emotional structures – no family, no role, no way to mourn. A range
of competing discourses jostle across her – all attempting to define her problems, her solutions, her femininity, her future. The text itself attempts a visual
representation of this process, whereby space is allowed to become, in Muriel
Spark's phrase, 'a pattern in itself'.[3] Syntactical utterances, which would appear
to imply order, disintegrate: space itself offers coherence and relief. Order, a
key term for this novel, is opposed to emptiness in two ways: we witness Joy's
attempts to restore order to her life, to fill in time, to give meaning – but we
also witness her being 'ordered' – by the health service, by friends and colleagues,
by the men in her life, by the sequences of memory itself. The only way in
which Joy can create meaning is to resist attempts at ordering her, to create
chaos, as the novel itself does, by listing, cataloguing, quoting; the emptiness
of such 'order' becomes evident.

Foreign Parts also explores characters trapped within institutionalised and
contradictory discourses. Cassie and Rona, with their clearly delineated and
often oppositional characters, operate with guidebooks bearing little relevance
to their own experiences, work with inadequate maps, and are confronted with
markers of history – cemeteries, churches, museums and memorials – that
appear to have little significance for them. The Guidebook, entitled *Potted-
France – An alphabetical guide for the traveller who needs to keep tight purse strings*,
appears to offer containment, control and order, but is hopelessly inappropriate to their needs and hectoring in tone: 'Don't Miss!' or 'Indefinable,
indefatigable, CHARTRES cathedral comes close to the impossible ideal of
perfection' (76). Again discourses of order are rendered ridiculous through
over-use and juxtaposition.

In both novels, then, we see the writer 'taking apart' mechanisms which oppress and contain. Galloway's novels are also, however, 'reconstructive' fictions, which attempt to offer a refashioning of concepts of identity linked to those material shapers of subjectivity: gender, class and nation. As others have recognised, both her novels have a positive trajectory.[4] 'BRICOLAGE' as a term therefore offers an apt description of their technique of building a text from fragments, of making something out of bits and pieces, forcing the reader to move between discourses and participate in the act of reconstruction. A further definition of 'bricolage' as 'rough repair' encompasses each book's unsteady movement towards assembling anew. Towards the end of *Foreign Parts* Rona ponders on the restoration of ancient buildings she has seen: 'I think it's wonderful they don't just leave things falling to bits. They put them back together again' (254). In the challenge to heterosexual conventions of lifestyle, in the possibility of a new form of relationship between Cassie and Rona, in the opportunities of leaving the past, of saying what has hitherto been unsaid, things are put back together but in a new way. In the hopeful ending to the narrative we are allowed a glimpse of new possibilities, of a way of living which might not be determined by all the old discourses. Likewise, although *The Trick Is to Keep Breathing* is a narrative of breakdown, it also takes fragments of experience and begins to move forward. By the end of the novel Joy is shown feeling more 'like herself', beginning to function within social rituals (buying a Christmas tree), and can offer a complete syntactical utterance to Michael (and to herself): 'I forgive you' (235). Ironically what leads her towards such recovery is acceptance of randomness, an absence of order, brought out by her Christmas horoscope which says 'Submit to chaos for once'. Joy continues: 'I have to learn to submit to terrifying chaos and not revert' (223). She has to accept that the narratives, the discourses in which she is entrapped, will always be partial, insubstantial, inadequate. Moreover, as Cairns Craig argues in *The Modern Scottish Novel*, the breaking down of the narrative is paralleled by the acquisition of control on the part of the author:

> Control over the page numbers becomes the signature of the character's refusal of the discourses by which she is controlled; it is also, however, the signature of the author, whose control over her text extends not just to the details of typographic layout but also to the details of the marginalia of the text.[5]

Through such a reading, both writer and reader become architects of an alternative power dynamic, a different narrative to that of the novel's ostensible plot.

A more technical use of the term 'bricolage', from the writing of the anthropologist Claude Lévi-Strauss, throws further light on Galloway's strategies of fragmentation.[6] Drawing on Lévi-Strauss's use of the term to describe the creative putting together of bits and pieces, of cultural and natural objects, transforming or subverting their original use, cultural studies has appropriated the word to analyse the ways in which subcultures rework every-day objects to produce subcultural styles and artefacts.[7] This quality of subversion, of making us look differently at objects, artefacts and words, is central to Galloway's writing. Her novels offer a transformative use of the everyday, but also a subversion of its original purpose. From the start *Foreign Parts* provides us a with a map reference to another country: the floating term 'BRICOLAGE' offers us a clue to the way in which we are being encouraged to read. This is fiction with a political and cultural agenda; through its 'bricolage', its 'making-do with' but also 'remaking' of myths of gendered and national identity, Galloway offers us new mappings of these intersecting territories.

Both Galloway's novels address, in their subject-matter, women operating within systems of oppression, but they also challenge the structures of 'patriar-chy' in three formal aspects: in their reluctance to endorse systems of binary oppositions, in their use of humour and in their typographical experimentation.

Foreign Parts very obviously challenges the binary oppositions that charac-terise our linguistic structures but also determine and are determined by hierarchies of power. As a text it appears to operate by oppositions but then interrogates or breaks them down: Cassie and Rona/Rona and Cassie are not interchangeable, as the frequent textual formation of

Cassie and Rona
Rona and Cassie

appears to suggest; they still have the capacity to surprise each other. Initially it would seem that Cassie is paralysed by thinking, by uncertainty, by a sense of chaos which prevents her from acting, whereas Rona, with her large bag full of sticking plaster, tissues, teaspoons and penknife, is exasperating but ready for anything. The 'Zodiac labour sign' for Cassie, we learn, is sitting by the fire, Rona's is mowing hay. But this apparent binary opposition does not hold: it is Rona, the well-prepared and ordered, who finds the unexpected and creates the novel's small epiphanies – the discovery of a puppy carved in golden stone, a field full of roses in the dark, a garden of sunflowers as a backdrop to break-fast. And Cassie, *cassé*, broken by the past, nevertheless moves into the present through her constructive ordering of snapshots until those with Rona, not just those from her relationships with men, become part of the narrative. *The Trick* also refuses to settle for fixed and oppositional categories: Joy, persuading the council to let her stay on in Michael's house, will not be 'mistress' as opposed to wife; in the hospital, by asking the doctor 'How are *you*?' (226), she attempts to break down the patient/doctor dichotomy. The novel itself also blurs categories: Myra is possibly Joy's sister, perhaps her mother; Joy, in the end, is neither 'joy' nor 'stone'.

Galloway's challenge to such oppositional systems is strengthened by her humour; in an approach characteristic of feminist narratives, she draws upon the carnivalesque, using inversion and parody to undermine the discourses of power. Hélène Cixous, commenting on the double meaning of 'voler' (to fly and to steal) notes:

> women take after birds and robbers just as robbers take after women and birds. They (*illes*) go by, fly the coop, take pleasure in jumbling the order of space, in disorienting it, in changing around the furniture, dislocating things and values, breaking them all up, emptying structures, and turning propriety upside down.[8]

Galloway's typographic experimentation functions to exactly that end, but her novels also work with a more direct use of humour, with 'a subversive spirit of feminine mischief'.[9] Although *The Trick*, focusing on breakdown, might be read as an account of yet another woman 'on the edge', it sustains its dark humour throughout: the repeated joke about psychiatrists changing a light bulb serves as ironic comment on the inadequacy of medical treatment; Marianne's letters from America – helping Joy to 'last' – are full of jokes; significant encounters between the Health Visitor and Joy, Joy and Paul (Harridan and ExLover), and Doctor and Patient are presented in a dramatic form which immediately highlights the farcical and stereotyped nature of the conversation. Even the list of 'THINGS YOU CAN DO IN THE EVENING' has its futility exposed by the elision of 'sew' and 'go out for a meal': 'Sewing and going for a meal. Tricky juxtaposition' (37). *Foreign Parts* offers more humour in its situations and is overtly funny. It relies on the mischievous, subversive laughter of woman to offer distance if not salvation: Rona, we know, 'had the dirtiest laugh in the world' (13) and it is her laughter, the shared laughter of 'Rona and me' – and the reader – that ends the novel, offering hope: 'I've no sense of direction, me. I haven't a bloody clue. Rona and me. We stand in separate places, looking out over water that is just water. Rona takes fresh aim, laughing. Defying gravity' (262).

The third aspect of Galloway's subversion, her typographical experimentation, has been closely analysed by a number of critics.[10] While it can be related to the influences of Gray and Kelman, it also owes much to *écriture féminine*. Hélène Cixous suggests:

> the use of the upper-case consists above all in expressing forces in the text: it is a kind of vectoring, lines of variable intensity: where *current* passes ... In such a way that putting an upper- or lower-case letter on a word gives it a different resistance.[11]

Galloway's texts resist typographical and syntactical convention, trailing words across the page, allowing phrases to slip off it at times of crisis, panic, sexual attack, but they are also novels written against the grand narratives and mastering discourses which shape us. These mastering narratives are directly related to the materiality of people's lives: Joy's status as 'mistress' rather than 'wife' nearly results in her being thrown out of the home she established with Michael. Her attempt to sustain a domestic environment without social legitimisation, her refusal to work within 'binary oppositions', almost results in homeless-ness. Likewise, her sense of being 'nothing' is manifested physically in her anorexia. In this novel the text not only becomes a paradigm of the discursive fragments which construct Joy's identity; experimentation functions beyond an aesthetic level as a commentary upon the ways in which discursive practices determine the materiality of our lives. Galloway thus presents a forceful chal-lenge to the apparent division between essentialist and anti-essentialist forms of feminist writing.

Feminist theory has been much engaged with debating the relationship between limited reflectionist models of textuality – 'mirroring' women's experience – and those which present aesthetic challenges to 'patriarchal' systems of discourse and knowledge.[12] Literature offering specific representa-tion of women's material circumstances is treated with suspicion because in delineating oppression it is still embodying patriarchal categories. To move towards an interrogation of linguistic and aesthetic systems through textual experiment, however, is to move towards another kind of marginality – not least in terms of readership. Galloway has developed a form of aesthetic experimentation that challenges established literary and linguistic conven-tions but is not 'purely verbal' subversion. Rather her writing offers a 'deconstruction' of gendered subjectivities and sexuality which takes into account the materiality of people's lives and, while remaining immensely read-able, takes the reader beyond shaping discourses.

Berthold Schoene-Harwood accuses the Scottish literary establishment of concerning itself 'primarily with the question of national identification at the expense of other, perhaps more fundamentally identity-bearing issues that have started to emerge in Scottish writing, such as gender, sexuality and non-white/non-Scottish ethnicity'.[13] Yet it is Galloway's concerns with the politics of gender and sexual identity that have preoccupied a number of critics.[14] The issue Schoene-Harwood raises, that problematic desire to codify Scottishness, nevertheless manifests itself in what seems a more worrying critical elision between feminism and the politics of national identity. While it may be tech-nically accurate to position her writing in terms of the influence of Kelman and Gray, it is dangerous to assume that her writing works within the same cultural paradigms of Scottishness. Douglas Gifford, for example, notes that 'she is merely working with what's out there in traditional urban-Scottish humour ... simultaneously reflecting and satirising the way in which it mingles the humane and the cruel, the sympathetic and the savagely sceptical',[15] yet in *The Trick* much of the laughter comes from outside – such as Marianne's jokes about Scottishness in America – or from being between, rather than working within, tradition. Even more problematically, at the conclusion of a perceptive analysis of the novel's relation to 'the regulations of patriarchy', Cairns Craig claims that the body of Joy Stone is representative of Scotland itself: 'That "black hole", that "nothing at all" is the image not only of a woman negated by a patriarchal society but of a society aware of itself only as an absence, a society living, in the 1980s, in the aftermath of its failure to be reborn' (1999, 199). Claiming the novel's subversive strategies for a nationalist agenda, Craig performs a manœuvre little different from the interpellation of Chris Caledonia in Lewis Grassic Gibbon's *A Scots Quair* (1932–4), yet another act of appropriation whereby both the body of the text and that in the text become representative of the motherland. A reading of *Foreign Parts*, however, shows that Galloway herself is highly alert to the dangers of women functioning as symbols rather than subjects, to the tradition whereby the exponents of art are men, the depictions in art are of women. Aileen Christianson offers a different perspective, arguing that Galloway intertwines with '"dark longings, hilarious despair" … confident assumptions of being female and various in contemporary Scotland'. She continues: 'The gaps in history where women were not, the lies about what women were, are refused by both, the notable silences are resisted and filled out'.[16] Although Christianson acknowledges 'Scottishness and femaleness may be problematised but they are also emphatically centralised', her desire to emphasise the fact of Scottishness leads to an endorsement of dominant models of nationality and history (140) that Galloway questions implicitly in *The Trick* and more explicitly in *Foreign Parts*.

The relationship between gendered and national identities is a notoriously complex one, and the Scottish context is no different. Susanne Hagemann notes that in the spheres of literature both women and Scots 'suffered from similar methods of peripheralisation and expressed their protest along similar lines', but her essay can only conclude that woman and nations are both 'constructs'.[17] Craig argues that in Lochhead's poetry, there is a parallelism between the suppressed nation and the repressed feminine – 'the negation of a female identity becomes an index of a lost national identity'[18] – but the connection is rarely so simple. As Marilyn Reizbaum suggests, women in Scotland and Ireland have been caught in but 'sought to alter this dynamic, seeing on the one hand the paternalistic nature of cultural marginalization (their identification with the nationalist cause) and, on the other, the patriarchal dimension of their own cultures' nationalist movement (their exclusion from it)'.[19] In *The Trick* and to an even greater extent in *Foreign Parts* Galloway casts doubts on these simple mappings: through her own method of 'making do' she takes myths of nationality and, with the materials available, redraws their intersections with patriarchy.

Although Scottishness is not an explicit concern of *The Trick Is to Keep Breathing* it is part of the exploration of identity and fragmentation carried on within it. It is too easy, however, to see Joy as representative of any particular kind of Scottishness, or Scotland. Her existence as a woman in Scotland, in a specific class context, produces certain markers of identity: she is a product of a culture in which women are silenced and marginalised in particular ways. Considering her reluctance to go to work, something which had previously 'defined' her, Joy muses, 'I can't think how I fell into this unProtestant habit. I used to be so conscientious. I used to be so *good* all the time. [where **good** = **productive/**

hardworking/wouldn't say boo]' (81). The Calvinist work ethic, whereby
work and productivity become earthly markers of salvation, is a familiar one,
but is here set in the context of a religion in which traditionally 'It was only
when under appropriate control that "true womanhood" could flourish'.[20]
'Goodness' therefore is equated not only with work but with submissiveness:
'[where **good = not putting anyone out by feeling too much, blank,
unobtrusive**]' (82). Goodness is also evaluated from a class context in which
meaningful labour belongs to the masculine sphere: Joy's reliance upon work
to 'define' her.

> This is my workplace.
> It tells me what I am. (12)

This becomes a grotesque parody of identity. Joy's workplace does not tell her
what she is: it is, in fact, the memorial service for Michael held there that
denies her any existence, asking for remembrance for wife and family but
obliterating his relationship with Joy. Just as in the much-quoted equation
that follows – '*Love/Emotion = embarrassment: Scots equation. Exceptions
are when roaring drunk or watching football. Men do rather better out of this
loophole' (82) – Joy is presented satirically observing but also caught within a
system which does not correlate to her own subjectivity. In each case the 'equation' renders her emotions doubly illegitimate.

Play with dislocated and dislocating myths of Scottishness continues
throughout: Joy describes holding her 'head up, up like Jean Brodie' in refusing
to book a hospital place, 'But I knew I'd phone sooner or later. I knew I'd be
back on Monday' (108). This caricature of Scottish womanhood is no more a
match for Joy's situation than any of the images constructed by diet sheets,
horoscopes or fashion magazines. All, nevertheless, contribute to the circulating
economy of discourses in which she operates. Her ambiguous relationship to
Scottishness culminates in another scene of misrecognition at the supermarket:
Joy is accosted by someone she went to school with, whose name she can't
remember. This man, who has acquired his 'own practice' (a lawyer/doctor/
dentist/vet?: worthily defining occupations for a Scottish lad o' pairts), living
in Stirlingshire (historic heart of Scotland), married and 'down to see the folks'
(secure with family), has a faltering conversation with Joy then leaves.

> A mirror spread out behind the space where he had been. There was a woman in
> the frame, gawping, the fountain bubbling up at her back. She was listening to
> a distant kiddy-ride playing Scotland the Brave. Her coat was buttoned up
> wrong so the collar didn't sit right, the boots scuffed and parting from the sole.
> The hair needed washed and combed and my eyes were purple. I looked like a
> crazy-woman/wino/raddled old whore. (191)

Joy's location within but mismatch with 'Scottish' masculine culture is made
evident, aurally and visually, as the music plays on. The man has asked her if

she is 'Making a name for yourself I expect?' but Joy can only reply 'I haven't been very well lately' (191). This hybrid creature, who misrecognises herself and has made no 'name', embodies the problematic relationship between gendered and national identities.

It would be a mistake, of course, to assume Joy's experience offers the novel's only comment on the relationship between nation and identity. The contexts in which we understand Joy's situation also sustain a dialogic relationship to 'Scottishness'. Background details reinforce our sense of 'in-betweeness' as inevitable in the negotiations of Scottish womanhood. Marianne, whose letters aid recovery, is also shown playing out a problematic relationship to her own national identity: from America, in 'exile', she recounts, with a strong sense of the absurd, the irony of having to teach country dancing, of living in the Bible Belt and talking about Burns and Shelley (197), the humour of someone playing Danny Boy to her because they thought it was Scottish (150), yet she still asks for cheddar and oatcakes to be sent. Marianne functions in the novel as a lost 'other' for Joy: she feels at her most secure when symbolically returned to the womb of Marianne's mother, Ellen: 'I lie in Marianne's bed, the warm milk her mother made for me forming skin' (206). It is significant, therefore, that the person with whom she has the clearest communication – which Marianne reinforces on the telephone, saying 'It's so good to hear you, not to have to say everything twice' (204) – is a Scotswoman out of Scotland. Putting together the artefacts of the culture – Burns, oatcakes, country dancing – can produce only a subversive version of Scottishness, offering a 'rough repair' of national identity.

Cassie and Rona also venture abroad: but rather than being 'lads o' pairts' traversing the world with confidence in a cohesive national identity, these 'heroines' are lasses both 'in parts', fragmented and dislocated in their social roles, and in 'foreign parts', unknown lands. 'Neither real nor proper: just fraudulent moochers in other people's territory, getting by on the cheap' (150), Cassie and Rona explore new regions with unhelpful and out-of-date maps; they are a product of both their gender and their ethnicity. 'Coming from a wee country you forget how big other places can be ... We thought backroads would be prettier. But coming from a wee country, we forgot' (63–4). The coordinates with which they attempt to plot their journey are inappropriate; they are 'fraudulent moochers' not only because they come from a 'small' Scotland, but because they come from a 'we(e)' country, women with specific and singular experiences who in the end might find some common ground between themselves. It is, however, a commonality which emerges from difference – differences not only between each other but from the grand narratives of geography and history.

Drawn into the mastering discourses of European history, and the grand narrative of the First World War in particular, Cassie and Rona are shown in an uneasy relationship to larger cultural patterns and to their 'own' Scottish history. Cassie's obvious response to the archivolts of Chartres in which, the guidebook asserts, the seven liberal arts are depicted 'allegorically by women and historically by the men considered to be the outstanding exponents of each art' is to cry 'Enough' (94). Her reaction to the war cemetery, however, is also one of alienation:

> The place was full of folk who belonged to somebody but none of them were hers. She had no right play-acting or making up wee sentimental fictions while her pal was busy. Or manufacturing spurious noble sentiments about it either. It was dubious territory indeed, the fantasy you could understand a bloody thing by looking at the likes of this. Rows of dead people. Dead men. Dead boys. (50)

Nor can she locate herself within Scottish 'history':

> Macbeth. St Columba. Your own country's medieval life restricted to an English play and a velcro shape off the felt table at Sunday school. Robert the Bruce. Kings and generals, Men of Letters. Of the mass of people, less than nothing. Women didn't come into the reckoning at all. (165)

The novel deepens its analysis of the tensions between gender and national identity, between patriarchy and post-colonial culture, through the figure of Cassie's ex-partner Chris, who, as his relationship with Cassie becomes more threatening, takes her to increasingly non-European holiday locations in which his money and status as a white male can be more forcefully asserted, distancing himself from an 'effeminate' less powerful Scotland:

> People tried to buy us breakfast every morning, desperate to practise their English. Chris loved all that, talking in a drawl about the Houses of Parliament and London Our Capital. It's Edinburgh his bloody capital only he didn't want to risk saying that and have them think he was less important than they thought. I was all ready to do that for him, to see their eyes blanking up when I said SCOTLAND ACTUALLY but he got there first. (179)

The structures of colonisation lead patriarchy to assert itself more forcefully in men whose political context has disempowered them. For Cassie, however, the 'power' gained by asserting Scottishness is that it weakens her already diminished status by its association with a supposedly 'emasculated' culture, forcing her to align herself with a nation and history that she does not necessarily feel is her own.

Further questions about the ways in which certain narratives retain meaning, while others oppress and exclude, are raised by a visit to Chenenceau when, carved into the wall of a room that housed the Scots guard of Mary Queen of Scots, they find the word

HAME.

The German tourists 'leave not seeing the best ... a whole word a dead man took the time to chip into resistant masonry, four-lettered, legible, clear' (227), but the resistant word of a 'dead man' speaks to Cassie, the very person who slept through a trip to 'Bannockburn maybe' (234). Grand concepts of a feminised motherland, or of a masculine narrative of struggle, are equally disempowering. The concept of 'hame', however, with its connotations of the self and the familiar, the 'heimlich', an antithesis of expansion and war, can and does speak to her. Through this incident the novel acknowledges (while it also questions) the desire to belong, that need to make stories and histories, which we witness in Cassie as she remakes her own history through 'insignificant' photographs: 'Rotten photo ... I've only kept it because I remember taking it ... That's what I like about this one. That I took it for me. Just for me' (232). An insignificant foggy field acquires 'historical' meaning because it marks Cassie's own transformation from passive to active, from viewed to viewer, from object to subject. A foggy field, ancient graffiti, can thus acquire counter-discursive power.

Writing of a number of significant Scotsmen who contributed to transformations of the modern world, Cairns Craig suggests they lived 'in a spatial traversal across cultural differences rather than in singular journey within the evolving history of an individual culture'. Scotland, nevertheless, 'was an origin which did not provide the *telos* of their life's narrative, but it provided the purposes by which they were guided' (1999, 236). In its technique of 'bricolage', in the subversion and transformation of cultural artefacts and objects, Galloway's fiction goes beyond this idea of spatial traversal which is still structured through national identification, with 'origin' and 'purpose', and calls into question models of history and national identity based upon such grand narratives; it questions the extent to which they can speak to women of 'hame'. Rather than filling in 'gaps' in history, the novel problematises predominant and confining notions of history and identity. *Foreign Parts* ends with Cassie and Rona looking at the Channel, throwing stones: 'Another scuds out, headed for where Dunkirk might be, or home. It could be going home. Godknows. I've no sense of direction, me ... We stand in separate places, looking out over water that is just water' (262). To believe there is a problem with being a 'fraudulent moocher' is to believe both in essential truth and linear direction, to hold to the grand narratives of geography and history: for Galloway's women, and Scottish women generally, a more positive reading of 'fraudulent mooching' seems a welcome alternative to the discourses of national identity by which we have been bound.

Notes

1. Janice Galloway, *Foreign Parts* (1994; London: Vintage, 1995), p. 13.
2. Janice Galloway, *The Trick Is to Keep Breathing* (1989; London: Minerva, 1991).
3. Muriel Spark, *The Driver's Seat* (1970; Harmondsworth: Penguin, 1974), p. 13.

4. See Douglas Gifford, 'Contemporary Fiction II: Seven Writers in Scotland', in D. Gifford and D. McMillan (eds), *A History of Scottish Women's Writing* (Edinburgh: Edinburgh University Press, 1997), pp. 604–29 (610).
5. Cairns Craig, *The Modern Scottish Novel* (Edinburgh: Edinburgh University Press, 1999), p. 196.
6. 'The "bricoleur" is adept at performing a large number of diverse tasks ... His universe of instruments is closed and the rules of his game are always to make do with "whatever is at hand", that is to say with a set of tools and materials which is always finite and is also heterogeneous because what it contains bears no relation to the current project, or indeed to any particular project, but is the contingent result of all the occasions there have been to renew or enrich the stock or to maintain it with the remains of previous constructions or deconstructions', Claude Lévi-Strauss, *The Savage Mind* (London: Weidenfeld & Nicolson, 1972), p. 17.
7. See, for example, Michel de Certeau, *The Practice of Everyday Life* (Berkeley, CA: University of California Press, 1984) and Dick Hebdige, *Cut 'n' Mix* (London: Comedia, 1987).
8. Hélène Cixous, 'The Laugh of the Medusa' (*Signs*, Summer 1976), reprinted in E. Marks and I. de Courtivron (eds), *New French Feminisms* (Brighton: Harvester, 1981), pp. 245–64 (258).
9. Pam Morris, *Literature and Feminism* (Oxford: Blackwell, 1993), p. 73.
10. See, in particular, Craig, *The Modern Scottish Novel*; and Josiane Paccaud-Huguet, 'Breaking through Cracked Mirrors: The Short Stories of Janice Galloway', *Études Écossaises* 2 (1993), pp. 5–29.
11. Hélène Cixous and Mireille Calle-Gruber, *Hélène Cixous Rootprints: Memory and Life Writing*, trans. E. Prenowitz (London: Routledge, 1997), p. 62.
12. Maroula Joannou, for example, talks of the difficulty of attempting to place early twentieth-century women's writing in historical context which would move beyond a 'reflectionist' model of textuality, while still finding some aspects of a more theoretical feminism problematic. See Maroula Joannou, *'Ladies, Please Don't Smash These Windows': Women's Writing, Feminist Consciousness and Social Change 1918–1938* (Oxford: Berg Publishers, 1995), p. 13. Likewise Rita Felski questions the challenge of a feminist aesthetics in *Beyond Feminist Aesthetics: Feminist Literature and Social Change* (Cambridge, MA: Harvard University Press, 1989), p. 39.
13. Berthold Schoene-Harwood, 'Dams Burst: Devolving Gender in Iain Banks, *The Wasp Factory*', *Ariel: A Review of International English Literature*, 30:1 (January 1999), pp. 131–48 (131). See also '"Emerging as the Other of Our Selves" – Scottish Multiculturalism and the Challenge of the Body in Postcolonial Representation', *Scottish Literary Journal*, 25:1 (May 1998), pp. 54–72: 'For instance, the works of contemporary Scottish writers like Janice Galloway, Edwin Morgan, Alasdair Gray or James Kelman are first and foremost lauded for their skilful literary encapsulation of an elusive, if ostensibly unmistakable Scottishness' (55).
14. See Margery Metzstein, 'Of Myths and Men: Aspects of Gender in the Fiction of Janice Galloway', in G. Wallace and R. Stevenson (eds), *The Scottish Novel since the Seventies* (Edinburgh: Edinburgh University Press, 1993), pp. 136–46; Paccaud-Huguet, 'Breaking through Cracked Mirrors'; Lavinia Greenlaw, *Times Literary Supplement*, no. 4753 (1994), p. 20; Glenda Norquay, 'The Fiction of Janice Galloway: Weaving a Route through Chaos', in G. Norquay and G. Smyth (eds), *Space*

& *Place: The Geographies of Literature* (1997), pp. 323–30 (to an extent this is an earlier version of this chapter).

15. Gifford, 'Contemporary Fiction II', p. 609.

16. Aileen Christianson, 'Lies, Notable Silences and Plastering the Cracks: The Fiction of A. L. Kennedy and Janice Galloway', in *Gender and Scottish Society: Polities, Policies and Participation* (Edinburgh: Unit for the Study of Government in Scotland, University of Edinburgh, 1998), pp. 136–40 (139).

17. Susanne Hagemann, 'Women and Nation', in Gifford and McMillan, *A History of Scottish Women's Writing*, pp. 316–28 (323).

18. Cairns Craig, *Out of History: Narrative Paradigms in Scottish and English Culture* (Edinburgh: Polygon, 1996), p. 199.

19. Marilyn Reizbaum, 'Canonical Double Cross: Scottish and Irish Women's Writing', in K. R. Lawrence (ed.), *Decolonizing Tradition: New Views of Twentieth-Century 'British' Literary Canons* (Urbana: University of Illinois Press, 1992), pp. 165–90 (168).

20. Lesley Orr Macdonald, '"Denied the Capacity to *Become*": Paradigms of Polity and Power in Scottish Presbyterianism 1830–1930', in *Gender and Scottish Society*, pp. 127–35 (130).

CHAPTER ELEVEN

A. L. Kennedy's Longer Fiction: Articulate Grace

Sarah M. Dunnigan

Alison Louise Kennedy (b. 1965) is an elusive rather than an evasive writer; elusive in her refusal to be pinned down to any literary 'philosophy' or credo of gender or nationalism, not evasive because she states clearly that, 'When I write, my aim is to communicate, person to person. I am a human being telling another human being a story which may or may not be true, but which hopefully has a life and truth and logic of its own'.[1] That comment, exemplifying Kennedy's rigorous intellectual honesty, perhaps contradicts the aim of this chapter. She refuses to endow her fictions with any 'literary terminology ... it will have nothing to do with the work' (100). Yet Kennedy's disavowals *do* constitute a gloss on her art: fictions of communication, identification (words she herself uses in her essay), and love – impossible, achieved, imagined.

Kennedy refers to the 'deliverance' which a work of fiction can achieve, releasing the reader 'from the limitations of my isolated individual reality'; the effort to escape the enclosures of intellectual and emotional solitude drives most of Kennedy's protagonists. Her writing has a measure of intellectual scepticism; but Kennedy's gift among her contemporaries is to combine an intelligence, political and moral, with an exquisite emotional sensitivity. For Kennedy, writing is a 'sensual rather than an intellectual process', a 'spiritual experience of enormous power' (100).[2] The sensuality of the word is always present: 'I love these words. These words are lovely.'[3]

A prolific writer, her first collection of short fiction – *Night Geometry and the Garscadden Trains* – was published in 1990; and in 1994 and 1997, further short story collections followed, *Now that You're Back* and *Original Bliss*.[4] She has written drama and screenplays for film and television (for example, *ghostdancing* for BBC Scotland TV, 1995, and the film *Stella Does Tricks*, 1997) as well as non-fiction (*The Life and Death of Colonel Blimp* and *On Bullfighting*), and cultural and literary journalism. In 1998, she produced a collection of poetry from her performance work *Delicate*, entitled *Absolutely Nothing*.[5] Her work has received extensive critical acclaim and earned numerous prizes. In 1993, she was voted one of *Granta*'s twenty best British novelists (along with Candia McWilliam and Iain Banks; unlike many other contemporary Scottish women writers, Kennedy has been critically subsumed into a larger literary

'Britishness' in certain circles). This chapter explores Kennedy's longer fiction, *Looking for the Possible Dance* (1993), *So I Am Glad* (1995) and *Everything You Need* (1999).[6] It takes its impulse from the way in which Kennedy has spoken of her own writing – the 'sensual' and the 'spiritual', the process of writing as emotion filling the spaces between words – and examines the formal artistry of her fiction and its inscriptions of desire, memory, loss (what might be called Kennedy's 'ghost writing'), estrangement and love.

All Kennedy's fiction is narratologically complex. Her characteristic stylistic trait is the use of free indirect speech and thought. Kennedy's deft use allows intimate access to characters' interiority, her prose often syntactically reca-pitulating the interior thought process while emphasising the ironic distancing of conventional third-person narration. For example:

> 'That's right'. He wiped his mouth with one hand, as if he didn't like the taste of what he'd said.
> *He's such a terrible liar, he really shouldn't even try.*
> She waited, although she could guess that he'd rather she didn't, that he'd hoped the conversation might be over with. 'Nathan ——' but she stopped herself from going on.
> *He doesn't even want me here ... (Everything*, 476)[7]

Kennedy's first novel, *Looking for the Possible Dance*, is less conceptually and formally experimental than her subsequent work but exemplifies a character-istic narratological device: the 'expendable' temporal framework. This might be defined as the instability of tense which renders the past and present lives of characters in intimate proximity. Two different narratives of time are braided seamlessly together so that the multiplicities of the narrative are worked through with those of identity and desire. The train journey from Glasgow to London undertaken by Margaret, Kennedy's central protagonist (ultimately ending in return), cuts a clear, linear narrative line. The motif of the journey, the acts of departure and return, underpins the book (Colin leaving Margaret; Margaret leaving her father) and lends it an overall pattern of circularity. The end of the journey is the end of the line narratively speaking – the book's end – and, figuratively, spells resolution for Margaret: 'Her track is beginning to bind itself under others' (249). Entwined around Margaret's journey are recollec-tions and memories. The complex, haunting constellations of memory – 'a ghost, with a time past restoring' (*Everything*, 5) – are a constant theme in Kennedy's work. Different strands of recollection constitute Margaret's interior journey, often in a sensuous, Proustian cluster: 'As tall, green barley smears across the windows of her train, Mr Lawrence walks across one of Margaret's dreams. She can feel his breath like dust ... Then her mind draws up the smell of hot, small gravel and the feel of it ... This is a memory from the summer' (*Looking*, 23).

The novel's central 'memorial' structure is Margaret's relationship with her father; the central narrative 'moment', which itself stems from the first paternal evocation, is the ceilidh. The recollected original dance evokes an innocence to contrast with the 'fall' of the ceilidh. Here, Margaret's boyfriend Colin meets the loan shark dealer who will try to kill him, and Margaret's débâcle with her misogynistic employer and his drunk, despairing wife ensures her dismissal. In both instances, Margaret is unwittingly complicit, as Richard Todd demonstrates; the ceilidh is a night full of narrative ironies.[8] In the novel's dissolution of past and present boundaries, Kennedy's narrator is playful, withholding yet also implying larger outcomes: 'In his future, Colin has this memory' (*Looking*, 91). *So I Am Glad* echoes this manipulation of readerly expectations where the narrator, Jennifer, guards Martin/Savinien's identity: 'I would love to tell you who he is right now' (39). In *Everything You Need*, Nathan Staples's seven stories together constitute the story of his daughter's life and his confession that he is her father.

In *Looking for the Possible Dance*, therefore, a non-linear but associative narrative is found; for Margaret, certain words spark associations. The most intricate interweaving occurs with the encounter with James on the train, a 'boy or perhaps a man, his face seems older than his body' (55). Interspersed with written communications (which chart their growing mutual attachment) are memories, chiefly of the ceilidh. The encounter is deeply moving but resists any sentimentalised assumptions or simplification. Their paper colloquies, tender, comic, ironic by turns, address the possibilities of communication. Through typographical experimentation, language – the evasions, ellipses, interpretations of words – is foregrounded: 'PEOPLE CAN TALK TO "Yes. You meet people you can talk to and be yourself with. Not often, but you do. Are you yourself now?" YES NO PILLS NO JAGS ALL MEEEE' (191). The connection, rare in James's life, ends when Margaret's address is blown 'along the platform out of sight' as James 'struggles out of the blanket to wave back' (170). Communication is won, only to end ironically in loss.

Kennedy's next novel, *So I Am Glad*, concerns an emotional intimacy which cannot ultimately survive; an erotic and spiritual dialogue between the seventeenth-century Cyrano de Bergerac, writer, soldier, *philosophe*, and Jennifer, a contemporary Glaswegian radio announcer. Love breaches the centuries but only gradually, for Jennifer must renounce her avowed emotional isolation. The figure of Jennifer, 'professional enunciator' (37), anticipates the contrast between professional articulateness and private inarticulacy which *Everything You Need* explores through the emotional solipsism of its community of writers. Her job is a combination of professionalised loneliness and one-way communication. Jennifer's calculated quiescence, however, is paradoxical; as a narrator she strikes an extraordinary intimacy with the reader of her 'testament'. There is a tender, playful and subversive bond which pivots, as in most of Kennedy's fictions, on the tension between disclosure and concealment. 'Do you still like me? Did you ever? Need to? Maybe not' she asks (129). Her narrative, the writing out of her love for Cyrano Savinien de Bergerac, is confessional. She strives for verisimilitude throughout her tale and her self-revelation: 'I am not emotional. You should know that about me ... I feel you should be better informed' (4–5). She lays bare yet denies the identities – sexual, social, familial – which constitute the self transformed by the loving encounter. Psychological admissions made to the reader(s) are retracted as if too compromising: 'I will tell you soon about my parents ... but when I do, you'll already know they played no part in making me how I am' (6).

Yet the act of writing, the process of recollection, is an emotional exorcism. It is a compulsive act, incumbent upon Jennifer for her own needs as much as any spurious reader's:

> Now this section, you needn't read or really bother with. It won't add to your understanding of the book, or of the story it's trying to tell. Here is where I'll put something down that's for me, a corner of all this writing which is only mine and not a confidence I'm going to offer, not part of my calculations. (69)

She then recounts the strangeness of her parents, their temporary need for her as a child for 'their own, closed reasons' (71), so that one 'reticence' becomes enfolded in another. Jennifer's possessive claim of certain narrative moments of sanctity or privacy intensifies the text's 'self-consciousness'; the tale as a whole questioning larger issues of temporal, spatial, sexual and moral identities. Jennifer's story is paradoxical in another way. She confesses to vacuity, being 'empty': 'I can dig down as deep as there is to dig inside me and truly there is nothing there, not a squeak' (7). This is both an excuse and a defence: if 'nothing terribly bad has ever happened' (6) to Jennifer, then from where does her pain come? This sense of herself as a *tabula rasa*, a blank sheet or canvas on which to be written, works with the text's underlying idea about the redemptive grace of love.

Kennedy's fictions take liberty with narrative structure and tense. *So I Am Glad* echoes the wilfulness of her first novel: 'Now I'm going to cheat. We are high on the lip of the new year. ...' (137). This section exemplifies many Kennedy traits: the defamiliarising description of the mundane or quotidian ('Each street lamp supported a kind of fish shoal halo' (139)); the philosophical 'vignette', infused with a shot of the narrator's quasi-satiric paranoia ('THE MEANING OF THIS SHAPE IS YOUR FUTURE, WHAT FUTURE WILL IT BE? PLEASE THINK IN THE SPACE PROVIDED' (139)). Jennifer dreams of Savinien: 'Back. With me. I was happy. We were happy' (140). The simplicity of this reunion is partly mocked by Jennifer, a dream neither labyrinthine nor Freudian. Despite this, the idea of the dream, and the ideal self-containedness of dream, is a leitmotif for the novel. Jennifer's story is a tale of love and reincarnation; a fable in which the miraculous is manifest among the ordinary. The imaginative or dreamt is part of the novel's intellectual and psychological fabric.

The entire novel, the kernel of Jennifer's story, is spun from the provisionality of its narrative, the assumption on Jennifer's part that its miraculous fiction will *not* be credible. Part of this desire to attain 'the truth' (19) is realised in the filmic or documentary style of the narrative. Jennifer, as narrator, uses visual frames: 'Now I want to show you someone else' (8). She concedes, 'So you have the full picture now' though she herself seeks literal and textual invisibility: 'I wouldn't leave a trace. Of course, that wouldn't be the only alteration now. This story will, among other things, form a record of various cuts' (10). The verity of the image, as it were, is also important in *Everything You Need* where the opening 'sequence' reconstitutes the visual memory of Nathan Staples's estranged wife whom he loves still.

Most of Kennedy's fictions construct their own metafictions or meta-narratives. This is exemplified not only by their artistic formalism but in the process by which the act of writing is deconstructed by Kennedy's protago-nists, usually for its emotionally sacrificial nature: 'the whole *writing a book* thing might make me wonder just what kind of a person I could be ... I should get a life' (*So I Am Glad*, 129). The novice writer, Jennifer, speaks of writing as 'paying [the] penalty' (186). This flippant existential and writerly angst is writ large in *Everything You Need* which satirises the London metro-politan literary world and the crass professionalisation of literature, the marketplace presided over by the benign but ultimately disillusioned and de-spairing Jack Grace, Nathan's agent and beloved, tragic companion. Mary Lamb's seven-year writing fellowship includes her 'baptism' into that com-mercial world from which Nathan strives to protect her; like Jennifer, she is a novitiate to writing. The process of becoming a writer lies self-referentially at the heart of *So I Am Glad* and *Everything You Need*.

Both novels also share a fascination with the text, the created object or artefact. Whether the earlier work is memoir, testament, fiction, document, there are other smaller 'texts' encompassed within the larger which play upon the concepts of writing, communication, language. Jennifer's letter to Savinien writes her miraculous love into being, textual shape or form, while she never allows Savinien, its recipient, to read it. Instead, as part of the interior narrative, she lays it bare upon the page for her voyeuristic readers or witnesses: 'Think of what follows as the letter I would have written then and it will serve you and the story perfectly well. Indulge me for a page' (203). In turn, Savinien inscribes his love for her in a letter written in French, a language incompre-hensible to Jennifer. In the elaborate baroque conceits of Savinien's language, the words *l'amour*/love are broken apart, the act of translation or spelling out the first transformation of that love into the death/*La Mort* which condemns it: 'I knew the love he meant, the one that included darkness and loving on alone' (236). Writing is the attempt to find presence, to restore an absence or, in Jennifer's words, an emptiness. It is also erotic: 'If I do not touch the paper often I hope that when I lift it out and warm it there will always be something about it like the scent of him' (236). Jennifer's 'marvellous' tale is a com-memoration of love but also enshrines both the loss and the indirection that separates the end of it from the beginning: 'You'll have read, I suppose, the opening of this book, about all of that calmness I no longer have. Sometimes the best beginning is a lie' (280).

Everything You Need is Kennedy's most recent fiction about fiction, a meditation on the agonistic and redemptive power of writing. The work is divided into seven 'sections' which span the seven years of Mary Lamb's fellowship before she emerges as 'Mary Lamb the writer'. Nathan gives Mary seven codified rules of writing, urging her to believe that 'no one can stop you being a writer' while he dreads the consequences of her creativity: 'they were both – quite willingly – at the mercy of their minds. He would know how much she was his daughter' (185). Mary fears Nathan's judgement at first but they both find communion 'in the imperfection of her words' (185). There are small ironic tendernesses to Nathan's role as tutor/father: he urges her 'to look after her words' so that the bond between the writer and the written is a loving shelter; and yet language is not 'own[ed]' (Rule Four, 325). Writing is also a dangerous vocation; Foal Island is a needful sanctuary for writers like Joe,[9] who has died in spirit (483), and Lynda who, to Nathan's horror, shows Mary her pierced labia and describes writing as a 'monster' needing to be controlled (163). This, together with Nathan's suicide attempts, draws correspondences between writing and mutilation, a creative act which can also be self-destructive.

The seven-year structure parallels the seven stories which make up Nathan's 'book' for Mary (this numerological symbolism underpins the text). This is Nathan's 'proper book', to make Mary 'proud' (105), replacing the letters 'with nothing definite to say' (297) which he writes to her, ironically shown to him by Mary. Typographically, this is set apart from but interwoven with the main fabric of the text, constructed not as a simple linear narrative but ranging from Mary's infancy to Maura's pregnancy (Mary / Maura: daughter / wife); from Nathan's intense desires for Maura to their final brutal separation in London. It is Nathan's part-fiction, part-testament, part-confession, a retelling or admission to his daughter of his past and his present love for her. It is the most important text he has ever written.

Nathan must learn to love, to give himself up to his daughter; the third of his narratives reveals this arduous task by presenting his own intrusions (Kennedy's stylistic marker of free indirect thought). Nathan interrupts himself, ironically confessing his fear of confession. He desires to change the narrative, 'his story', to efface its pain by the wilful act of 'editing out' or resorting to fictive inventiveness: '*And why the last two paragraphs? You don't need them ... You've even lost your **narrative** backbone now*' (403–4). Revelation of the text is the very revelation of love: '*Who is this for, really – do tell? Not the daughter, surely? Not ever anyone but the wife. Maura – who never liked to read you ... But Mary **will** read me. In the end, she'll read me and she'll know what I mean, because we're like each other. She'll take in what I give her and she'll add herself and we will fit*' (221). Mary observes him writing 'her story', noticing that as he writes in recovery from his final failed suicide attempt that there are only 'a handful of pages left' (547). Mary becomes the ultimate judge of Nathan's writing in a reversal of roles. The final page of the book is also that of Nathan's story: 'I've already written out everything I know'. It is both gift and plea: 'Please, my darling, have need of me' (567). Writing is the act and art of love – the final seventh rule when the other rules have become dispensable – while that of reading, no less, is a reciprocation of that love, an absolution according to the novel's metaphorical texture. Writing and reading in Kennedy is instilled with eroticism and may signify restoration or catharsis: 'If, in this world, I could, I would write you whole and well' (*Night Geometry*, 126).

In *So I Am Glad*, Kennedy writes about the repressive hurt of the family. To the child Jennifer, her parents maintain a conspiracy of silence, a veil of secrecy (22) so that she responds in kind by seeking to keep herself 'safe' from them (71). There is another, more significant 'fable', however, in Kennedy's longer fiction which explores familial unions rather than fragmentation. Her first and third novels present a triangulation of desire: the figure of the young woman (Margaret, Mary) and her two *loci* of desire, the father and the lover. The love between father and daughter is exquisitely drawn; no other contemporary Scottish woman writer explores the complexity of father-daughter devotion.[10] Perhaps such a desire remains largely unwritten because a conventional 'feminist' reading might perceive the daughter as a 'gift' of exchange in a male economy of desire (Mary Lamb claims she is caught between the two 'bookends' of Jonathan and Nathan (*Everything,* 160)). To speak (as a woman) of this love is immediately to invoke a taboo. The bond in *Looking for the Possible Dance* is not necessarily imbued with sexual import but in *Everything You Need* the daughter erotically (mis)recognises the father. Mary is unaware of Nathan's real identity so that only Nathan recognises the transgression and redresses it by arranging that Mary witness Lynda, another of the island writers, fellating him. Through the prevention of the incest taboo another is constructed in its place: the sexuality of the father is enacted before the daughter. Here, Kennedy articulates the unspeakable with an extraordinary sensitivity. The foregrounding of father and daughter is partly achieved by the elision in both novels of the mother figure. In *Looking for the Possible Dance*, Margaret barely knows the mother who left, the novel's one symbolic act of a journey without return. Margaret at one point desires to 'mother' her father but this is not oppressive. In *Everything You Need*, Mary is brought up in the loving tenderness of the Uncles, Bryn and Morgan; when she leaves them for the first time, there is pain but not that which had accompanied her mother's irreparable act of leaving (32). The earlier novel enshrines a daughter's love for her father but also depicts Margaret's mourning his ineffable loss; the retrospective narrative renders the vivid re-creations of her father *in memoriam*. At the Methodist dance, he asserts that: '"Everything else is a waste of time ..."' She ... wondered what he meant' (1, 2). This aphorism implies a profound sadness, a denial or loss on the father's part: he urges that Margaret be 'more alive than me ... You'll remember to do that for me' (5). The rest of the novel might be seen as Margaret's effort to fulfil the promise of that night, sustaining her early desire 'to please ... oblige' (4) him as a matter of keeping faith. It begins a web of recollection and association: as she begins to dream on the train (52), the sound of her father is constant; his injunction 'to live' haunts her until she is angry that he is no longer there to be told how she lives: 'Like, I can breathe fire. I learned how to do that. And other things ... her hands were throbbing. She thought of slipping them flat against her father's back and rubbing her chin into his shoulder as if they were going to start a slow dance' (175).

Here, the paternal is not linked with prohibition: 'Her father and her pleasure have always been close' (6). The relationship with her boyfriend Colin is charted against that with her father. His memory haunts her, 'like a cry springing up from out of clear water' (64): how he consoled her when Colin had left for London ('He hugged her, gave her that silence again' (67)). For Margaret, her father's death is eternally renewed (86): 'she would ... wake up in the morning with something she hadn't known before ... Sometimes she knew her daddy must have planted it' (101). Protectively, he tries to save her from the 'mistakes' he himself made in love (111): in the creation of her desire, Margaret paradoxically has the masculine 'point of view' as reference. She 'discovers' 'in her sleep' her father asking her to stay through love: 'We're more than family, we're the same. Two parts of one thing, do you see?' (154). This dreamt space of tenderness she deliberately withholds from Colin (155): the most articulate language of desire in the novel is spoken by father and daughter.

In *Everything You Need*, the daughter is also made in the image of the father, united in 'their capacity for longing' (345). The 'theft' of Mary from Nathan requires that he learn her history. Mary at first resents his inquisitiveness, the demanding nature of his literary tutelage. Because he is dead to her, Nathan must achieve a kind of resurrection. Another father and daughter exist within the novel: the young girl, Sophie, who belongs to the writer Joe and whom Mary ironically first sees cradled by Nathan (155). When she nearly drowns, her return is almost miraculous. Loss makes recovery more precious. This successful restoration of the child is countered by the story of the lost, dead child on the mainland. Between these two fables of loss and restoration, Kennedy charts a tale of daughter-father love which refuses silence. At the heart of the novel is the recovery of a fundamental symbiosis: '*When I bleed, she cries*', Nathan recalls of an incident when Mary had accidentally cut his lip (147). 'Please, God', he writes, 'never take me from this' (147).

Kennedy frequently invests sexual desire with violence. In the novella 'Original Bliss', she writes in visceral detail about the dark consolations of hard core pornography for Edward Gluck;[11] in *So I Am Glad*, the sadomasochism of Jennifer's relationship with her original 'partner' Steve is enacted. In this, Kennedy again invokes taboos of various kinds. The narrator is conscious of such transgression: 'Want to see it? Close your eyes now' (131). Sadism is performed by the female figure upon the male; as in 'Original Bliss', the masculine is the abject position. Part of Jennifer's sexual history in the novel exposes the banal mundanity of sex, a consolation to her because she can choose silence:

Oh, a few words now and then are unavoidable, of course. I can remember.
THERE
NOW
LATER
and NOT (THERE, NOW, LATER)
YES and NO
DID and YOU
and
HAPPY?
YET?
But that isn't speaking. (3)

The relationship with Steve is one of need, dependence, denial (50–2), and intercourse is computed as a tedious, meaningless equation ('Cunt + Cock =   ' (92)). Yet it seems a simplification of the erotic complexities of Kennedy's writing to suggest that in this novel, and in her work as a whole, there is a clear-cut polarity between 'bad' sex and 'good', nor is there simply suggested a distinction between 'articulate' and 'non-articulate' sexual desire, even though Jennifer confesses 'I've never liked public discussions of love' (90) and then announces her 'personal definition of love' or emblem as handcuffs. There might well be a ready connection between the verbal significations of the cuffs – 'Clickilicklick. STOP. Because you should stop' (91) – and her plea when a child to parents driving too fast 'to stop speeding, to stop being so together, to stop being' (104) before she witnesses their sexual caresses.

Above all, excess defines the novel's sadism: the fear and liberation of going too far. Jennifer is unable 'to stop' in the sexual persona of Captain Bligh which emancipates her from any 'feminine' inhibition (91). She is gratified by inscribing pain upon the body painlessly, as it were, when intimate recognition of that body is prevented: 'you need only look at him when you wish, you will already know where to strike' (94). The novel speaks the unspeakable in articulating female sadistic pleasure but it is also an acknowledged, then renounced, transgression, as Jennifer severely abuses a silenced Steve, as if 'finding an edge and stepping beyond it and gripping that edge and throwing it away' (127). The novel's heart of darkness provides an arresting, if ultimately 'censored', inscription of desire.

Though desire reaches its extremity here, that violent 'edge' is part of a 'gradient' or continuum of sexual desire in Kennedy's writing. The essence of desire is that it entails self-abnegation, a renunciation of some kind. Kennedy has been praised for writing about sexuality from both the female and male 'points of view', and of achieving a kind of 'genderless' fusion.[12] This seems curious, the kind of inverse commendation bestowed on Alan Warner, for example, for his female 'ventriloquism'. In fact, desire – and the significance of renunciation – is arguably written in the feminine: *Looking for the Possible Dance* and *Everything You Need* describe the loss of virginity for their main female protagonists. The 'rite' is more elaborate for Mary in the latter – as if to 'seal' her departure for Foal Island – when the Uncles discover her and Jonathan together (the 'masculine' again a circumference around female desire but in no way a repression or negation of it). Kennedy's writing depicts the sexual encounter as either alternately or a fusion of intense eroticism and violence (exemplified by the figure of Cyrano de Bergerac). For Margaret and Mary, their male lovers may hurt in their penetration but the characteristic fusion of assertion and abnegation on their part seemingly makes Kennedy's writing articulate the censored paradoxes of contemporary female desire; it redraws the permissable boundaries of the female erotic.

So I Am Glad is Kennedy's most intense and philosophical meditation on desire. An unknown or uncertain identity is erotically liberating: 'Good morning. Whoever you are' (66). In the act of first naming her strange 'guest', Jennifer partially invents her lover, and submits unquestioningly to the dissolution of his identity: 'I let Martin turn into Savinien' (84). Articulating his name, when 'the voice' is charged with erotic *frisson* throughout the novel, is an intimacy in itself (11, 77). Their love is a collision of historical, national and cultural identities so that in Paris Savinien re-enacts an extravagant seventeenth-century 'Exercise in Love' (88).

Several reasons may underlie Kennedy's choice of Cyrano de Bergerac (1619–55), soldier, lover, poet, playwright, philosopher, *libertin*; she has written that she grew to identify with him (in his roles as sceptic, satirist, iconoclast) (*Critical Quarterly*, 53). His writing was resurrected by the nineteenth century after a period of decline, and the 'mythologising' of Cyrano de Bergerac was cemented by Edmond Rostand in 1897.[13] His fictional status is punningly alluded to by Kennedy's novel so that her Cyrano sees himself as a kind of palimpsest (80). In the Paris Bibliothèque Nationale, Savinien reads for himself the expurgation and censorship of his writing, 'My words, my books' (270), until the library becomes a mausoleum, and writing a ghostly act. Kennedy's fidelity to Savinien's own writing is interesting: the journey which her fictional Cyrano describes seems to echo his own literary account of a fantastic voyage, *L'Autre Monde*, which drew philosophical relativism, *histoire comique* and social satire into its marvellous fiction.[14] Kennedy's 'invention' of Savinien's voice often emulates the philosophical *gravitas* and beauty of seventeenth-century discourse: 'my heart is clean … I can give you access to my soul' (250). The figure of Cyrano de Bergerac appositely licenses the 'philosophy' of love which the novel seemingly espouses: the duality of souls. Jennifer begins and ends in solitude but in-between she discovers 'that single moment when you truly touch another person' (78). 'I assumed … Savinien and I were the same' (102): in an echo of Renaissance Neoplatonism, Jennifer and Savinien are indivisible so that for the first time she can utter the charmed pronoun of lovers – 'We. That's Savinien and I. Us' (222) – and

the word 'love' meaningfully (233). Their dreams coalesce until that very si-
multaneity is a harbinger of Savinien's final departure.

That 'death' is anticipated throughout the novel, not simply in his violent,
near-death encounters in Glasgow, but in the sheer precariousness of his physical
existence. Jennifer must literally and metaphorically sustain him: he breathes
more easily 'Because of me' (31). His paradoxical fragility is erotically manifest in the shining trace or imprint which he leaves upon her skin yet which
inscribes the possibility of his disappearance. Jennifer preserves 'the sheer miracle of Savinien's existence' (261) in words, as if it is one of Cyrano de Bergerac's
fabled utopian worlds.

The very title of Kennedy's first novel deploys a present participle, under-
lining an unfulfilled act; the idea of longing or need binds together the
protagonists of her most recent novel. The typologies of longing so embedded
in all of Kennedy's longer fiction give them the structure of a quest. *Everything
You Need* explicitly uses the medieval romance metaphor of the Grail (396)
and retells the story of Nathan (the atheist) on a writer's tour to Jerusalem.
Kennedy is not an *overtly* religious writer but religious metaphors underlie, or
can be applied to, her fiction;[15] In *Looking for the Possible Dance*, Colin is literally
crucified for his attempts to defeat the loan sharks. Kennedy's fiction contains
an existential and philosophical darkness which co-exists with love's saving
grace; it also embodies the specificity of that affirmative process as rooted in a
quest structure, and the idea, most explicit in *Everything You Need*, of a secular
'deliverance'.

In this chapter Kennedy's fictional enactments of the intimacy, estrangement and eroticism of writing have been suggested. The 'intellectual' and the
'sensual' are married. Her work articulates verbal and psychological thresholds
between disclosure and revelation, and the trope of memory – the immanence
of the past within present lives – is a constant. Most Kennedy protagonists are
haunted by ghosts. The underlying structure of Kennedy's novels is loss and
their 'quest' a restoration, whether moral, sexual or spiritual. She writes uniquely
about the violence of desire, pleasure and transgression, and creates an almost
fabled beauty at the heart of her most tender fictions about lovers, and daughters
and fathers. While her work as a whole is about the emotionally and politically
disenfranchised and dispossessed, it also aims to discover the means of
(re)enchantment.

Notes

1. 'Not Changing the World', in Ian A. Bell (ed.), *Peripheral Visions: Images of Nationhood in Contemporary British Fiction* (Cardiff: University of Wales Press, 1995),
   pp. 100–2 (100).
2. See also Kennedy's essay in *Critical Quarterly*, 37:4 (1995), pp. 52–5.
3. 'Star Dust', in *Night Geometry and the Garscadden Trains* (1990; London: Phoenix,
   1995), p. 83.

4. A. L. Kennedy, *Now that You're Back* (London: Jonathan Cape, 1994); *Original Bliss* (London: Jonathan Cape, 1997).

5. A. L. Kennedy, *The Life and Death of Colonel Blimp* (London: British Film Institute, 1997); *On Bullfighting* (London: Yellow Jersey Press, 1999); *Absolutely Nothing* (Glasgow: Mariscat Press, 1998).

6. Editions referred to are *Looking for the Possible Dance* (London: Vintage, 1998); *So I Am Glad* (London: Vintage, 1996); *Everything You Need* (London: Jonathan Cape, 1999).

7. I am grateful to Kirsty Williams for allowing me to read her BA University of Strathclyde dissertation on this subject: 'A. L. Kennedy: A Dialogue of Theme and Style' (1999).

8. Richard Todd, *Consuming Fictions: The Booker Prize and Fiction in Britain Today* (London: Bloomsbury, 1996), pp. 160–1.

9. The novel's literal and imagined islands evoke traditional literary connotations of the marginal, the exotic, otherness, exile and enchantment. Foal Island is itself a history, a fable, as when Louis assumes 'the task of translating the island for her [Mary], unveiling all its little histories and dialects' (124). First 'sacked and burned' by a planted Tudor lord who exiled the monks and other inhabitants, the island evokes the paradigm of other clearances and plantations (the Scottish Highlands, Ireland) though this particular colonisation ends with a beautiful mythical reincarnation (125–6).

10. Dorothy McMillan, 'Constructed out of Bewilderment', in Bell, *Peripheral Visions*, pp. 80–99 (96).

11. A. L. Kennedy, 'Original Bliss', in Kennedy, *Original Bliss* (London: Jonathan Cape, 1997), pp. 151–311.

12. Eleanor Stewart Bell, 'Scotland and Ethics in the Work of A. L. Kennedy', *Scotlands*, 5:1 (1998), pp. 105–13 (108); Alison Smith, 'Four Success Stories', *Chapman*, 74–5 (1993), pp. 177–92 (192).

13. Edwin Morgan, *Edmond Rostand's Cyrano de Bergerac: A New Verse Translation* (Manchester: Carcanet, 1992).

14. See Edward W. Lanius, *Cyrano de Bergerac and the Universe of Imagination* (Geneva: Librairie Droz, 1967). See also Kennedy's film *ghostdancing*, BBC Scotland (1995).

15. In *Critical Quarterly*, 37:4 (1995), Kennedy alludes to her religiosity (55).

CHAPTER TWELVE

Scottish Women's Short Stories: 'Repositories of Life Swiftly Apprehended'

Alison Lumsden

In a recent introduction to the Macallan/*Scotland on Sunday* collection *Shorts*, Candia McWilliam writes:

> Short stories are a disputed phenomenon. Are they harder, or easier, to write than novels, writers are asked, as though short stories were front gardens and novels arboreta. There's a certain sizeism at play, and a bit of slack thinking. Short stories are shorter than novels and that's it. No proper writer approaches them as a thing to be dealt with frivolously, as it were, in the spare time left by a novel. Short stories are the repositories of life swiftly apprehended. Because they are short, they are often thought easy. There can be no more malicious misrepresentation.[1]

McWilliam highlights a long-standing set of attitudes towards the short story in Britain in general; it is, typically, regarded as the little, and often inferior, sister of the novel, a form of exercise on which writers cut their teeth before moving on to more challenging forms. We should, perhaps, be more ashamed of this attitude to short fiction in Scotland than elsewhere in the United Kingdom, since there is a long and fine tradition of short stories. Walter Scott developed the form in stories such as 'The Two Drovers' and it is a tradition which runs through R. L. Stevenson and on into Lewis Grassic Gibbon. Women have also written successfully in this genre; Violet Jacob, Naomi Mitchison and Jessie Kesson, to name only a few.

However, the method of publication of the short story – often in journals, periodicals and anthologies – means that they are more likely to go out of print than novels, and in many cases the work of their predecessors has been unavailable to the present generation of women writers. Naomi Mitchison's stories, for example, were unavailable until Isobel Murray's collection *Beyond This Limit*, where the title story is reproduced for the first time since its original, limited edition.[2] Violet Jacob's stories too have only recently come back into print.[3]

In spite of this history of neglect, recent years have seen considerable activity in the short story form among Scottish women writers. It is clear that the republication of work by writers like Mitchison and Jacob, and the fact that there has been a market for it, has contributed to this situation, but other factors have also been significant. There has, of course, been a general upturn in Scottish writing and publishing since the 1970s, and the role of James Kelman, whose work has been key in much of Scottish writing's rejuvenation, cannot be over-estimated. Kelman, who looks to the United States and continental Europe where the short story has always enjoyed greater status, is himself a master of the form and his collections demonstrate what can be achieved in the short story, highlighting the distinctively charged space it may occupy in contrast to the novel, and the extraordinary literary effects it can achieve. Kelman's work has given a new-found credibility to the short story in Scotland, and suggested ways in which it may be developed; his influence is evident on many of the women short-story writers working in Scotland today.

Looking further back, it is evident that the influence of Muriel Spark has also been considerable – an influence reflected in writers like Candia McWilliam and Shena Mackay. Spark, of course, launched her writing career with a short story, 'The Seraph and the Zambesi', and her collections of short stories – *The Go-Away Bird* and *Bang, Bang You're Dead* – provide fine examples of the form.[4] Spark's general success as a writer has ensured that these stories have remained in print and, perhaps more significantly, her emphases on well-crafted writing, brevity of vision and on 'life swiftly apprehended' in her novels as well as short stories have ensured a respect for these aspects of writing in Scotland.

Finally, short story writing has also benefited enormously from the publication of anthologies in Scotland in recent years. The Collins collection (published since 1973), the Association for Scottish Literary Studies *New Writing Scotland* (itself in its eighteenth year) and the Macallan/*Scotland on Sunday* short story competition and its related publication have all had a significant effect on both the writing and reception of short stories in Scotland today. These anthologies provide a site for discovering new talent Rose, Smith and Kennedy have all been published by *New Writing Scotland* – while often they provide the breakthrough which unknown writers need in order to gain publishing contracts – Dilys Rose, Ali Smith, Chris Dolan and Michel Faber, all past winners of the Macallan/*Scotland on Sunday* competition have each gone on to gain the much sought-after contract for a first collection of short stories.

Perhaps the most significant of all these writers is A. L. Kennedy whose *Night Geometry and the Garscadden Trains* (1990) was published to immediate acclaim, winning its author both the John Llewellyn Rhys Prize and the Saltire First Book Award.[5] It is a collection which maps out the territories which have repeatedly concerned Kennedy since she began writing, announcing her interest in both physical and emotional parameters and the spaces available to women within patriarchal 'geographies'.

Kennedy both acknowledges and downplays her role as a Scottish woman writer, stating 'I am a woman, I am heterosexual, I am more Scottish than anything else and I write. But I don't know how these things interrelate'.[6] This statement acknowledges that while her gender and nationality may be facts of Kennedy's identity, they do not set the agenda to which she writes. However, she continues:

> I can't tell you how exciting it was to read *Lanark* and recognize the atmosphere of a country I knew. A whole part of my life became three-, if not four-dimensional. When I saw the dialogue in *The Dear Green Place* I was delighted to find the humour and rhythm of something I heard around me ... I believe that fiction with a thread of Scottishness in its truth has helped me to know how to be myself as a Scot. ('Not Changing the World', 102)

While Kennedy may deny a direct correlation between nation and writing she aligns herself with the generation of writers who, for our times at least, have put a form of Scottishness back on the literary cultural agenda. So too, she stresses the role of language as an element by which we may recognise ourselves in terms of nationhood or, indeed, gender.

The roles available to women are often described in Kennedy's work spatially: 'Time divides me from my mother and her mother and beyond them there are lines ... of women who are nothing more than shadows in my bones' writes the narrator in 'Genteel Potatoes' 'and as you read this I am somewhere else' (*Geometry*, 42). Such positional signifiers are recurrent in Kennedy's writing, announcing an uneasiness in relationships, a desire for proximity and a knowledge of the impossibility of it. This is, of course, the significance of the 'geometry' in the title story of this collection, for as the narrator tries to negotiate the terms of her marriage this is expressed through the spatial parameters of their sleeping arrangements; 'this positioning, our little bit of night geometry, this came to be important in a way I didn't like because it changed. I didn't like it then, as much as I now don't like to remember the two of us together and almost asleep, because, by fair means or foul, you can't replace that. Intensity is easy, it's the simple nearness you'll miss' (*Geometry*, 27). In Kennedy's world such statements are significant, because the outward appearance of things does not belie, but usually illuminates the interior. 'The flat was very like him; in his colours, with his books' she writes in 'Tea and Biscuits' (*Geometry*, 1) and it is often by their relationship to such outward appearances that the roles available for women are inscribed.

Kennedy's explorations of the boundaries which contain and limit both men and women is subtle, and so too is her engagement with the implications of nation. In 'Friday Payday' for example, the girl sometimes longs to leave London for Scotland; 'Sometimes she just got dead homesick – adverts on the underground for Scotland, they lied like fuck, but they still made you think.'[7] She is not alone in Kennedy's world, for here characters frequently travel between Scotland and elsewhere, considering the place of Scotland as part of their identity, even subjectivity, as they do so. In 'Christine', for example, the narrator tells us:

> I went to a university in England and came back home as little as possible, because I could no longer be at home there. Scots down south either turn into

Rob Roy McStrathspeyandreel or simply become Glaswegian – no one will
understand you, if you don't. Rather than smile through a lifetime of simpleton
assumptions and kind enquiries after Sauchiehall Street in the frail hope of one
day explaining my existence, I chose to be English and to disappear. (*Now*, 15)

Suggestively, Homi Bhabha, in his work on literature and nation, comments
on the role of the stereotype in colonial discourse, suggesting that it is 'a form
of knowledge and identification that vacillates between what is always "in
place", already known, and something that must be anxiously repeated'.[8] Here,
Kennedy similarly interrogates the options open to those from a marginal
culture and expresses the impossibility of a Scot retaining any sense of identity
outside the usual clichés.

The 'lies' created by such clichés are also the subject of 'The Role of Notable
Silences in Scottish History'. Kennedy, in fact, is frequently concerned with
the relationship between story writing and lies and here the particular lies
which are being explored are those which we have invented to describe our
Scottish selves: the story of Glen Flasprog, for example, or 'seven centuries of
Scottish slaughter' (168) and the myth of the Glasgow hardman. Other lies
include those about the 'weather ... bridies ... culture ... socialists ... hogmanay
and Irn Bru' (*Geometry*, 71). However, Bhabha also describes the 'ambivalence'
of the stereotype (66) and here the story does not simply deconstruct and dis-
card the models we have constructed about Scotland's past, since the 'lies' also
suggest a sort of truth; while they may leave out 'the huge, invisible, silent
roar of all the people who are too small to record' (*Geometry*, 64), there are also
lies which may help us learn something about the society in which we live;
Scotland's myths are a kind of lie but they may also tell us something about
ourselves; like the grid of the city, where 'ugly things happen under a beautiful
light' (67), they may offer parameters which help us to negotiate our way around
ourselves. After all, as the narrator concludes, 'there's no point being Scottish if
you can't make up your past as you go along' (64). Within such parameters
Scotland's disrupted, junctured past, a source of anxiety for so many, becomes a
site, for Kennedy, where Scotland's identity can be creatively reinvented.

Kennedy's stories also interrogate both gender and Scottishness via language
for often her stories demonstrate a keen sense of the subtleties and nuances within
discourse, the spaces between words which help construct and maintain distance
or, occasionally, approach proximity. Language both shapes and is shaped by our
personal and national identities; in 'Christine' for example, the narrator states:

Like many of us, I already had a variety of accents for private and social use. I
found it remarkably easy to sound like almost anyone I met. In fact ease had
very little to do with it – I would echo whoever I spoke to quite automatically,
moving from neutral to bland imitation and back again. Today this makes all
situations alike to me – I am consistently slightly out of place, but never
uncomfortably so. And if we are ever stuck for conversation people can always
ask me where I come from and I can always fail to answer them. (*Now*, 15–16)

This may well describe the situation of being Scottish (feeling out of place but never uncomfortably so) but it also highlights the way in which identities may be constructed via cultural and ideological narratives. 'At other times and in another country, that space had been her cunt' states Suzanne in 'Rockaway and the Draw' but now 'Ben called it his beaver',[9] reminding us that sexuality may also be shaped, or appropriated, by the language which we choose or have imposed upon us.

While gender and Scottishness may be concerns which constantly underlie Kennedy's work, they seldom set the agenda. In Janice Galloway's short stories, however, these are issues which are engaged with more directly. Galloway's first collection of stories – *Blood* (1991) – for example, takes for its title story the most fundamental marker of female identity, menstruation.[10] As Margery Metzstein has noted, here this natural female process is described as abhorrent, a subject of both fear and embarrassment.[11] The young music student in the story, for example, runs away from 'this unstoppable redness seeping through the fingers at [the girl's] open mouth' (*Blood*, 9), suggesting a grotesque parody of menstruation and society's responses to it.

Galloway's stories have a far stronger sense of place than Kennedy's and engage more directly with the ways in which attitudes towards women are shaped by our national identity. At times this is signalled by language, for Galloway's characters often speak in the west of Scotland written prose made familiar by Kelman's experimentations. However, rather than simply echoing her male counterparts, Galloway's stories offer female perspectives on the parameters seemingly created by west of Scotland men and their constructions of Scottish society.

It is this negotiation of the interfaces between urban Scottish identity and gender which is explored in Galloway's story 'Frostbite'. The opening line 'Christ it was cold' (*Blood*, 20) may seem to announce itself as being in familiar territory for recent Scottish writing, but the protagonist of the story is, rather unexpectedly, a young girl on her way home from piano practice. She encounters another familiar character, 'a man lumping up and over the top of the hill, flapping after the buses' (21) who falls and lies 'in the gutter like an old newspaper' (22). But while much recent Scottish writing has concerned itself with giving voice to such characters, this story is about the attitudes they hold towards women, and the ways in which such attitudes shape experience within Scotland. The man's whine about his encounter with a 'bad woman' is articulated in familiar terms: 'O he'll be that angry hen. He will and am that ashamed. Am a stupit old fool a am' (23). But the girl recognises that his words also position her in a particular way as she is excluded and negated by this particularly male discourse: 'The story. A man's story about what he would call a *bad woman*, and he would tell it as though she wasn't a woman herself, as if she shared his terms ... And she wouldn't be expected to argue – just stand and listen' (25). As the story develops, however, his attitude is more than simply negating; it is an expression of an underlying misogyny within Scottish society.

As the man gets on the bus and the girl, passively resigning herself to missing the bus rather than get on it with him, reminds him to 'look after yourself' (27), the man suddenly superimposes his earlier quarrel with the bad woman onto her, revealing a hatred of all women which runs through Scottish society: 'Aye. Keep away from bastart women, thats what yi do. Filth. Dirty whooers and filth the lot a them, the whole bloody lot. Get away fi me bitchahell – and he lunged a fist' (28). For many Scottish men, this implies, all women are 'bad women', 'dirty whooers' to be avoided. Yet the story ends with an assertion of sorts as the girl acknowledges her own, justified, anger, and the possibilities available to her beyond male agendas and her own collusion with them:

> Then, unexpectedly, she felt angry; violently, bitterly angry ... Who did he think he was, lashing out at people like that? And what sort of bloody fool was she, letting him? What right had he? What right had any of them? ... To hell with this waiting. There were other ways, other things to do. Take the underground; walk, dammit. Walk. (28)

A similar kind of assertion of alternative possibilities available to women is also found in the short story 'Fearless' (*Blood*, 110). Again, the story shows a young girl having to deal with a male type common in most small Scottish towns:

> The thing about Fearless was that he lived in a state of permanent anger. And the thing he was angriest about was being looked at ... He would storm up and down the main street, threatening, checking every face just in case they were looking then if he thought he'd caught you he would stop, stiffen and shout WHO ARE YOU TRYING TO MAKE A FOOL OF and attack. Sometimes he just attacked: depended on his mood. (111)

But as in 'Frostbite' the small girl in this story refuses to collaborate, lashing out in the face of Fearless's aggression, and exposing him for the bully he is: 'All I saw was a flash of white sock with my foot attached, swinging out and battering into his shin' (114). As Fearless limps away shouting about liberty, and the girl is told off by her mother, the victory is limited. Yet Galloway has, in this story, both interrogated the complacencies by which misogyny is often composed, and identified the refusal of a younger generation of women to collaborate with them:

> My mother is dead, and so, surely, is Fearless. But I still hear something like him; the chink and drag from the close-mouth in the dark, coming across open, derelict spaces at night, blustering at bus stops where I have to wait alone. With every other woman, though we're still slow to admit it, I hear it, still trying to lay down the rules. It's more insistent now because we're less ready to comply, look away and know our place. And I still see men smiling and ignoring it because they don't give a damn. They don't need to. It's not their battle. But it was ours and it still is. I hear my mother too and the warning is never far away. But I never could take a telling.
> The outrage is still strong, and I kick like a mule. (115)

In many of Galloway's stories, as in her longer fiction, her female protagonists are fragile, their identities sometimes barely intact in the face of the relationships or environments in which they find themselves. But her characters are seldom so fragile that they cannot, as here, analyse the boundaries which are containing them and, in the end, 'kick' against them. And from this anger, or grief or bitterness new possibilities arise; tentative, vigorous possibilities by which women may find ways to affirm their lives and female subjectivities in a patriarchal, sometimes hostile Scottish society.

Ali Smith no longer lives in Scotland and her collections of short stories *free love and other stories* (1995) and *Other Stories and other stories* (1999) concern themselves little with national identity.[12] Many of them are about the seeming fragility and fleetingness of relationships and often they take as their subject-matter moments of affirmation or even epiphany which run just below the surface of the quotidian. Like A. L. Kennedy, Smith is interested in the nature of fiction itself and the ways in which it both conceals and reveals. 'Tell me a story' says the narrator in 'A story of love' and later 'there was once ... a story that was told by way of other stories' (*Other*, 176) suggesting that while Smith's stories may at times seem brief and slender (one is called 'A quick one' (*free*, 31)) they are in fact interconnected, suggesting that life, and indeed identity, is made up from such brief and fragmentary moments.

Smith's style is to write via surface rather than texture, by words which skim over the presence of their subject-matter leaving much that is unsaid, numinously absent. The consequence in terms of her Scottishness is that while some of the stories may be set in Scotland – Edinburgh and its Grassmarket in 'Jenny Robertson your friend is not coming' (*free*, 41) or somewhere in the Highlands in 'Miracle Survivors' (*Other*, 103) – this seldom implies any cultural significance. While some of her material is unmistakably Scottish in origin – such as the string of north-east superstitions in 'Cold Iron' (*free*, 84–5) – this is not used to effectively posit questions of national identity, but is, rather, simply part of the narrative bricolage which creates the surface of Smith's fictional world.

The narrator in 'A story of love' requests a love story and this is the subject of many of Smith's works. They are tales of both past and present loves and of brief encounters, but, perhaps unusually for contemporary fiction, they also attempt to capture the joy of love alongside its bleaker moments; moments of affirmation – 'you longingly hopelessly fearfully selfishly ... wordlessly kissed me' (*Other*, 177) – alongside moments when love can apparently transform – 'I ... thought ... she was surrounded with yellow light' (*free*, 4–5). Frequently these love stories also raise wider questions about sexuality and gender as they explore lesbian experience. While this is not overtly present in Smith's work it underlies nearly all of her fiction. In *free love*, for example, a first lesbian relationship is described as potentially 'sordid' while the narrator suggests that such attitudes are, of course, relative: 'But then, what people think is sordid is relative after all; the person who saw us holding hands between our seats at the theatre one night thought it sordid enough to tell our mothers about us in anonymous letters' (*free*, 9). In *Other Stories and other stories* these relationships are less fraught and more affirmative, suggesting that the problematics of sexuality and gender are not, in fact, what actually matter. What matters are the moments of love if you are lucky enough to find them: 'Does it have to be a boy? It's always stories of boys and dogs. Can't it be a girl? Yes, you said, it can be a girl; true love stories are always interchangeable' (167).

Dilys Rose has rejected any overt label as a woman writer. 'I'm certainly not writing for women only or feminists only' she states:

> I'm a woman writer because I'm a woman. I believe in feminism, but I'm not setting out to promote that in what I write. I write stories about men as well. I live with a man. I can't deny that part of my life. It's a big part of it. I don't think labels are useful. They restrict interest rather than create it.[13]

Nevertheless, while, as for Kennedy, gender may not be what shapes the agenda in Rose's writing, it is a presence in her work. In many instances her stories deal with women who are slightly disorientated by their circumstances – 'New York' in *Our Lady of the Pickpockets* (1989),[14] for example, or 'A Little Bit of Trust' and 'Friendly Voices' in *Red Tides* (1993)[15] – suggesting that for women fear lies just under the surface in everyday situations, or in many of their encounters with men.

Rose's short stories portray women of all ages and in many situations, frequently expressing the complexities and ambiguities which are often part of women's everyday lives. The first story in *Red Tides*, for example, explores the guilt, frustration, exhaustion and love implicit in being the mother of small children. In the story a woman, a mother of two (who is only ever referred to as the 'mother'), travels away for a day and night to attend a conference, 'the first opportunity to be a person in her own right, to have some kind of independent presence, to be more than just a buggy-pushing, bag-laden donkey' (9). However, she is so exhausted that she sleeps through the whole evening. The story ends with a telephone conversation with her small daughter, and a description of her 'raging love', a juxtaposition pertinent for the mixed emotions involved in motherhood (10).

Similar tensions are explored in the story 'All the Little Loved Ones' where a woman describes the way in which she is trapped by the parameters of her own domesticity:

> My house is where my life happens. In it there is love, work, a roof, a floor, solidity, houseplants, toys, pots and pans, achievements and failures, inspirations and mistakes, recipes and instruction booklets, guarantees and spare parts, plans, dreams, memories. And there was no need, nothing here pushing me. It is nobody's fault. (75)

The woman, however, is 'approaching a precipice' (71), faced with the possibility of having an affair, and terrified by the thought of the consequences; 'So simple, so easy. All I have to do is rock on my heels, rock just a shade too far and we will all fall down. Two husbands, two wives and all the little loved ones' (76).

On the other side of the coin, in the story 'Over her Head', Rose explores the life of an older woman, a mother of grown-up children with children of their own. Here, Rose describes the alienation involved in growing old; the woman is frustrated by her body which seems at odds with her mind:

> The cold had made her legs hurt – fiery twinges in the veins – and the hairy winter coat added to her bulk and made her feel like nothing but a fat old woman. It wasn't what you were supposed to feel and she wasn't old, not really. In her mind she felt much the same as when she was a girl but her body betrayed her and everything around her ... hammered it home that she was getting on. (*Red*, 79)

The woman has signed up for a course in self-discovery, yet the story suggests that in her life, all experience is, one way or the other, about self-development and confrontation:

> With the family or the group, it was no different. You couldn't have a talk, just a plain old conversation, it was always sparring, one way or another. And if you watched the television, whether it was the news, a nature programme or a drama, what did it all boil down to but confrontation? (79–80)

As in many of Rose's stories life for women can be both complex and bewildering; while they may inhabit only domestic situations, women's lives are fraught with hard choices and confrontation, discourses of challenge and sometimes negation which often threaten deconstruction of self and the self's tenuous social and familial securities.

Rose is as suspicious of the label 'Scottish writer' as she is of one which determines her in terms of gender:

> I've been too interested in other countries to feel that Scotland is my only frame of reference ... I would like Scotland to be a little more international. We're a small country and we have the advantages and disadvantages of that. I think nationalism is something we should shake off a bit. Not because there aren't a lot of things that are particular to Scotland to write about, but that being Scottish is not a virtue or a vice in itself. (*Monsters*, 213)

In many ways Rose plays out these attitudes in her writing for, of all the women short-story writers dealt with here, her work is most clearly international in flavour. Many of her stories are set outside Scotland – in the United States, Canada or, in particular in her latest collection *War Dolls* (1998), in more exotic locations such as Mexico or Morocco.[16] However, while many of Rose's narrators are well travelled, some find it harder to shake off Scotland than they might wish. The potentially vulnerable protagonist of 'New York'

(*Our Lady*, 21) half wishes 'she were back in Scotland, in that cold country cottage' even though she has 'put aside every spare penny for her escape' (22). Similarly, the woman in 'Drifter' (34) feels a strange homesickness for Scotland and while she hopes she has cast off her Scottish (Calvinist) heritage of guilt and sin she finds she has 'a hard dark seam' of Scottishness running through her (40).

Rose's presentation of Scottishness is often as complex and ambiguous as her portrayal of female experience. In some instances Scotland can be seemingly summed up in the old clichés – 'too much to drink – The national excuse for everything' (*Red*, 61). However, the hypocritical twin faces of Scotland and of Edinburgh in particular are also explored in the story 'Street of the Three Terraces' where the trendy, yuppyish aspects of the reconstructed Leith and Scotland in general are set against the 'poof bashing' near Calton Hill. In Leith 'tourists and city people go to these new places, to eat, drink and soak up the local atmosphere' (63) while outside 'is the atmosphere, bands of off-duty seamen and lorry-drivers, looking for bars, brawls, women' (63).

These stories suggest a rather bleak Scotland; one, as Rose herself suggests, still bound, in spite of its recent window dressing, by its parochial male-orientated macho parameters. However, one of Rose's most recent stories, 'Why Do the Hands not Weep' (*War Dolls*, 205), reminds us that these discourses may not be entirely sufficient to describe Scottish life. The setting is a bar somewhere in rural Scotland. The decor suggests the usual Scottish clichés – the barmaid wears a 'tummy-hugging tartan skirt' (207) and the coffee is predictably dreadful. The bar, too, is a male enclave, and the men 'larded with oil, fish scales, blood and other unidentifiable clart' (208). One of the men approaches the narrator and with his banal chat-up line of 'Blondie' seems ready to fulfil an expected role. The woman is not surprised that a 'lone woman ... was still considered fair game' (209). However, when the man begins to talk, his subject is his dead son: 'It could have been drink but it was a stag ... Four boys dead, the stag too, just before dawn on the coast road south' (213). The story is poignant, reminding us that in Rose's stories things are not always what they seem and Scotland, and what it is made of, cannot always be delimited by simple binary oppositions of gender and culture.

While Rose is possibly the most international of women writers working in Scotland today, a newer voice, Laura Hird, offers work specifically located in Scotland. In *Nail and Other Stories* (1997) neither Hird's Scottishness nor her gender are foregrounded.[17] Nevertheless, many of her stories are unquestionably set in Scotland and often in very specific areas such as Edinburgh's Tollcross. Hird portrays the seedier side of urban life in contrast to Edinburgh's new-found capital status; 'Routes', for example, describes a twelve-year-old boy travelling on city buses to escape his miserable homelife, the limits of his desires circumscribed only by Fife across the water and the parts of the city he can see from the bus but can never hope to live in: 'Aw the lights across in Fife look barrie at night. It's like a whole other place just across that wee bit water'

(89). The class divide that Hird describes is not of course specific to Scotland, but it is the way in which it is manifested in Scottish experience that seems to interest her here. The events of the story 'Tillicoultry/Anywhere', for example, could, as its title suggests, take place anywhere, but the narrative setting in Tillicoultry is a reminder that its circumstances (wife swapping) may also occur in the familiar territory of central belt post-industrial Scotland.

'Tillicoultry/Anywhere' also, however, explores the way in which the wife, Christine, collaborates in her own loveless and manipulative marriage, and many of Hird's stories explore this element of female collusion – 'Of Cats and Women', for example, turns the table on any notion of women as straightforward victims by describing the response of an ex-wife to her husband's new lover, concluding with her violently killing her husband's cat. Such behaviour is common in Hird's world where both men and women are manipulative and exploitative. In the collection's closing story 'There Was a Soldier', Hird's preoccupations with exploitation and the seedy underbelly of Scottish life are brought together. Here, Hird sets out to undercut any vestiges of a romantic image of Scotland we might still have at the beginning of the twenty-first century. The Highlands – 'Dalwhinnie, Kingussie and Aviemore' – are only places to be by-passed, the Grampian mountains 'loomed ominously above them like ferocious painful bruises on the skyline' and the Caledonian forest has become 'a dense, black bastard of a forest' (186). With a nod to Scotland's frequently vaunted 'heroic' past, 'Culloden Moor' becomes simply a 'resting place for the victim of a Scottish soldier' (190). Hird's stories take no hostages and the image she presents of Scotland in these days of its so-called rejuvenation is a bleak one where the possibilities for both men and women seem far from optimistic.

A more compassionate description of Scottish life is offered by Candia McWilliam. Like Muriel Spark and Shena Mackay, whose work often resembles her own, McWilliam lives outside Scotland. However, her collection *Wait Till I Tell You* (1997) engages directly with Scotland,[18] since it is divided into two sections, 'North' and 'South', with a transitional story in the middle where a character travels between Scotland and England. However, the relationship between north and south is not simply oppositional, since some stories bridge the divide. The story 'Homesickness', for example, is in the 'North' section but describes a woman living in England. Here she and her husband meet with the usual preconceptions about her own country:

> What made Sandy laugh was when folk down here said, 'You must miss all that delicious fish.' He knew they were thinking of sturdy fishing smacks and fresh cod like a steak of sea-meat ... Sandy had two aunties who gutted white fish on Barra and hadn't felt their hands in years. They couldn't fancy fish but when it was in finger form, out of the deep freeze in the post office.
> As for heritage foodstuffs, sod that. (81)

The Scotland which is portrayed in McWilliam's work is often a rural or island one and perhaps because of this offers a more kindly Scotland than that presented in urban fiction. This is not to say that the stories are without analysis; 'Carla's Face' (13), for example, offers both a compassionate response to the woman who has come home to her island with her strange 'orange' face and a critique of why she may have wanted to leave it in the first place. Similarly, 'Those American Thoughts' expresses a young man's desire to escape the boundaries of his Scottish life and his Scottish relationship:

> He saw himself, thinking in America, in his mind. Since they were taking place in America these thoughts were unusually pure and free and big, with enormous cactuses and skyscrapers surrounding them. Everything was important in America. Those American thoughts of his were very important. (42)

Often too, the stories carry gentle reminders of the parameters which define Scottishness; in 'Shredding the Icebergs', for example, 'Scottish people come off particularly poorly' on hot days, 'We're spare and sandy, or red and beety, or sweaty and soft with burning cheeks and meeting eyebrows, or blue-skinned blondes with the junkie posture who go old overnight at twenty-eight or the second baby' (3–4). Such half-comic, half-recognisable traits may be virtually intangible but they light-heartedly articulate shared Scottish experience.

As in Rose's stories, the complexities and ambiguities of women's roles are also explored. Being a wife can be stifling as women become shut in by domesticity and obligation. In 'Seven Magpies', Morag prepares her husband's breakfast:

> So as to prepare Edward's breakfast without distressing him, for he had washed his hair this morning as usual, she lit a candle, and set it in the sink to consume the frying smells from the children's breakfast. No one could say she had not colluded in her own demotion from love object to servant. The extravagant acts of obedience and enslavement had, she thought, been a conduit of intimacy between them. Now these actions had set into resented habits and their certainly fetishistic significance had fallen away. (138)

Marriage, however, is also at times life-affirming in McWilliam's work, an act of sustained compassion as it is 'With Every Tick of the Heart' (208), where the couple Denise and Norman make quiet allowances for each other after waiting years to marry. Motherhood also provokes complex and ambiguous responses. Children can be 'devious' with 'dissembling ignorance' (160) but the thought of losing them is the 'only only' as the mothers in the story of that name imagine their heads 'cut off at the neck, their frozen sweetness of face under the streaming curtailed hair' (31).

Kennedy, Galloway, Smith, Rose, Hird and McWilliam represent the most successful women short-story writers in Scotland today, but there are many new voices emerging, often via anthologies and competitions. Caroline Mack, for example, has been a runner-up in the Ian St James award, and appears in *Shorts*, while Linda Cracknell has also been a winner of the Macallan/*Scotland on Sunday* competition. Regi Claire's *Inside-Outside* was recently shortlisted for the Saltire First Book Award,[19] and Ruth Thomas's *Sea Monster Tattoo* has been shortlisted in the past. Thomas has recently published her second collection, *The Dance Settee and Other Stories.*[20]

These writers describe women in many roles, and are bound neither by the old parameters of women's experience nor by a particularly Scottish agenda. However, while gender and nation may not be foregrounded in their work, these are very much part of the texture. That we cannot discuss their work more fully is a marker of the fact that while short stories may be regarded by some as something of a second-rate genre in Britain, there are many Scottish women writers who are adopting the form to offer glimpses, diverse and complex, of 'life swiftly apprehended'.

Notes

1. Candia McWilliam (ed.), *Shorts 2: The Macallan / Scotland on Sunday Short Story Collection* (Edinburgh: Polygon, 1999), p. vii.
2. Naomi Mitchison, *Beyond This Limit: Selected Shorter Fiction*, ed. Isobel Murray (Edinburgh: Scottish Academic Press, 1986).
3. Violet Jacob, *Flemington and Tales from Angus*, ed. Carol Anderson (Edinburgh: Canongate, 1998).
4. Muriel Spark, 'The Seraph and the Zambesi', in Spark, *The Go-Away Bird* (London: Macmillan, 1958); Muriel Spark, *Bang-Bang You're Dead* (London: Granada, 1960).
5. A. L. Kennedy, *Night Geometry and the Garscadden Trains* (1990; London: Phoenix, 1993).
6. A. L. Kennedy, 'Not Changing the World', in Ian A. Bell (ed.), *Peripheral Visions: Images of Nationhood in Contemporary British Fiction* (Cardiff: University of Wales Press, 1995), pp. 100–2 (100).
7. 'Friday Payday', in Kennedy, *Now that You're Back* (London: Jonathan Cape, 1994), p. 142.
8. See Homi K. Bhabha, *The Location of Culture* (London and New York: Routledge, 1994), p. 66.
9. A. L. Kennedy, 'Rockaway and the Draw', in Kennedy, *Original Bliss* (London: Jonathan Cape, 1997), p. 10.
10. Janice Galloway, *Blood* (London: Secker & Warburg, 1991). Galloway's second collection is *Where You Find It* (London: Jonathan Cape, 1996).
11. Margery Metzstein, 'Of Myths and Men: Aspects of Gender in the Fiction of Janice Galloway', in Gavin Wallace and Randall Stevenson (eds), *The Scottish Novel since the Seventies* (Edinburgh: Edinburgh University Press, 1993), pp. 136–46.
12. Ali Smith, *free love and other stories* (London: Virago, 1995); *Other Stories and other stories* (London: Granta Books, 1999).
13. Dilys Rose in Gillean Somerville-Arjat and Rebecca E. Wilson (eds), *Sleeping with Monsters: Conversations with Scottish and Irish Women Poets* (Edinburgh: Polygon, 1990), pp. 208–15 (212).
14. Dilys Rose, *Our Lady of the Pickpockets* (London: Secker & Warburg, 1989), p. 21.
15. Dilys Rose, *Red Tides* (London: Secker & Warburg, 1993), pp. 45 and 11.
16. Dilys Rose, *War Dolls* (London: Review, 1998).

17. Laura Hird, *Nail and Other Stories* (Edinburgh: Rebel Inc., 1997).
18. Candia McWilliam, *Wait Till I Tell You* (London: Bloomsbury, 1997).
19. Regi Claire, *Inside-Outside* (Edinburgh: Scottish Cultural Press, 1998).
20. Ruth Thomas, *Sea Monster Tattoo and Other Stories* (Edinburgh: Polygon, 1997);
    The Dance Settee and Other Stories (Edinburgh: Polygon, 1999).

Selective Bibliography of Writing by Other Contemporary Scottish Women Writers

Lynne Stark

This selective bibliography has defined 'Scottish' in the broadest terms, including work by women writers born in Scotland, resident here, or, to use Muriel Spark's phrase, 'Scottish by formation'. Most but not all titles listed were published between 1990 and 1999. Publications referred to elsewhere in the book are not normally relisted here. Only parallel text Gaelic publications have been listed.

Fiction

Aboulela, Leila, *The Translator* (Edinburgh: Polygon, 1999).
Atkinson, Kate, *Behind the Scenes at the Museum* (London: Doubleday, 1995).
——. *Human Croquet* (London: Doubleday, 1997).
Broomfield, Janet, *A Fallen Land* (London: The Bodley Head, 1990).
——. *Australia Lane* (London: Little, Brown & Company, 1995).
——. *A Song in the Street* (London: Little, Brown & Company, 1996).
Bryan, Lynne, *Envy at the Cheese Handout* (London: Faber & Faber, 1995).
——. *Gorgeous* (London: Sceptre, 1999).
Burnett, Margaret, *Indians Don't Kiss: A Novel* (Edinburgh: Polygon, 1996).
Cherkawska, Catherine, *The Golden Apple* (London: Century, 1990).
Christie, Anne, *My Secret Gorilla* (London: Piatkus, 1981).
——. *Growing Wings* (London: Piatkus, 1993).
Claire, Regi, *Inside-Outside* (Edinburgh: Scottish Cultural Press, 1998).
Close, Ajay, *Official and Doubtful* (London: Secker & Warburg, 1996).
——. *Forespoken* (London: Secker & Warburg, 1998).
Crow, Christine, *Miss X, or The Wolf Woman* (London: The Women's Press, 1990).
Davie, Elspeth, *Creating a Scene* (London: Calder & Boyars, 1971).
——. *The High Tide Talker and Other Stories* (London: Hamish Hamilton, 1976).
——. *Climbers on a Stair* (London: Hamish Hamilton, 1978).
——. *The Night of the Funny Hats* (London: Hamish Hamilton, 1980).
——. *A Traveller's Room* (London: Hamish Hamilton, 1985).
——. *Coming to Light* (London: Hamish Hamilton, 1989).
——. *Death of a Doctor and Other Stories* (London: Sinclair-Stevenson, 1992).
Davis, Margaret Thomson, *A Woman of Property* (London: Century, 1991).
——. *A Sense of Belonging* (London: Century, 1993).
——. *Hold Me Forever* (London: Century, 1994).

——. *Kiss Me No More* (London: Century, 1995).

——. *A Kind of Immortality* (London: Century, 1996).

——. *Burning Ambition* (Edinburgh: B&W Publishing, 1997).

——. *Gallachers* (London: Century, 1998).

——. *The Glasgow Belle* (Edinburgh: B&W Publishing, 1998).

Dewar, Isla, *Keeping up with Magda* (London: Headline Book Publishing, 1995).

——. *Women Talking Dirty* (London: Headline Book Publishing, 1996).

——. *Giving up on Ordinary* (London: Headline Book Publishing, 1997).

——. *It Could Happen to You* (London: Headline Book Publishing, 1998).

Dunnett, Dorothy, *Moroccan Traffic* (London: Chatto & Windus, 1991).

——. *Scales of Gold* (London: Michael Joseph, 1991).

——. *The Niccolo Dossier* (London: Michael Joseph, 1992).

——. *The Niccolo Dossier 2* (London: Michael Joseph, 1992).

——. *The Unicorn Hunt* (London: Michael Joseph, 1993).

——. *To Lie with Lions* (London: Michael Joseph, 1995).

——. *Caprice and Rondo* (London: Michael Joseph, 1997).

Elphinstone, Margaret, *The Incomer* (London: The Women's Press, 1987).

——. *A Sparrow's Flight* (Edinburgh: Polygon, 1989).

——. *An Apple from a Tree* (short stories). (London: The Women's Press, 1990).

——. *Islanders* (Edinburgh: Polygon, 1994).

——. *The Sea Road* (Edinburgh: Canongate, 2000).

Fell, Alison (ed.), *The Seven Cardinal Virtues* (London: Serpent's Tail, 1990).

——. *Mer de Glace* (London: Methuen, 1991).

—— (ed.), *Serious Hysterics* (London: Serpent's Tail, 1992).

——. *The Pillow Boy of the Lady Onogoro* (London: Serpent's Tail, 1994).

——. *The Mistress of Lilliput* (London: Doubleday, 1999).

Fine, Anne, *Taking the Devil's Advice* (London: Viking, 1990).

——. *Telling Liddy: A Sour Comedy* (London: Bantam, 1998).

Galford, Ellen, *Moll Cutpurse* (Edinburgh: Stramullion, 1984).

——. *The Fires of Bride* (London: The Women's Press, 1986).

——. *Queendom Come* (London: Virago, 1990).

——. *The Dyke and the Dybbuk* (London: Virago, 1993).

Gerber, Mary, *Maiden Voyage* (Glasgow: Kailyards Press, 1992).

Gladstone-Millar, Lynne, *The Long Yesterday: The Story of Patrick and Rosie* (Bishop Auckland, Durham: Pentland Press, 1995).

Gray, Muriel, *The Trickster* (London: HarperCollins, 1994).

——. *Furnace* (London: HarperCollins, 1997).

Hayton, Sian, *Cells of Knowledge* (Edinburgh: Polygon, 1989).

——. *Governors* (Nairn: Balnain, 1992).

——. *Hidden Daughters* (Edinburgh: Polygon, 1992).

——. *Last Flight* (Edinburgh: Polygon, 1993).

Henderson, Meg, *The Holy City: A Tale of Clydebank* (London: Flamingo, 1997).

Heron, Liz, *A Red River* (London: Virago, 1996).

Heyman, Kathryn, *The Breaking* (London: Phoenix House, 1997).

Hird, Laura, *Born Free* (Edinburgh: Rebel Inc, 1999).

Hodgman, Jackie, *The Fish in White Sauce Incident* (Aberdeen: Keith Murray Publishing, 1992).

Holms, Joyce, *Festival of Love* (London: Hale, 1991).
——. *Love on the Way* (London: Hale, 1991).
——. *Payment Deferred* (London: Headline Books, 1996).
——. *Bad Vibes* (London: Headline Books, 1998).
——. *Thin Ice* (London: Headline Books, 1999).
Knight, Alanna, *Killing Cousins: An Inspector Faro Mystery* (London: Macmillan, 1990).
——. *A Quiet Death* (London: Macmillan, 1991).
——. *The Sweet Cheat Gone* (Wallington: Severn House, 1992).
——. *To Kill a Queen* (London: Macmillan, 1992).
——. *The Evil that Men Do* (London: Macmillan, 1993).
——. *Strathblair: The Novel* (London: BBC Books, 1993).
——. *This Outward Angel* (Sutton: Severn House, 1993).
——. *Inspector Faro and the Edinburgh Mysteries* (London: Pan, 1994).
——. *The Missing Duchess* (London: Macmillan, 1994).
——. *The Bull Slayers* (London: Macmillan, 1995).
——. *Murder by Appointment* (London: Macmillan, 1996).
Lillie, Helen, *Home to Strathblane* (Glendaruel: Argyll Publishing, 1993).
——. *Strathblane and Away* (Glendaruel: Argyll Publishing, 1996).
——. *The Rocky Island* (Glendaruel: Argyll Publishing, 1998).
Lingard, Anne, *Figure in a Landscape* (London: Headline Review, 1996).
Lingard, Joan, *After Colette* (London: Sinclair-Stevenson, 1993).
——. *Dreams of Love and Modest Glory* (London: Sinclair-Stevenson, 1995).
Livesey, Margot, *Criminals* (London: Secker & Warburg, 1996).
McCabe, Mary, *Everwinding Times* (Glendaruel: Argyll Publishing, 1994).
McDermid, Val, *Final Edition* (London: The Women's Press, 1991).
——. *Dead Beat* (London: Gollancz, 1992).
——. *Kick Back* (London: Gollancz, 1993).
——. *Union Jack* (London: The Women's Press, 1993).
——. *Crackdown* (London: HarperCollins, 1994).
——. *Clean Break* (London: HarperCollins, 1995).
——. *The Mermaids Singing* (London: HarperCollins, 1995).
——. *Blues Genes* (London: HarperCollins, 1996).
——. *Booked for Murder: The Fifth Lindsay Gordon Mystery* (London: HarperCollins, 1996).
——. *The Wire in the Blood* (London: HarperCollins, 1997).
——. *Star Struck* (London: HarperCollins, 1998).
——. *A Place of Execution* (London: HarperCollins, 1999).
McGregor, Iona, *Alice in Shadowtime* (Edinburgh: Polygon, 1992).
McIntosh, Isobel, *Menlove Affairs* (Bishop Auckland, Durham: Marionette Books, 1998).
Mackay, Rosemary with Sheena Blackhall and Wilma Murray, *Three's Company: A Collection of Stories from Aberdeen by Three Leading Writers*; selected and introduced by Jessie Kesson (Aberdeen: Keith Murray, 1989).
Mackay, Shena, *Dunedin* (London: Heinemann, 1992).
——. *The Laughing Academy* (short stories) (London: Heinemann, 1993).
——. *The Orchard on Fire* (London: Heinemann, 1995).
——. *The Artist's Widow* (London: Cape, 1998).
——. *The Worlds* [sic] *Smallest Unicorn* (London: Cape, 1999).

McKinlay, Margaret, *Double Entry* (London: The Crime Club, HarperCollins, 1992).
——. *The Caring Game* (London: The Crime Club, HarperCollins, 1993).
——. *Legacy* (London: The Crime Club, HarperCollins, 1993).
Mackinnon, Marianne, *The Alien Years* (n.p.: Lewes Book Guild, 1991).
——. *The Deluge: A Tale of Florence in Flood* (Glasgow: Hillcrest, 1993).
——. *The Quarry* (Glasgow: Hillcrest, 1995).
Milton, Saba, *Garganette, The Amazing Story of a Giant Female* (London: Open Gate Press, 1991).
Mina, Denise, *Garnethill* (London: Bantam, 1998).
Morin, Carole, *Lampshades* (London: Secker & Warburg, 1991).
——. *Dead Glamorous: The Autobiography of Seduction & Self-Destruction* (London: Gollancz, 1996).
Penney, Bridget, *Honeymoon with Death and Other Stories* (Edinburgh: Polygon, 1991).
—— with Paul Holman (eds), *The Invisible Reader* (London: Invisible Books, 1995).
Pilcher, Rosamunde, *The Blue Bedroom and Other Stories* (Sevenoaks: Coronet Books, Hodder & Stoughton, 1990).
——. *September* (Sevenoaks: New English Library, Hodder & Stoughton, 1990).
——. *Flowers in the Rain and Other Stories* (Sevenoaks: New English Library, Hodder & Stoughton, 1991).
——. *Coming Home* (London: Hodder & Stoughton, 1995).
Prince, Alison, *The Witching Tree* (London: Allison & Busby, 1996).
Randall, Deborah, *White Eyes, Dark Ages* (Newcastle-upon-Tyne: Bloodaxe, 1993).
Reynolds, Siri, *House of Rooms* (Edinburgh: Polygon, 1997).
Ross, Bess, *A Bit of Crack and Car Culture and Other Stories* (Nairn: Balnain Books, 1990).
——. *Those Other Times* (Nairn: Balnain Books, 1991).
——. *Dangerous Gifts* (Nairn: Balnain Books, 1994).
——. *Strath* (Edinburgh: Canongate Books, 1997).
Scott, Manda, *Hen's Teeth* (London: The Women's Press, 1996).
——. *Night Mares* (London: Headline, 1998).
——. *Stronger than Death* (London: Headline, 1999).
Stewart, Isobel, *A Time to Trust* (London: Robert Hale, 1994).
Stewart Mary, *The Prince and the Pilgrim* (London: Hodder & Stoughton, 1995).
Stirling, Jessica, *The Penny Wedding* (London: Hodder & Stoughton, 1991).
——. *The Welcome Light* (London: Hodder & Stoughton, 1991).
Tuttle, Lisa (ed.), *Skin of the Soul: New Horror Stories by Women* (London: The Women's Press, 1990).
——. *Memories of the Body: Tales of Desire and Transformation* (London: Grafton, 1992).
—— (ed.), *Crossing the Border: Tales of Erotic Ambiguity* (London: Indigo, 1998).

Poetry

Alderson, J. M., *The Pearl Seekers and Other Poems* (Edinburgh: School of Poets, 1997).
Allan, Elizabeth, *Ballater Bairn and Other Poems by Betty Allan* (Skene, Aberdeen: Elizabeth Allan, 1985).
——. *Awa' Fae Ballater; Scots Verses by Betty Allan* (Skene, Aberdeen: Elizabeth Allan, 1987).

Andrew, Moira, *Summer Child: A New Poem by Moira Andrew*, illustrated by Lillian Elliot (Sanction, nr. York: Santone Press, 1988).

Armstrong, Kate, *Wild Mushrooms* (Carnoustie: Blind Serpent Press, 1993).

Baker, Rosemary, *From Both Sides Now: Poems by Rosemary Baker* (Kirkcudbright: Markings, 1997).

Batchelor, Glynda, *Our Voices to the Wind: Poems from Shetland* (Brae, Shetland: Glynda Batchelor, 1993).

Bateman, Meg, *Aotromachd agus Dain Eile / Lightness and Other Poems* (Edinburgh: Polygon, 1997).

—— and Kathryn Heyman (selected by), *Getting Lippy: An Anthology of Poetry Challenging Male Violence. Poems from the 1995 Edinburgh Peace Festival's Poetry Competition* (Edinburgh: Democratic Left Edinburgh, 1996).

Beattie, Kath, *Tangihana and Other Korero*, illustrated by Lyn Youngson (Kirriemuir: Peter Youngson, 1992).

Beckett, Mavis Duncan. *A Wee Keek intae the Past: History in Verse by Mavis Duncan Beckett* (Kirkcaldy: Jedu Press, 1996).

Bourne, Kay, *Now and Again: Poems by Kay Bourne* (Edinburgh: Stockbridge Press, 1991).

Brackenbury, Rosalind (ed.), *Riches of Writing: A Collection of Prose and Poetry Put Together by Members of Her Creative Writing Classes during the Session 1985–6* (Edinburgh: University of Edinburgh Extra-Mural Studies, 1986).

——. *Telling Each Other It Is Possible* (Stamford: Taxus Press, 1987).

——. *Making for the Secret Places* (Exeter: Taxus Press, 1989).

——. *Going Home the Long Way round the Mountain* (Exeter: Taxus Press, 1993).

——. *The Beautiful Routes of the West* (Santa Barbara: Fithian Press, 1996).

—— and Brian Johnston (eds), *The Golden Goose Hour: The First Shore Poets' Anthology* (Edinburgh: Taranis Books, 1994).

Brown, Eleanor, *Maiden Speech* (Newcastle-upon-Tyne: Bloodaxe, 1996).

Brown, Elspeth, *Skifter: Poetry by Elspeth Brown* (Kirkcudbright: Wider Eye Publications, 1996).

Brown, Janet, *Childhood Memories of East Wemyss* (East Wemyss: Janet Brown, 1991).

Brown, Margaret Gillies, *Looking towards Light* (Dundee: Blind Serpent Press, 1988).

——. *Footsteps of the Goddess* (Edinburgh: Akros Publications, 1994).

—— and Caroline MacKay, *Errol: Poems of the Village* (Errol, Tayside: Silver River, 1997).

Butler, May, *Half in Hauf: Book of Poems* (Hawick: May Butler, 1990).

——. *A Teri Treasure* (Hawick: May Butler, 1992).

Butler, Rhoda, *Snyivveries: Shetland Poems By Rhoda Butler*, illustrated by the author (Lerwick: The Shetland Times, 1986).

Carnegie, Agnes C., *The Timeless Flow: The Selected Poems of Agnes C. Carnegie* (Aberdeen: Aberdeen University Press, 1985).

Cartmell, Fiona, *Stagefright*, illustrated Morag Stevenson (Aberdeen: Keith Murray, 1988).

Cook, Margaret Fulton, *Spell Bound* (Gourock: Itinerant, 1989).

——. *Good Girls Don't Cry* (Edinburgh: Chapman, 1996).

Crowe, Anna, *Skating Out of the House* (Clastock, Cornwall: Peterloo Poets, 1997).

Daiches, Jenni, *Mediterranean* (Aberdeen: Scottish Cultural Press, 1995).

De Luca, Christine, *Voes & Sounds: Poems in English and Shetland Dialect* (Lerwick: The Shetland Library, 1995).

Doubell, Patricia, *A Taste of Scotia* (Perth: Seil Publications, 1995).

Evans, Irene, *Slim Volume 1* (Muthill, Perthshire: Patchwork Press, 1997).

Evans, Sally, *Some Sunny Intervals: Poems by Sally Evans* (Edinburgh: Sally Evans, 1985).

——. *Millenial; or, The Far Side of English: A Poem* (Edinburgh: Diehard, 1994).

——. *Looking for Scotland: Poems by Sally Evans* (Salzburg: University of Salzburg, 1996).

Everill, Joyce, *Granny's Button Box: Poems and Memories by Joyce Everill* (Aberdeen: Aberdeen City Libraries for Aberdeen District Council, 1989).

——. *Knit One – Purl One: More Poems and Memories by Joyce Everill* (Aberdeen: Aberdeen City Arts Libraries, 1990).

Fell, Alison, *The Crystal Owl* (London: Virago, 1988).

——. *Dreams, Like Heretics: New and Selected Poems* (London: Serpent's Tail, 1997).

Fellows, Gerrie, *Technologies* (Edinburgh: Polygon, 1990).

Ferguson, Gillian, *Air for Sleeping Fish* (Newcastle-upon-Tyne: Bloodaxe, 1997).

Forbes, Lillias, *Turning a Fresh Eye* (Kirkcaldy: Akros, 1998).

Forrest-Thomson, Veronica, *Collected Poems and Translations* (London: Allardyce Barnett, 1990).

Forsyth, Moira, *What the Negative Reveals*, ed. Angus Dunn, drawings by Joyce W. Cairns (Inverness: art.book, n.d.).

Fraser, Bashabi, *Life* (Edinburgh: Diehard, 1997).

Frater, Anne, *Fon t-slige: Under the Shell* (Glasgow: Gairm, 1995).

Galloway, Kathy, *Love Burning Deep: Poems and Lyrics* (London: Society for Promoting Knowledge, 1993).

——. *Talking to the Bones: Poems, Prayers and Meditations* (London: Society for Promoting Knowledge, 1996).

Garry, Flora, *Collected Poems* (Edinburgh: Gordon Wright Publishing, 1995).

Gibson, Magi, *Kicking Back* (Glasgow: Taranis Books, 1993).

—— with Helen Lamb, *Strange Fish*, illustrated by Suzanne Gyseman (Glasgow: Duende, 1997).

Gilles, Valerie, *The Chanter's Tune*, illustrated by Will Maclean (Edinburgh: Canongate, 1990).

—— with Will Maclean and William Gillies, *St. Kilda Waulking Song* (Edinburgh: Morning Star, 1998).

Harbour, Josephine Singleton, *My World* (Rothesay: Writers Rostrum, 1986).

——. *Verse from the Bible* (Rothesay: Writers Rostrum, 1986).

Hardie, Kath, *Was Your Mother's Name Jocasta?* (Edinburgh: Rookbook, 1997).

Hendry, Diana, *Making Blue* (Calstock, Cornwall: Peterloo Poets, 1995).

Herd, Tracey, *No Hiding Place* (Newcastle-upon-Tyne: Bloodaxe, 1996).

Holland, Vincenza, *Mrs Turnbull's Tree: Poems by Vincenza Holland* (Sandyford, Newcastle: The Mote Press, 1990).

Hood, Assunta Arrighi (publishes under the name Assunta), *Whetted Wisdom: A Collection of Poems & Short Stories* (Scotland: Viaduct Press, 1994).

——. *A Field of Poppies: Popular Poems* (Scotland: V.A., 1995).

Howden, Elizabeth, *Leaves in the Wind* (St Andrews: Elizabeth Howden, 1985).

Johnson, Alison, *The Wicked Generation* (Belfast: Blackstaff Press, 1992).

Kermack, Alison, *Restricted Vocabulary* (South Queensferry, Edinburgh: Clocktower Press, 1991).

——. *Writing Like a Bastard* (Edinburgh: Rebel Inc, 1998).

Lamb, Sarah and Magi Gibson, *Strange Fish*, illustrated by Suzanne Gyseman (Glasgow: Duende, 1997).

Lumsden, M. S., *Affirmations: Poems in Scots and English*, ed. Evelyn E. Gavin, illustrations by Heather Rae (Aberdeen: Aberdeen University Press, 1990).

McCammond, Christine, *Vinegar and Brown Paper* (Gourock: Itinerant, 1988).

MacDonald, Anna, *Dundee Pride* (Dundee: Temperance Productions, 1987).

———. *The Endless Search: Collection of Poems, Limericks and Nonsense Verse* (Dundee: Temperance Productions, 1989).

———. *Apron Strings* (Dundee: Temperance Productions, 1990).

———. *Happy Birthday Dundee* (Dundee: Temperance Productions, 1991).

Macdonald, Jean, *A Skirt with Pockets: A Lifetime of Poems* (Watt, New Lanark: Geddes & Grosset, 1995).

McGee, Kate Sweeney, *Still Lips Moving* (Glasgow: Pussycat Press, 1998).

MacInnes, Fiona, *To Step among Wrack* (Kirkwall: The Orkney Press, 1988).

MacInnes, Mairi, *Elsewhere and Back: New and Selected Poems* (Newcastle-upon-Tyne: Bloodaxe, 1993).

Mackay, Caroline and Margaret Gillies Brown, *Errol: Poems of the Village* (Errol, Tayside: Silver River, 1997).

Mackinnon, Rayne, *Northern Elegies* (Edinburgh: Netherbow Centre, 1986).

———. *Orpheus* (Edinburgh: School of Poets, 1986).

MacLeod, Anne, *Standing by Thistles* (Edinburgh: Scottish Cultural Press, 1997).

———. *Just the Caravaggio* (Salzburg: Poetry Salzburg at the University of Salzburg, 1999).

McMenemy, Varry, *Beseeching Paradise Lost* (London: Excalibur Press, 1992).

Macnaughtan, Maureen, *The Kissing Game* (Kirkcaldy: Akros, 1997).

MacNaughtan, Moira, *Kuala Lumpur Traffic* (Farcham: National Poetry Foundation, 1997).

Malfatti, Teresina, *First Collection* (Rothesay: Writers Rostrum, 1986).

Middleton, Joanne M. *The Impending Desert* (Bedfordshire: New Millennium Books, 1998).

Miller, Pat, *Whistling in the Dark; Poems by Pat Miller*, images by Tom Heatley (Jedburgh: Out of Bounds, 1989).

Mitchell, Elma, *People Etcetera: Poems New and Selected* (Calstock, Cornwall: Peterloo Poets, 1987).

Nelson, Gillian, *Walking in the Garden* (Sutton: Severn House, 1994).

NicDhomnail, Mairi, *Mo Lorgan Fhin / My Own Footprints* (Inverness: Crois-Eilein, 1985).

Nicholson, Marjory, *'Ah Wish ah Hid a Fiver': A Collection of Poems by Marjory Nicholson* (Banff & Buchan: Banff & Buchan District Council, 1994).

Nicneill, Siusaidh, *All My Braided Colours* (Edinburgh: Scottish Cultural Press, 1996).

Niven, Liz, *Past Presents* (Kirkcaldy: Akros, 1997).

Paisley, Janet, *Pegasus in Flight: Poems and Illustrations* (Edinburgh: Rookbook, 1989).

———. *Biting through Skins: Poems and Illustrations* (Edinburgh: Rookbook, 1992).

———. *Wildfire* (Edinburgh: Taranis Books, 1993).

———. *Alien Crop* (Edinburgh: Chapman, 1996).

———. *Reading the Bones* (Edinburgh: Canongate, 1999).

Pitman, Joy, *Telling Gestures* (Edinburgh: Chapman, 1993).

Pogson, Patricia, *Rattling the Handle* (Todmorden, Lancs.: Littlewood & Arc, 1990).
——. *The Tides in the Basin* (Newcastle-upon-Tyne: Flambard Press, 1994).
Prince, Alison, *Having Been in the City* (Edinburgh: Taranis Books, 1994).
Ransford, Tessa, *Shadows from the Greater Hill*, photographs by Edwin Johnston (Edinburgh: Ramsay Head, 1987).
——. *A Dancing Innocence* (Edinburgh: MacDonald, 1988).
——. *Seven Valleys* (Edinburgh: Ramsay Head, 1991).
——. *Scottish Selection: Poems by Tessa Ransford* (Kirkcaldy: Akros, 1998).
Rich, Lilianne Grant, *The Pink Rose of Chenonceaux: A Pot-Pourri of Verses and True Stories* (Aberdeen: Rainbow, 1988).
Robertson, Jenny, *Beyond the Border* (Blackford, Perthshire: Chapman, 1989).
——. *Ghetto: Poems of the Warsaw Ghetto* (Oxford: Lion, 1989).
——. *Coroskirr* (Oxford: Lion Publishing, 1992).
——. *Insignia: A Gathering of Poems* (St Petersburg: Jenny Robertson, 1993).
——. *Loss and Language* (Edinburgh: Chapman, 1994).
Robertson, Laurna, *The Ranselman's Tale* (Lerwick: Shetland Publishing, 1990).
Roxman, Susanna, *Broken Angels* (Edinburgh: Dionysia Press, 1996).
Salt, Chrys, *Daffodils at Christmas* (Kirkcudbright: Markings, 1996).
Sangster, Maureen, with Kenny Storne and Colin Kerr, *Different People* (Edinburgh: Straightline, 1987).
——. *To Christ* (Glasgow: Galdragon Press, 1994).
——. *Out of the Urn* (Edinburgh: Scottish Cultural Press, 1997).
Saunders, Margaret, *Bridging the Gap: Immigrant Poems* (Goderich, Ontario: Moonstone, 1990).
Shaw, Brenda, *The Cold Winds of Summer* (Dundee: Blind Serpent Press, 1987).
Simmons, Jenni, *I Was Glad about the Butterfly*, photographs by Iain Robertson (Brae, Shetland: Nelson Smith Printing, 1988).
Simpson, Elizabeth, *It's Twilight at St. Fergus: A Collection of Private Verse by Elizabeth Simpson* (Fyvie: New Concept Publishing, 1995).
——. *Let Sleeping Dogs Lie* (Fyvie: New Concept Publishing, 1995).
——. *Let's Pretend Some More* (Fyvie: New Concept Publishing, 1995).
——. *A Scottish Retreat: Simple Verse, A Compilation of Poetry by Elizabeth Simpson* (Fyvie: New Concept Publishing, 1995).
Sinclair, Margaret, *Windae Hingin' and Busker Singin': The Poetry of old Glasgow* (Latheronwheel, Caithness: Whittles, 1991).
Smith, Morelle, *Deepwater Terminal* (Edinburgh: Diehard, 1998).
Steele, Judy, *The Aikwood Cycle: Poetry by Judy Steele*, calligraphy by Iain Black (Selkirk: Aikwood Press, 1995).
Stewart, Edie, *Fair Maids of February* (Eskdalemuir: Kagyu Samye-Ling, 1985).
Sulter, Maud, *As a Black Woman* (London: Akira Press, 1985).
——. *Zabat: Poetics of a Family Tree; Poems 1986–89* (Hebden Bridge: Urban Fox, 1989).
——. *Necropolis* (London: Urban Fox, 1990).
Sutherland, Stella, *A Celebration* (Bressay, Shetland: Stella Sutherland, 1991).
Symms, Dorcas, *Six Poems* (Edinburgh: School of Poets, 1997).
Warner, Val, *Before Lunch* (Manchester: Carcanet, 1986).
——. *Tooting Idyll* (Manchester: Carcanet, 1998).

Whamond, Dorothy, *Fifteen Minutes in Carthage* (Edinburgh: Rookbook Publications, 1996).
Wilkie, Pamela, *Voyager* (Calstock, Cornwall: Peterloo Poets, 1997).
Wyness, Lys, *Salty City* (Aberdeen: Langstane Press, 1994).
Young, Judith, *The Glen and Other Places* (Perth: Seil, 1995).

Drama

Di Mambro, Ann Marie, 'The Letter Box', in Alasdair Cameron (ed.), *Scot-Free: New Scottish Plays* (London: Nick Hern, 1990).
——. *Tally's Blood* – rehearsal script (Edinburgh: Traverse Theatre, 1990).
Downie, Anne, *The White Bird Passes*, adapted by Anne Downie from the novel by Jessie Kesson (Glasgow: Anne Downie, 1994).
——. *The Witches of Pollock* (Glasgow: Anne Downie, 1994).
——. *Waiting on One*; music by D. Andrews and D. McLellan (Glasgow: Anne Downie, 1996).
Hendry, Joy, *Gang Doun wi a Sang: A Play about William Soutar* (Edinburgh: Diehard, 1995).
Kerr, Ann, *The Last Threads* (Glasgow: Clydeside Press, 1990).
McLean, Linda, *Riddance* (London: Nick Hern, 1999).
MacPhail, Andrea, *Dead Nice: A Black Comedy in One Act* (Malvern: Kenyon-Deane, 1995).
——. *That Old Black Magic: A Black Comedy in One Act* (Malvern: Kenyon-Deane, 1995).
Millie, Gray, *Bare Bones Have No Bite* (Glasgow: Brown, Son & Ferguson, 1997).
——. *Burning Issues: A Hilarious Black Comedy* (Glasgow: Brown, Son & Ferguson, 1997).
Rae, Isabella C., *Bedbaths and Broomsticks* (Cumbernauld, Glasgow: Pedersen Press, 1992).
——. *Happy Death Day* (Cumbernauld, Glasgow: Pedersen Press, 1995).
——. *The Deil's Bargain* (Cumbernauld, Glasgow: Pedersen Press, 1997).
Ritchie, Aileen, *The Juju Girl* (London: Nick Hern, 1999).
Smith, Grainne *'Limmer': A Collection of Work by Grainne Smith* (Banff: Banff & Buchan District Council, 1995).
Watson, Alison Linklater, *Dying with Laughter* (Cumbernauld, Glasgow: Pedersen Press, 1996).

Useful Anthologies

The Cat's Mother: Maryhill Women Writers Group; An Anthology, ed. Linda McCann (Glasgow: Maryhill Women Writers Group & Maryhill Community Education, 1991).
Different Boundaries, ed. Barbara Weightman and Elsie MacRae (Glasgow: Smeddum Press, 1995).
Gold Star Salad: Glasgow Women Writers Group Anthology, ed. Linda McCann (Glasgow: Glasgow Women Writers Group, 1995).
Internal Landscapes: An Anthology of Poetry by Scottish Women, ed. Sheena Yule (Pittsburg: Dorrance, 1991).
Original Prints 2: New Writing from Scottish Women, introduction by Elspeth Davie (Edinburgh: Polygon, 1987).

Original Prints 3: New Writing from Scottish Women (Edinburgh: Polygon, 1989).
Original Prints 4: New Writing from Scottish Women, ed. Elizabeth Burns, Sara Evans,
    Thelma Good, Barbara Simmons (Edinburgh: Polygon, 1992).
Our Space: Kirkcaldy Women Writers Workshop (Kirkcaldy: Kirkcaldy Women Writers
    Workshop, 1986).
Pomegranate: Poems by Pomegranate Women's Writing Group (Edinburgh: Stramullion, 1992).
Special Reserve: New Writing from Women in Aberdeen, ed. Yvonne Spence (Aberdeen:
    Scottish Cultural Press, 1996).

Contributors

Carol Anderson teaches Scottish literature at Glasgow University. She has edited Violet Jacob's *Diaries and Letters from India 1895–1900* (1990), *Flemington* (1994) and *Flemington and Tales from Angus* (1998), and co-edited *Scottish Women's Fiction 1920s to 1960s* (2000). She is currently editing a volume of essays on Catherine Carswell. She has also written on nineteenth-century female novelists, fiction by contemporary Scottish women, and Scott and Stevenson.

Barbara Bell lectures in drama at Queen Margaret University College, Edinburgh. Her publications include 'The Nineteenth Century', in *A History of the Scottish Theatre* (1998), and articles on the Scottish National Drama. Her research interests include Scottish theatre, issues of national identity, contemporary popular theatre and actor training.

Helen Boden lectures in English and Scottish literature at Edinburgh University. Her research interests include late eighteenth- and early nineteenth-century English and Scottish literature, travel writing and autobiography, and contemporary Scottish writing and culture. She is currently writing *Travel Writing in the PostEnlightenment Age*.

Aileen Christianson lectures in Scottish literature at Edinburgh University. She is co-editor of *Scottish Women's Fiction 1920s to 1960s* (2000) and is an editor of the Duke-Edinburgh edition of *The Collected Letters of Thomas and Jane Welsh Carlyle*. She also publishes on Jane Welsh Carlyle.

Sarah M. Dunnigan is British Academy Postdoctoral Fellow at Edinburgh University. She is the author of a forthcoming book from Macmillan: *Eros and Poetry at the Courts of Mary Queen of Scots and James VI*.

Ksenija Horvat is a research fellow at the Drama Department, Queen Margaret University College, Edinburgh. A graduate of the University of Zagreb, 1990, her Ph.D. in 'Female Identity and Language in the Plays of Five Contemporary Scottish Women Playwrights', 1999, was at Queen Margaret University

College. Since 1990, she has also worked as a playwright and translator (translating *The Anthology of Contemporary Scottish Drama* (1999) into Serbo-Croatian). She has also published on contemporary Scottish women playwrights.

Alison Lumsden is employed by Aberdeen University as research fellow for the Edinburgh Edition of The Waverley Novels and is co-editor of Scott's *The Heart of Mid-Lothian* and *The Pirate*. She also publishes on R. L. Stevenson and twentieth-century Scottish fiction, including Nan Shepherd and Alasdair Gray.

Glenda Norquay is reader in Literary Studies at Liverpool John Moores University. She is editor of *Voices and Votes: A Literary Anthology of the Women's Suffrage Campaign* and *R. L. Stevenson on Fiction*, and has published widely on Scottish fiction.

Margery Palmer McCulloch teaches Scottish Literature at Glasgow University. She is the author of *Edwin Muir: Poet, Critic and Novelist* and *The Novels of Neil M. Gunn*, and is currently exploring the contribution of women authors to Scottish writing in the twentieth century.

Lynne Stark is currently completing a Ph.D. at Edinburgh University on contemporary Scottish fiction and its depiction of the body. She also teaches Scottish literature as a postgraduate teaching assistant.

Susan C. Triesman is Director of Drama at Strathclyde University and Artistic Director of the Ramshorn Theatre, Glasgow. She is a pioneer of Theatre Studies and Performing Arts degrees.

Index